Stopford Augustus Brooke

The History of Early English Literature

Vol. 1

Stopford Augustus Brooke

The History of Early English Literature
Vol. 1

ISBN/EAN: 9783337778347

Printed in Europe, USA, Canada, Australia, Japan

Cover: Foto ©ninafisch / pixelio.de

More available books at **www.hansebooks.com**

THE HISTORY

OF

EARLY ENGLISH LITERATURE

BEING THE HISTORY OF ENGLISH POETRY FROM
ITS BEGINNINGS TO THE ACCESSION
OF KING ÆLFRED

BY

STOPFORD A. BROOKE

Look unto the rock whence ye are hewn,
And to the hole of the pit whence ye are digged.—Isaiah li. 1

IN TWO VOLUMES

VOL. I

London
MACMILLAN AND CO.
AND NEW YORK
1892

PREFACE

This book is the history of the beginnings of English Poetry. It is the beginning also of a history of that poetry which, I hope, with perhaps too bold an ambition, to finish in the years to come. Life gives too short a time now for a long work, but it is a pleasure to have at least brought to an end this tale of the origins of English verse.

It begins in the older England over the sea. It ends with the accession of Ælfred. When he came to the throne in 871, literature, both Latin and English, had perished, after a career of two hundred years. The final home of both had been Northumbria. A few years after his accession the last unplundered seats of learning were destroyed. All the Muses were now silent. But before Ælfred died a new English literature had begun, and in a new land, and the King was himself its origin. What had been was poetry; this was prose. The country of English poetry had been Northumbria; the country of English prose was Wessex. At this date, then, the curtain naturally falls on the first act of this history. At this date, in the intervals of Ælfred's wars, it will naturally rise on the beginning of the second act.

The English literature of this period is entirely poetry, and this book is mainly dedicated to that poetry. I have not put aside the life of the people, the Latin literature, or the political history of England; but I have only spoken of them so far as they bore upon the poetry or illustrated it. That poetry is certainly not of a very fine quality, but it is frequently remarkable. It has its own special qualities, and with the exception of perhaps a few Welsh and Irish poems, it is the only vernacular poetry in Europe, outside of the classic tongues, which belongs to so early a time as the seventh and eighth centuries. The Welsh and Irish poems are few, problematical, and their range is limited; but the English poems are numerous, well-authenticated, and of a wide and varied range. In these two centuries our forefathers produced examples, and good examples for the time, of religious, narrative, elegiac, descriptive, and even, in some sort, of epic poetry. This is a fact of singular interest. There is nothing like it—at this early period—elsewhere in Europe. But the interest is even greater when we consider this poetry in connection with the whole of English song. It will be seen that a great number of the main branches of the tree of English poetry had already opened out at this time from the stem, and that the ideal and sentimental elements of the earliest poetry have continued, with natural changes, up to the present day. Here, then, in the two hundred years between 670 and 870, the roots of English poetry, the roots of that vast over-shadowing tree, were set; and here its first branches clothed themselves with leaves. Here, like the oaks of Dodona, it began to discourse its music; and there is not a murmur now of song in all its immemorial boughs which does not echo from time to time with the themes and the passion of its first melodies. Here, too, we can best discern, and here isolate most easily, those elements in English character which, existing before the race was mixed, have been, not the cause of our poetry, but the cause why the poetry has been of so high an excellence,—that steady consistency of national character, that clinging through all difficulty to the aim in view, that unrelenting curiosity, that desire to better what has been done, which, though not art themselves, are the effectual powers which enable art to strive, to seek, and at last to reach its goal.

Moreover, no national art is good which is not plainly that nation's own. In this Anglo-Saxon poetry of which I write we grasp most clearly the dominant English essence. The poetry of England has owed much to the different races which mingled with the original English race; it has owed much to the different types of poetry it absorbed—Greek, Latin, Welsh, French, Italian, Spanish—but below all these admixtures, the English nature wrought its steady will. It seized, it transmuted, it modified, it mastered these admixtures both of races and of song.

Of what kind the early English poetry is, what feelings inspired the poets, what imaginations filled their hearts, how did they shape their work—that is the vital, the interesting question; and to answer it, the poetry itself must be read. I have therefore not written much about the poems, but I have translated a great quantity of what seemed to me not only their best, but also their most characteristic passages. I have also, when they were short enough, translated whole poems like the fourth *Riddle* and the *Wanderer*.

How to translate them was my chief difficulty. It was necessary, above all, that the translation should be accurate, but it was also necessary that it should have, as far as possible, the rhythmical movement of verse. Of all possible translations of poetry, a merely prose translation is the most inaccurate.

The translations here given are as accurate as I could make them. I do not mean that there are no mistakes in them,—which would be an insolence I should soon repent,—but I mean that there is nothing out of my own fancy added to the translation. The original has been rigidly followed, and, for the most part, line for line. I have nearly always bracketed inserted words; and the only licence I have taken is the introduction of such words as *then* and *there* and *all*, when I needed an additional syllable for the sake of the rhythm which I adopted. Permission to do this was, I may say, given to me by the Anglo-Saxon poets themselves; it is their constant habit.

Then I felt that the translation should be in a rhythm which should represent, as closely as I could make it, the movement and the variety of the original verse. A prose translation, even when it reaches excellence, gives no idea whatever of that to which the ancient English listened. The original form is destroyed, and with it our imagination of the world to which the poet sang, of the way he thought, of how he shaped his emotion. Prose no more represents poetry than architecture does music. Translations of poetry are never much good, but at least they should always endeavour to have the musical movement of poetry, and to obey the laws of the verse they translate.

A translation made in any one of our existing rhyming metres seemed to me as much out of the question as a prose translation. None of these metres resemble those of Anglo-Saxon poetry; and, moreover, their associations would modernise the old English thought. An Anglo-Saxon king in modern Court dress would not look more odd and miserable than an Anglo-Saxon poem in a modern rhyming metre. Blank verse is another matter. It frequently comes near to the "short epic line" of Cynewulf, but it fails in the elasticity which a translation of Anglo-Saxon poetry requires, and in itself is too stately, even in its feminine dramatic forms, to represent the cantering movement of old English verse. Moreover, it is weighted with the sound of Shakspere, Milton, or Tennyson, and this association takes the reader away from the atmosphere of early English poetry. I felt myself then driven to invent a rhythmical movement which would enable me, while translating literally, to follow the changes, and to express, with some little approach to truth, the proper ebb and flow of Anglo-Saxon verse.

The Anglo-Saxon line is divided into two halves by a pause. The first half has two "measures," and the first syllable of these is accented, or "stressed." The second half has the same number of measures and accents. The binding together of these two halves is done by alliteration. Generally speaking, the two accented syllables in the first half and one of the accented syllables in the second half begin with the same consonant or with any vowels; almost always with different vowels. Frequently, however, there is only one alliterated syllable in the first half of the line. Unaccented syllables, the greater number of which were placed at the beginning of the second half line, after the pause, filled up the line. One school of poets, of whom Cynewulf was the chief, used a short line, with few slurred syllables. Another school which has been called the Caedmonian School used a line with a varying number of unaccented syllables, and as a great number of these were often inserted, the line has been called the "long epic line" in contrast with Cynewulf's shorter line. A poet of this school could use the shorter line when he pleased. He might have a line of only eight syllables, or one of three times that length, expanding it to express his swelling passion, or contracting it to suit a sharp question or a concise description. The variety then of the line was great, and its elasticity. It was capable of rapidity and solemnity; and its harmony and order were secured by the last alliterated stress being on the first syllable of the last word but one of the full line.

In order to be able to fulfil these needs and follow these peculiarities, I chose, after many experiments, the trochaic movement used in this book, each half-line consisting of trochees following one another, with a syllable at the end, chiefly a long one, to mark the division of the line. I varied the line as much as I could, introducing, often rashly, metrical changes; for the fault of this movement is its monotony. I have sometimes tried an iambic movement, but rarely; for this trochaic line with a beat at the end of each half-verse seemed to me to get the nearest to the sound of the Anglo-Saxon line, even though it is frequently un-similar to that line itself. I used alliteration whenever I could, and stressed as much as possible the alliterated words, and I changed the length of the line with the changes of the original. But when I could not easily alliterate my line or stress the alliterated word, I did not try to do so. It was better, I thought, to give literally the sense and the sentiment of the original than to strain them or lose them by a rigid adherence to alliteration and accent. I have made clear the division of the Anglo-Saxon line by leaving a space in the midst of each line of my translation. The two half lines are, of course, intended to be read right across the page, with a slight pause upon the space between them. I think the method used is on the whole the right method, but I am by no means satisfied with what I have done. I submit it with much deference to those who understand the difficulties of such a translation.

This book is written from the literary point of view, and desires, above all, to induce English-speaking folk to reverence, admire, and love the poetry which their fathers wrote in old time, since it is worthy. I have not therefore, except when I thought it necessary, entered into the critical or scientific questions which hum like bees around the poems. On these questions a great number of books, reviews, and pamphlets have been written. I have not avoided this side of the matter from any want of gratitude to the critics, or from any lack of appreciation of the work of Anglo-Saxon scholars. On the contrary, it is my duty and my pleasure to acknowledge, that were it not for the intimate and exhaustive labour of German, English, and American scholars, a book like this, which views the poetry of the ancient English only as literature, could not have been written at all, or, at least, not on any sure foundation. No translation worth reading, or giving a clear representation of what the Anglo-

Saxon poets thought or felt, could have here been made, had it not been preceded by the long, careful and penetrating labour of the philologists; nor could any just literary estimate of the poems or any useful arrangement of them have been worked out in this book, without the minute and accurate toil expended on them, and on their subjects, sources and dates by a multitude of critics among whom the Germans are pre-eminent. Moreover, had it not been for the labour and genius of the later historians of early England, especially of Mr. Green, I could not have had the materials for binding up, as I have tried to do, the poetry of England with the history of England.

I cannot, so numerous are they, mention the many scholars to whom my thanks are due, but my gratitude to them is none the less. Where I have specially used the work of any one of them I have acknowledged it in the text. Two, however, above all, ought to be thanked by me, as they have been thanked by all who have cared for ancient English poetry. Professor Grein is gone from us, but he will never be forgotten. To his *Dictionary* I owe my first interest in the Anglo-Saxon language, my first understanding of its power and charm. To his translation of the poems into German I owe my first appreciation of the poetry of early England. The reading of that translation made me eager to read the poems in the original, and I could not rest till I was able to do so. When I had read them I could not rest till I had written this book. The other scholar to whom this book owes so much is Professor Wülker. He needs no praise, but he may take gratitude from me. Had it not been for his *Grundriss zur Geschichte der angelsächsischen Litteratur*, one like myself, who late in life began to read the Anglo-Saxon literature, could never have found his way through the tangled mazes of Anglo-Saxon criticism, nor known what to look for, nor where to find his wants fulfilled. I cannot understand why the University Professors of Anglo-Saxon in this country do not have that book translated, and edited up to date.

I was fortunate enough while these pages were passing through the press to be in time to see Professor Earle's book, *The Deeds of Beowulf*, and though I do not agree with his theory of the origin of the poem, I wish to thank him for having, by his translation and notes, made *Beowulf* a more literary possession for the English people. I have also to thank Mr. Gollancz for permitting me to use the early proof sheets of his edition of the *Christ*. I saw these sheets after I had made the translations of the *Christ* contained in this book, and before he had re-written his translation as it now appears. I made some changes in my translation and adopted some of his phrases. I also adopted his new division of the poem, and his ending of it at line 1663. Since then his book has been published, and my personal thanks are now mingled with those due to him from all who care for English literature. To Miss Kate Warren, an accomplished student of Anglo-Saxon poetry, and an excellent teacher of our modern literature, I am also indebted for steady and valuable help frankly given to me throughout the writing of this book. She made the map which accompanies these volumes, and the Index is also her work. I have had the map drawn to illustrate the chapter which treats of the question—Why Northumbria was the special home of English Poetry. It represents the general relation of the English kingdoms to the Welsh, Irish and Pictish peoples, and it follows, in its main divisions, the map at p. 21 of Mr. York Powell's *History of England*. It does not pretend to give the boundaries between the several English kingdoms or between the English and the Welsh at any particular period from 600 to 800. Maps which explain the to-and-fro of those boundaries from time to time will be found in Mr. Green's *Making of England*. I have also had placed in this map, and underlined in red, the names of the most famous monastic centres of learning which had been set up before the death of Baeda.

And so, I bid this book farewell. It has tried, with many others, to save for remembrance and seclude for thought the neglected lands of early English poetry. Like the ancient places of this country where our forefathers met together for religion or war or council, they seem to appeal to England to take care of them, to give them interest and affection. Far too few of them remain, far too many of them have perished. The silent stream of time, with mordant and quiet wave, washed into forgetfulness those pleasant fields,

    rura quae Liris quieta
    mordet aqua taciturnus amnis.

       STOPFORD A. BROOKE.

August 2, 1892.

CONTENTS

CHAP.		PAGE
1.	Widsith, Deor, and the Scôp	1
2.	Beowulf—Introduction	17
3.	Beowulf—The Poem	37
4.	The Episodes of "Beowulf," and the "Fight at Finnsburg"	83
5.	The Mythical Elements in "Beowulf"	104
6.	Waldhere	132
7.	The Conquest and Literature	143
8.	Armour and War in Poetry	169
9.	The Settlement in Poetry	185
10.	The Sea	223
11.	Christianity and Literature	250
12.	Monasticism and Literature	30
	Notes	323

THE MATERIALS FOR THE HISTORY OF ANGLO-SAXON POETRY UP TO THE ACCESSION OF ÆLFRED THE GREAT

The Exeter Book formed part of the library which Leofric, the first bishop of Exeter, collected and left to his cathedral church. He catalogued it himself as a *Mycel Englisc boc be gehwilcum þingum on leoð-wisan geworht:* "A mickle English book on all kinds of things wrought in verse." It is still kept in Exeter Cathedral, and has been there, since Leofric died in 1071, for 821 years. It is a varied anthology, and contains poems which range from the eighth to the tenth or eleventh century. One or two may belong to the seventh century, and some may be of even higher antiquity. *Widsith*, for example, may contain verses which were made in the old Angle land over the seas. Of the poems mentioned in these volumes, it holds (and I give them in the order they are in the *Book*): *The Christ, Guthlac, Azarias, The Phœnix, Juliana, The Wanderer, Gifts of Men, The Seafarer, Widsith, Fates of Men, Gnomic Verses, The Panther, Whale and Partridge, The Soul to its Body, Deor, Riddles* 1-60, *The Wife's Complaint, The Descent into Hell, Riddle* 61, *The Message of a Lover, The Ruin, Riddles* 62-89. Others, either of little value or later than the eighth century, are also contained in it.

The Vercelli Book was discovered in the capitular library at Vercelli in Upper Italy by Dr. Blum in the year 1832. No one knows how it got there, but Wülker conjectures that a Hospice existed in that town for Anglo-Saxon pilgrims who went on pilgrimage to Rome, and who crossed by the Mont Cenis or the Great or Little St. Bernard Passes. A scanty library may have grown up there, and this manuscript have been left to it by some English voyager. The book is a volume of Anglo-Saxon homilies, but interspersed among them are six poems—*The Andreas, The Fates of the Apostles, The Address of the Soul to the Body, The Dream of the Rood, The Elene*. The last is a fragment on the *Falsehood of Men*. The handwriting is of the eleventh century.

The Manuscript of Beowulf is in the British Museum (Cotton Vitellius A. xv.), and the same MS. contains the poem of *Judith*.

The Junian Manuscript, of the Caedmonian poems.—It contains *Genesis, Exodus, Daniel, Christ and Satan*, and is in the Bodleian.

Two fragments.—(i.) *The Fight at Finnsburg*. It only exists in a copy of it made by Hickes from a leaf of parchment used in the binding of a manuscript of homilies. This leaf, found in Lambeth Palace Library, is now lost. (ii.) Two vellum leaves found by Professor Werlauff in the National Library at Copenhagen contain two fragments of a poem to which the name of *Waldhere* has been given.

CHAPTER I

WIDSITH, DEOR, AND THE SCÔP

"WIDSITH told his tale, unlocked his word-hoard," is the beginning of the earliest poem we possess in the English tongue. *Widsith*—that is, "the Far-Traveller"—may be the actual name of the writer, or a name which as a wandering poet he assumed; or, as it occurs only in the introduction, which was probably written much later than the body of the poem, it may be a title given to the poet by the writer of the introduction, and this seems the best explanation of the term. The suggestion that it is another name for Woden, and that Widsith is therefore a mythological person, does not seem to have sufficient ground for its adoption. He is rather the "poetic representative of the singer" who loved to wander from court to court and land to land; and his name, whether assumed by himself or given to him by an after-writer, expresses this very well.

The poem begins with an introduction of nine lines. This is followed by a catalogue, from the tenth to the seventy-fifth line, of the various places and kings and tribes that Widsith had visited. An interpolation then of twelve lines succeeds, and may have been inserted in the seventh century, and in England. The conclusion contains a personal account of the poet's way of living and of his last journey, and this runs on from verse 87 to the close.[1] The catalogue and the personal account are very old, older than anything else we have of Anglo-Saxon poetry, and may date from the time when the English as yet kept their seats upon the continent. The theories concerning the origin and date of the poem are numerous, and I place in a note at the end of this volume a short discussion of them. To treat of them here would confuse the personal impression which the poem was certainly intended to make.

The Preface (lines 1-9) which may have been written in the old Angle-land, tells us that Widsith, " who most of all men visited kindreds and nations, received in the hall for his singing memorable gifts." Born among the Myrgings,[2] he became the singer of the court, and while still young went, in this capacity, " with Queen Ealdhild the weaver of peace," the daughter of Eadwine and the wife of Eadgils King of the Myrgings, to seek the home of Eormanric (Hermanric), King of the Ostrogoths who lived "east from Ongle "; and this was his first journey.

Here the Introduction ceases, and at the 10t line Widsith himself, writing in his old age, describes his journeys.[3] "Many men and rulers I have known," he says; "through many stranger-lands have fared, throughout the spacious earth, parte from my kinsmen. Therefore I may sing in th mead-hall how the high born gave me gifts." Tw

---

[1] Verses 131-134 are, it is supposed, a later interpolation.
[2] The Myrgings, the dwellers near the *mark*, lived perhaps in the Elbe-lan between the Elbe and the Eyder, and were neighbours of the Angles.
[3] I assume here, for literary purposes, that the poem was written by one ma and that it is a personal account of his wanderings. In that way we can see t thing as Elfred saw it, and it is the first way in which we should look at it. T critical consideration of its genuineness comes in afterwards, and will be found a note at the end of this volume.

among the rest were most gracious to him, Guthere the Burgundian, "who gave me an arm-ring, no sluggish king was he, and Ælfwine[1] in Italy, Eadwine's bairn. He was of all men swiftest of hand in winning of honour, and freest of heart in the dealing of rings."

These names occur in the long list of kings and tribes whom he visited—a list which has certainly undergone some later interpolations. Many of the ancient names belong to the North German cycle of romance. A special place is given to Offa of Ongle. We hear also of personages known to us from the poem of *Beowulf*, of Finn, and Hnaef, of Hrothgar, Ingeld, and of the town of Heorot. It is a list of great importance for the history of the ancient tribes of Germany and for the heroic sagas of that country, but it has no literary value, and no personal interest. The personal interest comes in at line 87, after an interpolation of twelve lines. Widsith tells of his voyage to Eormanric, of his return, of the welcome his lord gave him, and of the songs he sung at home with his brother bard Scilling. The little tale is so simple, so direct, and so full of the detail of memory, that here if anywhere we seem to get to the genuine matter.

> For a longish time   lived I with Eormanric ;
> There the King of Gotens   with his gifts was good to me ;
> He, the Prince of burg-indwellers,   gave to me an armlet,
> On the which 600   seats of beaten gold
> Scorèd were,   in scillings reckoned.[2]

---

[1] On the supposition that this list is the genuine work of Widsith, that is, of a poet who, in his early youth, visited Hermanric, this "Ælfwine in Italy" cannot be Alboin, but, as Guest conjectures, some Chief fighting in Italy, probably during the inroad of Alaric and under his banner, in the beginning of the fifth century. If that explanation be rejected, the name Ælfwine, *unless* we advance the date of the poem to the seventh century, must have been interpolated, for Alboin died in 572, two hundred years later than the death of Hermanric (375) whom Widsith says he visited in his youth.

[2] The portions of a *baig*, outlined on the gold, would be called *scillings* ; when these were adjusted to a fixed scale upon the weight of the *solidus*, the

> This I gave to Eadgils, to my lord who guarded me—
> When I homeward came— for his own possession,
> For my Master's meed, Lord of Myrgings he—
> Since he granted land to me, homeland of my fathers.
>
> And another gift Ealdhild gave to me,
> Folk queen of the doughty men, daughter of Eadwine.
> Over many lands I prolonged her praise,
> When so e'er in singing I must say to men
> Where beneath the sky I had known the best
> Of all gold-embroidered queens giving lavishly her gifts.
> Scilling then and with him I, in a voicing clear,
> Lifted up the lay to our lord the conqueror;
> Loudly at the harping lilted high our voice,
> Then our hearers many, haughty of their heart,
> They that couth it well, clearly said in words
> That a better lay listed had they never.

The poem now represents his further wanderings among the Gothic tribes that, one after another, fought and began to settle in the provinces of Italy; and again, when he grew older, his visits to the Gothic princes while they were still fighting with the Huns in the dark woods about the Vistula. "Often was battle fierce," he sings, "when with hard swords the host of the Hreads had to guard the old fatherland against the bands of Ætla (Attila) all about the Wistla Wood." He names many of the warriors with whom he companied, and in whose camps he sang, but most "Wudga and Hama" (both of whom become personages in the hero sagas), "not the worst of my friends, though I name them the last." Then in four lines he sketches that long and dreadful war which the East Goten waged with the Huns, and so great is the power, even of poor poetry, that we see, as if they were alive, Wudga and Hama whirling the spear for wife and child in Wistla Wood.

---

scilling would become (1) a definite division of a ring, (2) a division equal in weight to a *solidus*, and this is the meaning here; but see, for the whole matter, *English Coin*, British Museum.

> Oft from their hosting   hurtling through air
> Midst the fierce folk   flew the spear yelling.
> Exiles, they ruled   o'er their women, their men ;
> Gold-wreathen warriors,   Wudga and Hama.

Then, leaving out verses 131-134, which are an interpolation, the Traveller ends his verses by a description of the wandering singer and of the glory of his art. Thus, drifting on, the gleemen rove through many lands—

> Say (in song) their need,   speak aloud their thankword!
> Always South or Northward   some one they encounter,
> Who,—for he is learned in lays,   lavish in his giving—
> Would before his men of might   magnify his sway,
> Manifest his earlship.
>   Till all flits away—
> Life and light together—   laud who getteth so
> Hath beneath the heaven   high established power.

The poem has but little literary value, but a certain literary charm is diffused over it by the names it enshrines—names of men concerning whom great sagas were written, and whose gests and government made a noise which filled the ear of the world. If the writer really saw Hermanric and Attila before they became heroes of Teutonic saga, we transfer to him and to his poem our pleasure in their cycle of stories. The very possibility that he saw these men excites us. Moreover, if we consider the poem to be of the fifth century, the light of four cycles of lays is reflected backwards upon it. Its names bring before us the sagas of Hermanric, of Alboin, of Gudrun, and Beowulf ; the story of Offa, and of the fight at Finnsburg. We may be said to be present at the birth and to watch over the cradle of these great Teutonic sagas. Even if the poem be of the seventh century, and these sagas are behind it and not before it, this reflected literary charm is still present. All the great figures rise before our eyes as we read their names in the dry detail of the catalogue. We may also bind it up with another fancy for which we have a good foundation. We may fairly imagine the delight of Ælfred when he read this poem. The catalogue of tribes and kings, the geographical details it contains would fall in with the temper of the king who translated and added to Orosius, who wrote down from Ohthere's and Wulfstan's lips their voyages to the North Sea, and to the mouth of the Vistula. Moreover, the passion for roving, for adventure, which is keen above all other nations in the people of our island, makes this poem representative of the English. Widsith is our Ulysses. "I have fared through many stranger lands, through the spacious earth; good and evil have I known." It is the true description of a common type of Englishman in every period of our history. Nor is Widsith's pleasure in his art or his practical pleasure in the receipt of gifts, less characteristic of the English. But the gifts are little in comparison with his joy in his work, and his reverence for it. Even great kings are but little, he thinks, without their singer. In his hands their history lies, and their honour. Horace did not feel more strongly the need of a sacred bard to chronicle great actions than did the earliest of English poets.

The poem is then not only the story of wanderings, it also sketches the life and the repute of the Scóp— the name given to the singer and poet who was retained in the court of a king or the hall of a great noble. He was frequently one of the thegns, and received money and landright from the king. He may have been, if not a thegn, on an equality with them;

and was often, as we see in *Beowulf*,[1] a renowned captain. Sometimes, like Widsith, or perhaps like Cynewulf at one period of his life, he took to roving, and singing from court to court. In this fashion he became the travelling geographer and historian, the bringer of news, the man who, by singing the great deeds of warriors in various lands, knit together by a common bond of admiration the heroes of diverse peoples, and made the great stories the common property of the Teutonic tribes.

As *Widsith* is the picture of the poet in his happiness, singing his life in a lyrical fashion (it has been attempted to arrange the poem in strophes), so the *Lament of Deor* images the Scòp in his sorrow. This song is much later, I think, than *Widsith*. It belongs to a time when the Gothic cycle of lays had at least well begun. Hermanric has become legendary. Theodric has become the fabulous hero. But the prominence of the story of Weland, and the mention of Geat, localise the poem among the Northern Teutonic tribes. From these it was brought to England, perhaps by some belated Angles, if Sweet be right in his conjecture that it may have been composed before the English migration. I think it is likely to be much later, and to have been made in England—it is put by some as far on as the eighth century,—but no decision can be come to on the matter. Its form is remarkable. It has a refrain, and there is no other early English instance of this known to us. It is written in strophes, and Sweet thinks that it may be a solitary remnant of a

---

[1] Beowulf is the name of a poem, and of the hero whose deeds are sung in the poem. Whenever I mention the poem, I print its name in italics, and whenever the hero is meant, his name is in ordinary type.

number of English strophic lays which belonged to the same class as some of the old Scandinavian lays which were rudely strophic.[1] One motive, constant throughout, is expressed in the refrain. This dominant cry of passion makes the poem a true lyric, and we ought to look upon it with pleasure, for it is the Father of all English lyrics.

Deor is not like Widsith, a treasure-gifted singer, always in favour of his lord. Like the *Wanderer* who looks back with mourning on the time when he was his master's favourite, he has been deprived of his rewards and lands, and has seen a rival set above his head. It is this whirling down of Fortune's wheel that he mourns in his song, and he compares his fate to that of others who have suffered, so that he may have some comfort. But the comfort is stern like that the Northmen take. Others, he thinks, have gone through great griefs, and come out on the other side of them—so also may he win through his pain.

Here is the song, and the legendary woes of which he speaks show that the English knew the story of Weland well, the story of Geat, of Hermanric, of Theodric, and the tale which became in after years the saga of Gudrun—

> Weland for a woman [2]   knew too well exile!
> Strong of soul that earl,   sorrows sharp he bore;
> To companionship he had   care and weary longing,
> Winter-freezing wretchedness.   Woe he found again, again.
> After that Nithhád   in a Need had laid him
> Staggering sinew-wounds-   sorrow-smitten man!
>   *That* he overwent; *this* also may I.

---

[1] German critics have rearranged the first four strophes, and put strophe 4 into the place of strophe 3. The order will then be harmonious. A strophe of six lines will be followed by one of five, twice over; but I think Müllenhof gave up this needless change.

[2] There are many readings of this obscure line. As to Weland, Hild, and Geat, a note at the end of the volume treats of them.

Not to Beadohild   was her brothers' death
On her soul so sore   as was her self-sorrow,
When that she was sure,   with a surety far too great,
That with child she was.   Never could she think,
With a clear remembrance,   how that came to be.
         That she overwent; *this* also may I.

Of this meed of Hild   we've from many heard;

.   .   .   .   .   .

And so bottomless   was the passion Geát felt,
That Love-sorrow stole   all his sleep away!
         That he overwent; *this* also may I.

For a thirty winters   did Theodric fast
Hold the Maerings' burg.   Many knew of that.
         That he overwent; *this* also may I.

We in songs have heard   of the wolfish thought
That Eormanric had!   Far he owned the folk
Of the Gotens' realm.   Grisly was that king.
Many a warrior sat,   with his sorrows cloaked,
Woe within his waiting!   Wistfully he longed
That the kingdom's king [1]   overcome should be!
         That he overwent; *this* also may I.

I omit here what seems a Christian interpolation of the ordinary gnomic character. We may, however, give thanks to it, for I suspect we owe the preservation of this lyric to the zeal of the interpolator who saw in the sadness of Deor an opportunity for introducing his gentle phrases on the vanity of life and the mercy of God. The rest is Deor's own. The Heorrenda who conquered Deor may be the Horant of the Gudrun saga of whom it is said that he bound all men with his song, that the beasts who listened to him ceased to graze in the woods, and the worms and fishes forgot their daily work in his singing. "Now," he says, "I will say concerning myself"

     Whilom was I Scôp   of the Heodenings:
     Dear unto my Lord!   *Deor* was my name.
     Well my service was to me   many winters through;

---

[1] I have introduced *king* into the text.

> Loving was my Lord ;   till at last Heorrenda,
> Skilled in song the man !   seized upon my land-right
> That the guard of earls   granted erst to me.
>   *That* one overwent ; *this* also may I.

With this song begins and ends the Old English lyric. We have in Anglo-Saxon a few elegiac poems of fine quality, but the true lyric—short, at unity with one thought, with one cry of joyful or sorrowful passion—does not occur again till long after the Conquest.

We have yet another sketch of the Scôp which we may well set beside the sketches in *Widsith* and in *Deor*, though it belongs to a later time in Anglo-Saxon literature. It is the eighty-ninth riddle of Cynewulf which Dietrich has happily solved as the Wandering Singer—

> Ætheling am I,   and to earls am known ;
> And not rarely do I rest   with the rich and with the poor ;
> Midst the Folks I'm famous.   Widely fares (through hall) —
> And for me a foreigner,[1]   rather than for friends—
> Loud the plunderers' applause,   if that I should have
> Glory in the Burgs   or the goods that shine.
> Also very great the love   that well-witted men
> Have of meeting me.   I to many folk
> Wisdom do unveil.   Not a word on earth
> Then is said by any man.   Though the sons of men,
> Though the Earth-indwellers,   eagerly seek after
> Footprints that I leave,   frequently I hide,
> From all men that are,   my (unfollowed) way.

If this riddle be by Cynewulf, as I think it is, he sketches in it his own position and temperament, and with that, the position and temperament of the Scôp. He was not only ennobled and at home with the rich, but also sang with the poor and stayed in their houses. He loved to win gifts and rings, and to

---

[1] The passage is most difficult. It means, according to my translation—and I read *fremdum* instead of *fremdes*—that the warriors enjoy the singing of a stranger, since he is new to them, more than the singing of their own bards.

excite the warriors who roved for plunder; but he sang a different kind of song to the elder and wiser men. And we may judge from all that is left to us that these songs of "wisdom" were the great sagas like *Beowulf*, tales of law and justice and noble war; sometimes riddles and gnomic verses fitted for well-witted men; even songs of history like that of *Widsith*; and, when he had so sung, all men sat silent, listening. Moreover, he was eagerly sought after, but it was often his habit, like many of his clan, to hide himself in solitude, musing like his fellow in *Beowulf* on new poems; or indulging the melancholy found in the *Lament of Deor*, and which lay deep in the temperament of Cynewulf. Of this there is ample proof at the end of the *Elene*. In that poem Cynewulf sketches his early life as a poet. Once he received treasures and appled gold, — once his youth was swift and happy, but now all joy was fled away, and sore had been his trouble. But at last, when he seemed to have lost the art of weaving words, God "unbound his breast, unlocked the craft of song, and again he practised with delight his versing." Cynewulf had been then a Scôp attached to a court, and also a wandering singer. He had had his pleasure and also his pain—had been Widsith and Deor in one.

When, however, we meet with the *wandering* Scôp we meet with that which is not usual. His place was, generally, like Deor's, a fixed place, with an appointment of food and money or land which attached him to the court of the chieftain or king. When he wandered, it was either from a roving spirit, or as an attendant on an embassage, like Widsith, or because misfortune had befallen his lord, like the "Wanderer," or because, like Deor, he was dispossessed by a rival.

Below the Scôp there were a great number of inferior singers who made it their business to go from place to place, to whom the name of Scôp was not given—who did not shape, but sang that which had been shapen by the Scôp. These were the gleemen, though their name is sometimes given to the Scôp— and in later Anglo-Saxon times, they were not unfrequently accompanied by jugglers, tumblers, and wrestlers. These two—the Scôp and the gleeman— were professional persons, but they were not the only singers. Almost every one made verses or sang them. Heroes in the midst of battle sang as they advanced, like Harold Hardrada at Stamford Bridge; Vikings, as they drave their ships through the gale or stormed a town on the river, shouted their hymn of defiance to the sea, or their praises of their ship, or the battle-stroke of the moment. Warriors chanted their deeds of the day in the hall or the camp at night, as Woden's chosen did in Valhalla. The old chiefs sang the glory of their youth. Their very swords and spears were thought to sing. The spear yells, the sword shouts in battle. Then, the wanderer who came into the hall to claim hospitality sang his stave of thanks, or versed for the chief in the high seat, who he was. The king himself often broke in with his tale, and seized the harp as Hrothgar did in Heorot. Even the preachers afterwards, like Ealdhelm, sang ancient songs in the public ways to draw the people round them. In the women's chambers, also, the old lays were sung. Ælfred, we are told, sang the ballads of his people at his mother's knee. At the feasts of the commoner folk it was the same as in the noble's hall. Freedmen, peasants, even the serfs, sent round the harp, (as we hear from the Caedmon story in Baeda), telling, as Greek and Roman did, alternate tales. The player beat the harp in time with the thoughts and images of his song; his voice rang out the alliterated words and the accented syllables of the verses. Gesture accompanied and exalted the things described. The listeners often joined in, moved to excitement, and a whole chorus of voices filled the hall, the monastery, or the farm-building.

As the practice of the art was widely spread, so was it greatly honoured. The very name of Scôp, like the independent word Poet, brought the minds of those that heard it back to the Shaper of the universe, who himself gave the art of song. Saga was Odin's daughter among the Northmen. The view of the Greeks, of Homer, that the minstrel's inspiration and invention were divinely-given, was held by our English forefathers. We are told in Baeda's story of the poet Caedmon that all men held his gift to be divinely given him of the Lord. Cynewulf, as I have quoted above, says that "God unlocked his breast and gave him back the power of song." In the *Gnomic Verses* this opinion is combined with the thought that the poet is less troubled with selfish and tormenting thought than other men, because he has so many human things to think of. "To all men," the versifier says, "wise words are becoming; a song to the gleemen and wisdom to men. As many as men are on the earth, so many are their thoughts; each to himself has a separate soul. So, then, he who knows many songs and can greet the harp with his hands, hath the less of vain longing, for he hath in himself his gift of joy which God gave to him." The joyousness of the gift is expressed by many words. Song and music are almost synonymous with *gleo* and *wynn* and *dream*, with glee and delight and joy. The lay is in *Beowulf* the *healgamen*, the rapture of the hall. The harp is the wood of social joy, the wood-beam of delight. Playing and singing are—"to awake the joyous wood, the rapture of the harp, to rouse the happy lay," to practise the "glee-craft," to have the "jocund gift of poesy." Wisdom and prophecy are by other words connected with song and poetry.

When we travel as far back as we can go with certainty—to the times when literary men in Rome discussed the *Germania*, we find the Teutonic tribes harpists and singers of verse. "They are a fair-haired folk," says Tacitus, "blue-eyed, strongly built," and he tells of their love of song. "They celebrate, in ancient lays, Tuisco, their earth-born god (that is, whom the Germans thought to have sprung out of the earth where they dwelt, so long was it since they had settled there), and Mannus his son, the forefathers and founders of their race." "Their legends say that Hercules had been among them, and they call on his name above all others in their war-songs when they march to battle." Other battle hymns were accompanied by the loud beating of the spears of the host against their shields, or by the roaring sound the warriors made when they laid their lips to the upper rim of the shield and hummed into it and over it. With this music they kindled themselves to battle, and according to its tone they foretold the issue of the fight. In the *Annals*, we hear of the larger type of poetry, of the beginnings of the sagas. They have songs, Tacitus writes, in honour of their deliverer

Arminius ;[1] there are other pieces also which they sing in their bivouacs and at their feasts.

All this music and verse was, as we see, already old in the time of Tacitus, and belonged to religion and to war—a music of solemn ceremonies, sorrowful or festival. "Of all ceremonies, going into battle was the most religious," save perhaps that other great ceremony which was always attended by songs—the burial of a king or hero, an instance of which we have in the closing lines of *Beowulf*.

For 1900 years, then, we know that the English race has been a singing folk, and though we are not alone in that characteristic, we are almost alone in this, that we possess in our own language products of that singing temper in poems like those of *Widsith* and *The Fight at Finnsburg* which may range from the fifth to the seventh century. Moreover, there are lays imbedded in the *Beowulf* which seem to go back to a still more remote antiquity.

If this be true, if we may venture to speak of any of our poetry as continental, the poems make us understand, better than any historical statement can do, that the first English were not in Britain, but in the Low Dutch lands and Denmark—that there was an England there before our England. The first emigration was to Britain, the second to America. And as the Pilgrims—and I use a fine comparison of Freeman's —"took with them to America the Bible, an old Shakspere, their ballads, the Gesta of English soldiers

---

[1] Vigfusson has written a short essay in the supplement to the *Corp. Poet. Boreale*, in which he more than suggests that Arminius is identical with Siegfried. If this be true, and there is much probability in the argument, it adds another charm to the great story, and a new interest to the statement of Tacitus. The Roman soldiers may then have heard the earliest lays of the Volsung and Niblung saga. Arminius "canitur adhuc barbaras apud gentes."

and sailors, in the memory of nurses, children, and women, so the English brought to Britain, in that first pilgrimage, *Widsith, Beowulf, The Fight at Finnsburg*."[1] Many other lays, no doubt, came with them, but their verse, Time, too greedy of the excellent, "devoured with privy paw, and nothing said."

---

[1] I cannot find the passage; I quote from memory. I may as well say in this note that the mention of Attila in *Widsith*, in our earliest English poem, written perhaps before the English left for Britain, adds an additional interest to Mr. Hodgkin's theory that it was the pressure of the Huns at the back of the north-German tribes which was the cause of the English migration. Two great sea-ruling peoples arose then from the fierce driving of the Huns—the Venetians and the English.

CHAPTER II

BEOWULF

Introduction

THE Beowulf MS. (Cotton Vitellius A. xv.) was one of those collected by Sir Robert Cotton. It was in Little Dean's Yard, Westminster, when the fire which, in 1731, destroyed so many manuscripts took place, and was fortunately among those which were not fatally injured. In 1753, having spent some time in the old dormitory at Westminster, it was transferred to the British Museum.

In 1705 Wanley, employed by Hickes, the Anglo-Saxon scholar, to make a catalogue of the old northern books in the kingdom, discovered the poem of Beowulf in the Cottonian library and calls it a *tractatus nobilissimus poeticè scriptus*. It is a parchment codex, and the handwriting of the two copyists is of the beginning of the tenth century. Thorkelin, a Danish scholar, had two copies of it made in 1786, and published the whole of it for the first time in 1815. This edition made the poem known, and it was discussed in English and foreign reviews. Meantime, in 1805, Sharon Turner gave the first account of the poem in his history of the Anglo-Saxons. Turner again, in 1823, and Conybeare, in 1826, filled up that account and translated portions of *Beowulf* into English verse, and in 1833 and 1837 John M. Kemble edited, with historical prefaces, and translated the whole of the poem. This scholarly book increased the interest of foreign scholars in the poem; and, since then, a great number of editions and translations have been published, while the essays, dissertations, articles, and notices on the poem and the subjects contained in it, fill a long list, and are written by English, French, German, Dutch, Danish, and American scholars.

The poem, consisting of 3183 lines, is divided into two parts by an interval of fifty years, the first containing Beowulf's great deeds against the monster Grendel and his dam, the second Beowulf's conquest of the Fire-drake and his death and burial. The first division may be again divided into two—the fight with Grendel, and the fight with Grendel's mother—and some suppose that they are due to different hands. Several episodes are introduced which are linked on, often very roughly, to the history of Beowulf, and two or three of these seem to be taken from other sagas of even an earlier date than the original lays of the legend.

The same kind of controversy which has raged over the composition of the *Iliad* and *Odyssey* has raged also over *Beowulf*. It is said that it is a single poem composed by one man; and, on the contrary, that it is a poem built up, in process of time, by various hands, and consisting of various lays of different ages; and this opinion, to take one instance, has been worked out by Müllenhof with a minuteness which makes the most severe demands upon our credulity. We are to conceive first of two old lays by different authors, then of a continuation of one of these, and then of an introduction to the whole by two other authors. The fifth—a reviser—added another portion and altered the previous work to suit his addition, and another reviser, the sixth in the series, increased the poem by episodes from other sagas and by Christian interpolations. Elaborate arrangements of this kind are as doubtful as they are interesting. The main point, however, seems clear. *Beowulf* was built up out of many legends which in time coalesced into something of a whole, or were, as I think, composed together into a poem by one poet. The legends were sung in the Old England across the seas, and brought to our England by the Angles, or by that band of Jutes or Saxons whom many suppose to have settled, at an early time, in northern Northumbria. They were then sung in Northumbria, added to by Northumbrian singers, and afterwards, when Christianity was still young, compressed and made into a poem by a Christian singer.

The first question we have to ask is with regard to the date of the story. Is it entirely mythical and legendary, or is there any actual history contained in it which will enable us to date its composition? Such a connection with known history has been suggested. The Hygelac of the poem, Beowulf's lord, has been identified with the King Chochilaicus, who is mentioned in the *Historia Francorum* of Gregory of Tours, and in another chronicle—the *Gesta Regum Francorum*.

About 512-520, when the conquest of Britain had but begun, when the victory of the Britons at Mount Badon caused a long pause in the advance of the English, we are told that Chochilaicus made an expedition from the modern Götaland to the Attuarii of the Frisian shore—the Hetware of the poem—to plunder and to slay. When he was about to leave, having laden his ships with slaves and spoil, the Frankish king Theodoric sent his son to attack him with an army of Franks and Frisians. In the battle Chochilaicus fell and all the booty was recovered.

This affair is four times mentioned in the poem of *Beowulf*, if we identify Hygelac with Chochilaicus. We are told that fate carried away Hygelac in feud against the Frisians. He fell under his shield. His life and the jewelled collar he had from Beowulf passed into the power of the Franks. Beowulf himself, before he goes down to fight with the dragon, tells of this fight; how Hygelac fell, how he avenged his lord's death. Two other allusions are made in the poem to the same expedition and battle. It is said, therefore, that it must have been after the date of 520 that the main story of the poem arose. Of that there can be no doubt, but we have also to remember that parts of the poem are drawn from lays older than 520 ; lays, some of which, as the preface about Scyld, may go back to a remote antiquity. But the poem itself carries us past the death of Hygelac in 520 to Beowulf's death in 570. Only after that date, then, could the last part—the fight with the Dragon—begin to be welded to the first part of the story, and this would take at least thirty years to accomplish. This would bring us to the year 600. If we take that date, and if we make the poem Northumbrian, this first interweaving of the lays would be made about the time of Æthelfrith, before Northumbria had become Christian.[1]

---

[1] This argument is based on the supposition that Beowulf was, at least partly, an historical personage. But the supposition is a doubtful one, and we can come to no certainty with regard to the date of the story. I have almost assumed that the poem arose into shape in Northumbria, but Professor Earle thinks that Mercia was the place of its birth, and Ten Brink endeavours to establish West

The second question to ask is, Where is the scene of the poem laid? It has been supposed by some, who hold that it was composed from end to end in England, that the scenery is English, and Mr. Haigh has ingeniously endeavoured to identify its descriptions with places on the coast of Yorkshire. But there is not one word about our England in the poem, not a single hint that the original singers knew of the existence of such a people as the English in Britain. The personages, the tribes are all of the continent— North, South, East and West Danes, the Geats, the Sweons, and the Frisians. The Danes dwelt in Seeland, and their chief town was there; the Geats in Scandinavia, in Götaland, and their king's town was on the west coast near the mouth of the Götaelf. The name Wederas and Weder-Geatas suggested to Grein a connection with the Island Väderöe or Veiröe, and with the group of islands Väderöane. The scenery then is laid on the coast of the North Sea and the Kattegat, the first act of the poem among the Danes in Seeland, the second among the Geats in South Sweden.

It is held then that the earliest lays of the story arose among the Geats and the Danes, and it is chiefly with these tribes, their manners, and their customs, that we are here concerned. But their manners and their customs were the same as those of the Angles. Angle and Geat and Dane spoke the same language, and were all kinsmen—and I am not sure whether we might not with propriety call Angle the tribes of South Sweden, or at least the Geats of the poem. At

---

Saxon connections for it. Professor Earle's interesting book, *The Deeds of Beowulf*, has just been published, and his theory of the origin of the poem is fully expounded in it.

any rate *Beowulf* became English. The earliest lays of the poem were adopted by the older England on the mainland,[1] the scenery of the poem was scenery with which the elder English were well acquainted before they came to Britain. However we may hold that the poem was altered and edited, its foundation lays were sung by a people who lived in South Sweden, in Denmark, in the Isles, and about the Elbe. Having thus conjectured the date at which the story began to take shape, and the place in which it arose, we may ask what theory we may form concerning its upbuilding. A multitude of theories have been put forward, differing here and there in minor points from one another. But the main lines are almost the same in the greater number, and I have brought them together here into as compact a form as I can.[2] The account is eclectic; I have added a few conjectures of my own, and I must risk some repetition for the sake of clearness.

The date of the death of Hygelac (512-520) is taken

---

[1] There is a theory of Ettmüller's which is interesting. In his view the story arose in the sixth or seventh century among the Geatas, inhabitants of South Scandinavia, who along with the Danes set up a Dano-Gautic kingdom which lasted till 720 or 730 A.D. But there were Danish and Geat settlers from this kingdom in Northumbria in the eighth century, and these brought the Song of Beowulf with them. Then some English poet, a layman, perhaps a pagan, put it into vernacular English. Afterwards, in the eighth or ninth century, this poem was redone by a clerical person in the West Saxon dialect.

Another suggestion may be made. If it should ever come to be clearly established—as some believe—that a branch of the same Jutish folk who seized on Kent in 450, had, about the same time, settled on the coast of Scotland, south of the Forth, so that Eadwine when he came there found English already spoken in the country—why then, the mythical lays of Beowa (added afterwards to the Beowulf legend) may have been brought to this part of England and sung in English there as early as the fifth century—and by the very folk, the Jutes, among whom they originally rose. The Angles would then have found them there, heard them sung, and adapted these mythic lays to their Beowulf story.

[2] They will all be found with all their differences in Wülker's *Grundriss*, pp. 269, etc. etc. The above account follows, on the whole, the analysis Ten Brink, following others, makes of the origin of the lays; but it does not disallow, but rather avers, that the poem, as we have it, was put into form by one poet, and with a distinct effort at unity of effect and purpose.

as the starting-point of the poem, and it is supposed that there was a Beowulf—an historical personage—who was present at his overthrow, a relation of Hygelac's, a mighty warrior and seaman, whose strength was very great—so that in tradition it was said to be as the strength of thirty men—and who slew the slayer of Hygelac in the fight. The fame of this great warrior (unmentioned in the *Chronicle* of Gregory of Tours) had been, according to the poem, spread far and wide among the Geats, the Island Danes, and the Angles, but now it became still greater. In every hall, at every feast, while he was alive, his gests were sung, and out of these rude songs was formed the germ of the story. After his death in 570 he grew into the legendary hero; wonderful tales collected round his boyhood, like the story of the swimming match with Breca, and his manhood's deeds became more and more marvellous. These legends entered into the original historic lays or became separate lays. A hero saga had begun, and was spread all over South Sweden and Denmark, among Geats, Danes, Angles, and it may be among the Saxons. That is the first step. The second is the addition to the legend of already existing myth, and of lays which were older than the historic Beowulf, older, that is, than the sixth century. It is suggested that there was among these Scandinavian, Danish, and Angle tribes an ancient myth concerning a divine hero whose name was Beowa, whom the introduction of the poem describes as one of the ancestors of Hrothgar the Dane. Beowa is the son of Scyld, son of Sceaf, who appears in the Anglo-Saxon genealogies as one of the ancestors of Woden. Beaw is his name in these genealogies, and we find traces of him in some names of places in England, such as Beowanhamm and Grendlesmere. This mythic hero was the real conqueror of Grendel and the conqueror of the Dragon. As time went on, these mythic deeds were transferred to the historic Beowulf. The subject had now grown into almost epic proportions. Not very much later the second part of the Grendel story was added to the first—the fight with Grendel's mother. The additions afterwards made—the episode of Scyld, of Finn's battle, of the Swedish war, of Thrytho,[1] and others—were such as might easily be foisted in by different bards, to fill up the portions of the saga which they chose out for their evening song to the warriors. Many more, no doubt, crept in, but those that remain are those which Time has selected. The lays in this condition were developed in our England and continued to be sung, even after the introduction of Christianity, in their ancient pagan shape. The warriors in hall were not likely to ask for any Christianising of these songs. Lastly, some poet, with much sympathy for heathen sagas and with as much Christianity as belonged to a man of the world, took all the lays, recast them in his own mind, formed them into a whole, embodied the episodes out of other sagas, conceived the character of Beowulf afresh, and with an ethical purpose, made it the central motive of the whole, and wrote the poem, for the most

---

[1] The episode of Thrytho, for example, and all the allusions to the Offa legend in the latter part of the poem might very easily have been intruded into it by some singer of Offa's court, in order to please or admonish the king, or Ecgferth his son. The poem reads in the special place where this episode occurs as if this had been done. It is there in much confusion, and the insertion seems never to have been harmonised with the original. I should conjecture that this episode was the very last which was introduced into the poem. This is very different from saying, as Earle does, that the Offa episode gives the key to the formation of the whole poem; and that the poem was made, as it stands, at the court of Offa, with the distinct purpose of instructing Ecgferth in the duties of a prince.

part, as it is. This is different from saying, as so many do, that it was a fortuitous congeries of lays; but, at the same time, it asserts—and it is necessary to assert this—that there were separate Beowulf lays existing, of different ages, long before this continuous poem was composed by a single poet with a single aim. He used these lays, and sometimes, it seems to me, inserted their very words. Existing thus in Northumbria from the beginning, as I think, of the eighth century, it passed through England, and I imagine that now and again slight additions were made to it by those who wished to Christianise it more than the original writer had done. To such persons, we owe, it may be, the homiletic parts of the poem. The final fortune that befell it was its translation into the Wessex dialect, and it is in that dialect that we possess it.

The last thing to say with regard to these questions of date, origin, and place is that we may fairly claim the poem as English. It is in our tongue, and in our country alone that it is preserved. The memory of it seems to have died out of South Sweden and the Danish isles. It was kept alive by the Angles, and those who preserved it and the country that sheltered it may claim the honour of its possession. In its pages are our folk, their ways of life and fashion of thought; and not only ours, but those of all North Teutonic folk from the end of the fifth century to the end of the seventh, to the end, I daresay, of the eighth. Any record of the manners and customs of the Teutonic peoples of those centuries is of great historical value. We have in the ancient Teutonic laws hints which throw light upon the habits of that time; but we have little that vividly represents the daily life of the North Teutonic peoples. It is this very want which is supplied by *Beowulf*. That tale gives us a picture of human life at this early time—let us say from the sixth to the eighth century—full of detail, painted in colours fresh and vivid, in which we see the works of war and peace, the king's hall, the harbour and the coast, the ships a-sailing, the life of the rovers, the settled town, the moorland round it, the hunt, the feast, the relations of the chief to his thegns and to his people, the customs of the court, of land and of gifts, the position of women, the burial of great personages. Behind the wars and tribal wanderings, behind the contentions of the great, we watch in this poem the steady, continuous life of home, the passions and thoughts of men, the way they talked and moved and sang and drank and lived and loved among one another and for one another. This is the value of *Beowulf* as history, and it is of especial worth to us. It is a record of the way our forefathers lived both on the continent and in our own country, and the record ought to be of surpassing interest.

There are other matters of interest which belong to the poem, matters religious, mythical, and literary, but they will be better discussed in another place. At present only one thing more remains before we come to the poem itself. It is to collect out of it the early history of its hero, and to bring that history up to the point at which the poem begins. There are materials enough for this work. Many allusions are made to the hero's youth. He gives an account of his early years in his death song. His dearest comrade, Wiglaf, speaks of his early wars. To collect all these scattered hints into one continuous story will make the whole poem clearer, and will enable me to sketch the character of Beowulf as he appears in youth and manhood. It is the English ideal of a hero as it was conceived by an Englishman some twelve hundred years ago.

Among the thegns who served Hrethel, King of the Geats, was Ecgtheow, of the family of the Waegmundings, a wise and great warrior; and Hrethel, seeing his prowess, gave him his only daughter to wife, and of these two came Beowulf whom his grandfather loved, for he left to him a famous coat of mail that Weland the great forgeman had smithied. Now Hrethel had three sons, Herebeald, Haetheyn, and Hygelac, and these were uncles of Beowulf. The first two perished before the action of the poem opens, and only Hygelac was left alive to be King of the Geats. Hygelac had a daughter who is scarcely in the story, and, by his second (?) wife Hygd a son called Heardred, Beowulf's cousin. Not one of these is left alive at the conclusion of the poem. On his mother's side all Beowulf's kindred are gone.

On his father's side, that is among the Waegmundings, none are left but Wiglaf, son of Weohstan; the last thus of all the hero's race, for Beowulf died childless. This fewness of kindred, this solitariness, is one of the pathetic points of the poem. Beowulf speaks of it again and again; to Hrothgar, to Hygelac, to others; and it is the last of his thoughts when he is dying. This, as well as his immense strength, isolates the hero, and the inward pathos of it—always great to a Northman—gave him, it may be, some of that gentleness for which, among a violent race, he is celebrated in the saga. Mildness and more than mortal daring meet in him, and the mildness, even more than the daring, separates his figure from the rest.

Ecgtheow, his father, had in his younger days

great praise among the coasts and isles for the mighty fight he had with Heatholaf, a Wylfing, whom he slew with his own hand. Then he took to roaming the seas and reached in his roaming the court of Hrothgar, King of the Scylding Danes, when Hrothgar was still young, and he became the king's man. For Hrothgar healed, for his sake, Ecgtheow's feud with the Wylfings, sending old-time treasures to them over the water's ridge. Afterwards, Ecgtheow went back to the land of the Geats, taking with him his son Beowulf, who seems to have been known, perhaps born, at Hrothgar's court, and settled in his home, "living many winters ere he died, and all the wise men, far and wide on earth, remembered him." This wisdom descends to Beowulf. Though he is young when he comes to Hrothgar to conquer Grendel, it is of his counsel as much as of his strength that we hear. Wealhtheow, the queen, begs him to be friendly in counsel to her sons. Hrothgar says to him, "thou holdest thy fame with patience, and thy might with prudence of mind. Thou shalt be a comfort to thy people and a help to heroes." When he gives an account of the patched-up truce between the Danes and the Heathobeards, his political vision of the end shows how clear and experienced was his judgment of human nature. When Hygelac his lord is dead, Hygd the queen begs him to rule the kingdom because its foes were many, and none could order matters more wisely than he. When he is dying, he looks back on his life, and that which he thinks of the most, is not his great war-deeds, but his patience, his prudence, his power of holding his own well, and of avoiding new enmities. Nowhere is this temper better shown than in the words he speaks to

Hrothgar when the king bursts out into an old man's passionate sorrow for the death of Æschere, his dearest thegn—"Sorrow not, wise man," says Beowulf, "it is better that a man should avenge his friend than mourn him overmuch. Each of us must await the close of life. Let him who can, gain honour before he die. That is best for a warrior, when he is dead. But do thou, throughout this day, have patience of thy woes; I look for that from thee."

Gentle like Nelson, he had Nelson's iron resoluteness. What he undertook to do, he went through without a thought save of getting to the end of it. His very words when he spoke made those who heard him conscious of his firm-set purpose (line 611). "Firm-minded Prince" is one of his names. The heights his character gained he was able to keep; and a similar phrase to that is twice used of the hero. Fear is wholly unknown to him, and he seems, like Nelson, to have inspired his captains with his own courage. It is a notable touch that when his thegns go to bed in the hall that Grendel haunts, it is said of them "that none of them thought that he should ever again seek his well-loved home, the folk in the free burg where he was brought up"—and with this thought they all fell asleep. It is a trait worthy of the crew of the *Victory*.

But his gentleness did not keep him back from fierce self-defence. When Hunferth accused him of being beaten in his match with Breca, his answer is full of scorn, of mocking, and of savage retort. "Drunken with beer, my friend, hast thou spoken of Breca—thou who wast thine own brother's murderer. Grendel, the grisly monster, had never wrought so many ills for thy king, nor such a shame in Heorot, had thy courage been as fierce as thou claimest!" Yet afterwards, when Hunferth, sober, lends him the old-world sword, Hrunting, he forgets his wrath and asks, if he die in his fight with Grendel's mother, that Hunferth may have one of his own swords. This swift wrath, forgetfulness, and generosity, are all of Nelson's character. The boastfulness was not. Beowulf always boasts before a battle of what he has done and will do against the foe. When he is going to die he sings a death-lay of his own glories. This, of which in some writer I have seen blame, is the fashion of the Northmen. Every Icelandic story is full of it, and all who hear Beowulf boast are as much pleased as the above writer is displeased.

Nor was he less prompt in the blood-feud than in speech, but the vengeance was not private or hasty. It is specially said of him that he did not like some others, "kill his drunken hearth-companions; nor was his mind cruel." So also his sense of honour, of which he was so jealous, was not held in a nice readiness to take personal offence, but in absolute truthfulness —"I swore no false oaths," he said when dying. So also he kept his honour in faithfulness to his lord —"on foot, alone in front, while life lasted, he was his king's defence." He kept it in an equal faithfulness when his lord was dead, and that to his own loss; for when Hygd offered him the kingdom he refused; and trained Heardred, Hygelac's son, "to war and learning; guarded him kindly with honour," and avenged him when he was slain. He kept it in generosity, for he gave away all the gifts he received; in courtesy, for he gave gifts even to those who had been rude to him, and he is always gentle and grave with women. Above all, he kept it clean in war, for these things are said of him—"So shall a man do when he thinks to gain praise that shall never end, and cares not for his life in battle." "Let us have fame or death!" he cries; and when Wiglaf comes to help him against the dragon, and Beowulf is wrapt in the flame, Wiglaf recalls to him the aim of his whole life. "Beowulf beloved, bear thyself well. Thou wert wont to say in youth that thou wouldst never let Honour go. Now, strong in deeds, ward thy life, firm-souled Prince, with all thy might; I will be thy helper."

These are the qualities of the man and the hero, and I have thought it worth while to dwell on them because they represent the ancient English ideal, the manhood which pleased the English folk even before they came to Britain; and because, in all our history since Beowulf's time, for 1200 years or so, they have been repeated in the lives of the English warriors by land and sea whom we chiefly honour. The type, especially, of the great sea-captains has been the same throughout. But it is not only the ideal of a hero which we have in Beowulf, it is also the ideal of a king; the just governor, the wise politician, the builder of peace, the defender of his own folk at the price of his life; the "good king, the folk-king, the beloved king, the war-ward of the land," the winner of treasure for the need of his people, the hero who thinks in death of those who sail the sea; the gentle and terrible warrior who is buried amid the tears of his people.[1]

When Ecgtheow, to return to the tale, from whom this prudence and wisdom of Beowulf came, had settled

---

[1] At this point of view we may fall in with Professor Earle's contention that the poem was intended to set up an heroic example of a king and warrior. "It is, in short," says Earle, "the institution of a prince."

down at home. Hrethel, Beowulf's grandfather, took the boy at seven years old into his court, gave him treasures and the daily feast; and remembering his kinship, made him equal to his own sons, Herebeald, Haetheyn, and Hygelac. But the boy was at first slothful, and the Geats thought him an unwarlike prince, and long despised him. Then, like many a lazy third son in the folk-tales, a change came; he suddenly showed wonderful daring, and was passionate for adventure. In this youthful prime he challenged Breca to the swimming match and the slaying of sea-monsters, and proved himself the master of the stormy sea. After that, tragic sorrow fell upon his grandfather's house. Haetheyn, Hrethel's second son, slew by mistake his eldest brother, piercing him to the heart with "an arrow from his hornèd bow," and Beowulf, more than sixty years afterwards, recalls in a pathetic passage the terrible grief of Hrethel, and compares it to the grief of an aged freeman who lives to see his young son hung on the gallows tree, a joy of ravens. Old and gray-headed, he can give his boy no help. Morning after morning he remembers his dead.

2456.
 Sorrow-laden does he look,   in the Bower of his son,
 On the wasted wine-hall,   on the wind-swept resting-places.
 Now bereft of joyous noise.
            Far the Riders sleep :
 In their howe the heroes lie.   Clang of harp is there no more,
 In the dwellings no delight,   as in days of old.[1]

So Hrethel mourned; "dirge after dirge he sang. All too empty meadows and dwellings seemed to him,"

[1] These verses have the look of an insertion, as if the poet knew of this mournful song and used it for this place. I should like to be able, in this fashion, to class it as an old English lyric. It has picturesqueness, simplicity, and passion; and a sweet movement. Compare—

    He saddens, all the magic light
    Dies off at once from bower and hall,
    And all the place is dark, and all
    The chambers emptied of delight.

and of that pain he died. And Haetheyn his brother's slayer became king, and strife broke out between him and the Sweons over the wide water. For Haetheyn had borne away the young wife of Ongentheow, the Sweon king, in vengeance of the raiding Ohthere and Onela, Ongentheow's sons, had done on his land at Hreosnabeorh. Then Ongentheow, old and terrible, pursued and hewed down the sea-chief Haetheyn, and took again his wife. He drove his foes before him into Raven's-wood, and they were weary of wounds, bereft of their king. All the night long he laid siege against them, taunting them that in the morning he would slay them with the sword or hang them on the gallows for sport to the fowls of the air. But in the dawn they heard Hygelac's horn and trumpets sounding, and took comfort. Brother came to avenge brother, Hygelac to avenge Haetheyn, following the bloody tracks of yesterday's battle. And Ongentheow sought the heights, fearful of the seamen, warding his wife and sons, and refuged in the earth fort. But victory was to Hygelac; Ongentheow's gray hairs did not save him from death. Wulf, son of Wonred, met the Sweon king, and smote so hard that the blood spurted in streams under his hair. Fiercely the old hero struck back, and Wulf fell, his helmet cleft, on the earth, but was not yet fated, and stood up, though his wound pained him. Then Eofor, Wulf's brother, rushed in on Ongentheow, and let his broadsword—an old sword of the giants—break over the shield-rim on the helmet of Ongentheow, and the king bowed down, struck to his life. And Eofor took from him his byrnie of iron, his hard-hilted sword and his helm, and carried them to Hygelac. So Hygelac became king, and gave gifts to Wulf; and to Eofor he gave his only daughter. That is the feud and that the enmity between the Sweons and the Geats.[1]

In some of these wars Beowulf took part. "He had avenged," he says, "the sorrows of the Weders." But he had also roamed the seas and undertaken many adventures, and by the time he went to Hrothgar, when the poem opens, he had seen many of the fates of men. We are told that his strength was spoken of "from hall to hall by the sea-farers," and his fame widespread, through distant ways. Though he was still young then, he had known life, and it seemed to him grim; needing fortitude rather than joy. To deepen this, came the Teutonic doctrine of the fate-goddess Wyrd, whose hand arranged the destinies of men, and had settled their death-day. The name of the goddess passed to the thing she ordained, and in the later interpolations of the poem the word is used in this sense, as well as in the sense of a personal Being. We hear of Wyrd herself, and we hear of the Weirds of men. The doctrine naturally acted differently on different types of men, and the poet makes it act with distinction on Beowulf himself. It settles his courage with firmness in the midst of desperate adventure. "'Wyrd' goes ever as it must," he says, when he thinks he may be torn by Grendel to pieces. "It shall be," he cries, when he goes to fight the dragon, "for us in the fight as Wyrd shall foresee." Yet his position is not that of pure Fatalism. The goddess may save a man if only his courage keeps his might at full strength in the

---

[1] Nor then did it end, for the grandsons of Ongentheow—Eanmund, and Eadgils came into the land of the Geatas, and Eanmund slew Heardred, Hygelac's son, at a feast. Weohstan the Waegmunding, Wiglaf's father, then took up the feud and slaughtered Eanmund. Long afterwards Eadgils, invading again the Geatas, is slain by Beowulf. Three generations the quarrel lasted, and when Beowulf dies, one of his warriors declares that the deadly hate will break out again.

battle. "Wyrd often preserves a hero from death if his power is at its best. Nor yet was I fated," he says to Hygelac when he describes his fight with Grendel's mother. While this sense of a fixed fate made him resolute to put into battle all his strength, it also established in him, combined as it was with his gentleness and tenderness, that grave melancholy of life so characteristic of the Northmen. However men fought and endured, Wyrd had doomed them. This appears all through the poem, and Beowulf's last words are, "Wyrd carried away all my kinsmen at the fated time."

It was, then, not only the mighty aspect of the man, with his thirty-fold strength, but it was also the grave conception he had of life written on his face, which made the warden of the coast, and Wulfgar, when they beheld him, say, " Never saw I greater earl, nor one of a more matchless air." With this went also the passion for new life, for movement, which Tennyson has drawn in *Ulysses*, but which is far more English than Greek; the inability to remain at ease, the longing "to strive, to seek, to find, and not to yield," which has always been the mark of English seamen.

Hygelac was now at peace; all the wars were over; and Beowulf could not stay feasting in the hall. Some wandering sailors told him of the trouble of Hrothgar from Grendel. I will go on adventure, he thought, as Drake would think years afterwards, and deliver the Danish king. His thegns "whetted him" to the deed; the sea-chief sailed away, and the poem begins. We approach it with a reverence which it deserves for its great age, and with a delight which is born of its association with the history of our people and our poetry. It is a moment of romantic pleasure when we stand beside the long undiscovered sources of an historic river, beside whose waters a hundred famous cities have arisen. It is a moment of the same romantic pleasure when we first look at the earliest upwelling of the broad river of English poetry, and think of the hundred cities of the imagination that have been built beside its stream.

CHAPTER III

BEOWULF

The Poem

THE poem opens with an account of the forefathers of Hrothgar the Scylding, King of the Danes. He is the builder of Heorot, the hall where Beowulf contends with Grendel. Hrothgar is the second son of Healfdene, who is the son of another Beowulf than the hero of the poem; and this other Beowulf is the son of Scyld, from whom the dynasty of the Scyldings takes its name. In ancient days, so ran the legend, Scyld, when he was but a child, was drifted in an open boat to the shores of the Danes. When coming thus out of the secret of the sea the bark touched the land, the folk found the naked child lying asleep in the midst of arms and gems and golden treasure, and took him up and hailed him king. With as many treasures as he brought, with so many they sent him away when he died.

As he came alone and mysteriously out of the sea, so he passes away alone and mysteriously into the sea, and the introduction to the poem describes his burial. It is the burial of a hero who had passed into a divine being, but it is also the burial of a great sea-king, the earliest record by some hundred years—for the introduction is probably from an ancient song about Scyld—of many burials of the same kind among the Northern lords; but touched with so poetic a hand that it is first of all accounts in art as it is first in time.

When the hour of fate had come, Scyld departed. Then his faithful comrades bore him down to the flowing of the sea,

> There at haven stood,   hung with rings,[1] the ship.
> Ice-bright, for the outpath eager,   craft of Æthelings!
> So their lord, the well-beloved,   all at length they laid
> In the bosom of the bark,   him the bracelet-giver,—
> By the mast the mighty king.   Many gifts were there,
> Fretted things of fairness   brought from far-off ways!—
> Never heard I of a keel   hung more comelily about
> With the weeds of war,   with the weapons of the battle,
> With the bills and byrnies.   On his breast there lay
> A great heap of gems   that should go with him,
> Far to fare away   in the Flood's possession.
>
> . . . . . .
>
> Then they also set   all of gold a standard,
> High above his head;   let the heaving ocean bear him,
> Gave him to the sea.   Sad was then their soul,
> Mourning was their mood.   None of men can say,
> None of heroes under heaven,   nor in hall the rulers,
> For a truthful truth,   who took up that lading.
>
> *Beowulf*, ll. 30-40, 47-52.

Thus, into the silence of the sea the hero went alone, lying dead among his treasures, and the wind in his banner of battle. It is a later heathen belief that the souls pass over an unknown water to the realms beyond, and it may be that this belief was one of the reasons why the Northmen sometimes buried their dead in boats, so that when they came to this great sea they might have carriage. Odinn, in after-myth, receives those who are buried like Scyld. When Sigmund bears Sinfiötli to the seashore, he lays him in a skiff which a gray-mantled pilot brings to the beach. This is

---

[1] *Hringed-stefna* is sometimes translated "with curved prow," but it means, I think, that in the prow were fastened rings through which the cables were passed which tied it to the shore.

Odinn, and he sails away with the body. Balder himself, whose myth is later than this of Scyld, is buried in a great ship. The gods place his body on a pyre in the midst of the bark; it is set on fire, and pushed into the sea.[1] Even a living man, in later times, buried himself in the way of Scyld. Flosi, in the Njal saga, weary of life, puts out to sea in a boat that all men called unseaworthy. "'Tis good enough," he said, "for a death-doomed man." Of him, too, it might be said, "none of men could tell who took up that lading."

As the poem begins with this burial, so it ends with the burial of Beowulf. His burial has nothing mythic, nothing mystic surrounding it. It might be that of an historical personage; and the contrast between the shore-burial and the sea-burial is worth making immediately. Beowulf, dead after his fight with the dragon, and his gray hair lying round his head, is borne to the top of the great cliff that overlooks the sea, to the very edge, where the wanderers on the sea may hereafter mark his lofty barrow. The cliff has its own name. Men saw from its height the whales tumbling in the waves, and called it Whale's Ness (Hrones-naes). There then the folk of the Geats made ready a funeral pyre, firm-fixed on the earth, and they hung it with helms and with shields of the war-host, with shining shirts of battle, as the hero had asked of them—

> In the midst thereof   the mighty-famous king,
> Their belovèd lord,   mourning, laid the warriors.
> Then the hugest of Bale-fires   'gan the heroes waken

---

[1] In the Ynglinga Saga, the burial of Haki is nearer to that of Scyld. Sore wounded, he had one of his ships loaded with dead men and weapons, and the sail hoisted. Then he let tarred wood be kindled, and a pyre made on the ship, while the wind blew seaward. Almost dead, he was laid on the pyre and the burning ship sailed out to sea. None of these, however, quite resembles the burial of Scyld, the most romantic, I think, of them all.

> High upon the hill,   and the reek of wood arose
> Swart above the swimming fire,[1]   while the hissing sound of flame
> Was with weeping woven—   for the wail of wind was still—
> Till the fire had broken   house of bone in twain,
> Hot upon his heart   .   .   .
>   Heaven devoured the smoke.
>   *Beowulf*, l. 3143.

This was the burning; after the burning the barrow is raised; and it shall be told at the end how the people of the Weders built up on the point of the Ness a mound, high and broad, to be seen from far by the sailors whom Beowulf loved. There is yet another burial told of in the poem. The bard at Hrothgar's table sings of the death of Hnaef, kinsman of Hildeburh (perhaps her brother), and of the burning of Hildeburh's son on the same pyre as Hnaef. "The blood-stained battle-sark, the golden helm, the boar crest, iron-hard, were piled on the wood; and, with the two chieftains, many another Ætheling who had fallen, writhing on the field of slaughter."

> Then beside the pyre of Hnaef   Hildeburh bade
> Lay her well-beloved son   all along the blazing flame,
> For to burn the bone-chest—   on the bale to place him.
> Wretched was the woman,   wept upon his shoulder,
> Sorrowed in her dirges,   and the smoke of war arose![2]
> Curling to the clouds   went the greatest of corpse-fires,
> Hissing round the burial-howe.   Then the heads were molten,
> Gaped the gates of all the wounds;   then out gushed the blood
> From the foe's bite on the body;   and the blaze devoured all,
> Greediest it of ghosts.   *Beowulf*, l. 1114.

This is an inland burial, but the other two are by the sea; and the sea-note struck thus at the beginning and close of the poem is heard constantly sounding

---

[1] *Swiodole* is here, I think, the quivering clear space of vaporous flame between the burning body and the dark-rolling smoke above it; at least this is the way I here understand *swadul* or *sweodol*, which is taken to mean "vaporous flame," sometimes "smoky flame," but the word is obscure.

[2] The other reading is *Gudrinc*, which would mean "the hero of battle passed upwards in the flame."

through its verse. The men are sea-folk. Beowulf in his youth is a sea-rover, a fighter with sea-monsters, a mighty swimmer of the sea. All the action is laid on the sea-coast. The inland country, not the sea, is the unknown, the terrible. Grendel and his dam are more sea-demons than demons of the moor. Their cave is underneath the sea. Nor in the last part of the poem are we without the all-prevailing presence of the ocean. The dragon lives in a cavern on the edge of the sea. The king and the dragon fight in the hearing of the waves. Beowulf's barrow, heaped high on the edge of the sea-ness, is a beacon for "those who sail through the mists of the sea." The background of all the action is the great deep — the chorus, as it were, of this story of the fates of men. Thus the ocean life, the ocean mystery, the battle with the ocean and on the ocean begin the English poetry, and they are as vivid in it now as they were in the youth of our people. The *Battle of the Baltic*, the *Fight of the Revenge*, the *Sailor Boy*, *Hervé Riel*, Swinburne's sea-songs, a hundred ballads, taste of the same brine and foam which the winds drove in the faces of the men who wrote *Beowulf*, the *Seafarer*, and the *Riddles* which concern the sea. Nay, more, the very temper of mind which pervades modern poetry of the sea — a mingling of melancholy and exaltation — is to be found in English poetry before the Conquest, and strange to say it is not found again, except in scattered ballads, till we reach our own century.

The action of the poem now begins with the voyage of Beowulf to the Danish coast. The hero has heard that Hrothgar, the chief of the Danes, is tormented by Grendel, a man-devouring monster. If

Hrothgar's warriors sleep in Heorot—the great hall he has built— they are seized, torn to pieces, and devoured. "I will deliver the king," thought Beowulf, when he heard the tale from roving seamen. "Over the swan-road I will seek Hrothgar; he has need of men." His comrades urged him to the adventure, and fifteen of them were willing to fight it out with him. Among the rest was a sea-crafty man who knew the ocean-paths. Their ship lay drawn up on the beach, under the high cliff. Then

>   There the well-geared heroes
> Stepped upon the stem,   while the stream of ocean
> Whirled the sea against the sand.   To the ship, to its breast,
> Bright and carvèd things of cost   carried then the heroes,
> And the armour well-arrayed.   So the men outpushed,
> On desired adventure,   their tight ocean-wood.
> Swiftly went above the waves   with a wind well-fitted,
> Likest to a fowl, the Floater,   foam around its neck,
> Till about the same time,   on the second day,
> The up-curvèd prow   had come on so far,
> That at last the seamen   saw the land ahead;
> Shining sea-cliffs,   soaring headlands,
> Broad sea-nesses.   So the Sailer of the Sea[1]
> Reached the sea-way's end.   *Beowulf,* l. 211.

This was the voyage, ending in a fiord with two high sea-capes at its entrance. The same kind of scenery belongs to the land whence they set out. When Beowulf returns over the sea the boat groans as it is pushed forth. It is heavily laden; the hollow, under the single mast with the single sail, holds eight horses, swords and treasure and rich armours. The sail is hoisted, the wind drives the foam-throated bark over the waves, until they see the Geats' cliffs—the well-known sea-nesses. The keel is pressed up by the wind on the sand, and the "harbour-guard, who had looked forth afar o'er the sea with longing for

---

[1] I have taken *sand-lida*, for 'the ship'; but *sand lidan*, which is Wülker's reading, makes the line "then was the *Sea sailed over*, at the end of the sea-way."

their return"—one of the many human touches of the poem—"fastens the wide-bosomed ship with anchoring chains to the strand, lest the violence of the waves should sweep away the winsome boat."

I have brought the two voyages together that we may see the customs of embarking and disembarking twice over, and realise the kind of sea and coast the shipmen of the poem sailed by—brief stretches of sea, between short bays protected on either side by capes rising from the mainland till they became cliffs above the open sea. At the end of the bay into which Beowulf sails is a low shore, on which he drives his ship, stem on. Planks are pushed out on either side of the prow; the Weder folk slipped down on the shore, tied up their sea-wood; their battle-sarks clanged on them as they moved. Then they thanked the gods that the wave-paths had been easy to them.

The scene which follows is almost Homeric in its directness and simplicity, and in the clearness with which it is presented. On the ridge of the hill above the landing-place the ward of the coast of the Scyldings sat on his horse, and saw the strangers bear their bright shields over the bulwarks of the ship to the shore. He rode down, wondering, to the sea, and shook mightily in his hands his heavy spear, and called to the men—

> Who are ye of men having arms in hand,
> Covered with your coats of mail who your keel afoaming
> O'er the ocean street thus have urged along.
> Hither on the high sea
> . .
> . .
> Never saw I greater
> Earl upon this earth than is one of you :
> Hero in his harness. He is no home-stayer,
> 'Less his looks belie him, lovely with his weapons.
> N.. is his air ! *Beowulf*, ll. 237, 247.

Beowulf replies that he is Hrothgar's friend, and comes to free him from "Grendel, the secret foe on the dark nights." He pities Hrothgar, old and good. Yet, as he speaks, the Teutonic sense of the inevitable Wyrd passes by in his mind, and he knows not if Hrothgar can ever escape sorrow. "If ever," he says, "sorrow should cease from him, release ever come, and the welter of care become cooler." The coast guard shows them the path, and promises to watch over their ship. The ground rises from the shore, and they pass on to the hilly ridge, behind which lies Heorot. What do they see as they look backward and forward from the ridge? This is the place to collect together all that can be said of the scenery in which the action is laid, and I shall not say anything of it, not even use an adjective, for which I have not some authority in the poem.[1]

Behind them lay the head of the bay, the low sandy shore on which they had driven their ship; the ship itself tied by cables to the strand. The deep blue water beyond spread out, between two rising nesses, to the entrance of the fiord through which, as through a gate, they saw the open sea. Only one figure animated this landscape, the Coast-ward, sitting high on his horse, with his spear resting on his thigh. Below them, as they looked landward, about a mile away, the great hall, Heorot, rose in the midst of a cultivated plain, which years of labour had reclaimed from the moor and fen. On every side of it the wild land climbed slowly upwards, on one side towards the coast, on the other to the savage and uninhabited inland country.

[1] The sole exception to this is what I say about the gard r 1-land, and the women tending the cattle.

The hall was a rectangular, high-roofed, wooden building, its long sides facing north and south. The two gables, at either end, had stag-horns on their points, curving forwards, and these, as well as the ridge of the roof, were probably covered with shining metal, and glittered bravely in the sun. Round about it lay the village, scattered houses, each in its own garth, with apple-trees and beehives and outhouses. Outside these was the corn-land, and the meadows on which sheep, oxen, and horses were grazing. Paths went in and out among the houses, and there was a wide meadow, like a village green, in the midst, between the hall and the houses of the hamlet, down which in the morning walked the king and queen from the sleeping-chambers to the hall, attended by their young men and maidens. On the outskirts of the meadow, and out into the open, the young men rode, breathing their horses; and in a place apart, as poets love it, walked to and fro the bard, framing his songs for the evening feast. The women sat spinning at their doors, or moved hither and thither, carrying water or attending to the cattle. This then was an island of tilled and house-built land at the edge of a wild waste of fen, but at a short distance from the sea. It is the image of a hundred settlements such as the Angles and Danes and Geats had built, and whence their young men ran out their ships to harry richer shores.

When Beowulf and his men looked inland beyond the dwellings, they saw nothing but the great moorland where the wolf and the stag and the wild boar roamed at will. Patches of wood were scattered over it, and these grew thicker towards the horizon, where the whole moor lifted into low hills. Over it, in ceaseless movement, the gray mists rose and fell, and among them, as night drew down her helm, dreadful creatures seemed to stalk, and the loathsome light of their eyes burned through the mist like flame.[1]

When, turning from the inland, the men looked towards the sea, they saw that the coast was broken into short bays and headlands, down to which the moor ran from the hills. Between each headland there was a narrow valley, hollowed out by descending streams, and each stream finally fell over a ledge of rock into the head of a bay. The slopes rising into the nesses were "steep and stony," and the trees that grew along the bed of the streams were rough and blasted by the sea salt and the wind—"a joyless wood." And among these fiords, at the head of a cavernous sea-gorge, there was close to Heorot a deadly place which they were afterwards to do with, of which a clear description is given in the text. It is the dwelling-place of Grendel and his dam—"the mickle mark-steppers who hold the moors"— the sea-end of a "hidden land, wolf-haunted, full of dangerous morasses." This was the scene they saw, but it was scarcely new to the men, for they daily looked on a similar landscape in their own land.

What they had now to do was to reach Heorot,

---

[1] I may as well, to illustrate this description, quote the passage from Ælfred's Orosius where Ohthere gives an account to the king of the scenery of the Northmen's coast. In his time there was, no doubt, in South Sweden and Jutland a wider fringe between the sea and the moor than that which Ohthere gives to the upper coast of Norway. But when *Beowulf* was first sung, it is more than probable that the coasts of the Geats and Danes were sparsely populated. At any rate this following passage is interesting: "Ohthere said that the coast of the Northmen was very long and very narrow. All that is fit either for pasture or plowing lies along the sea-coast, which, however, is in some parts very cloddy. Along the eastern side are wild moors, extending a long way up parallel to the cultivated land. The Finlanders dwell in the moors." The distance varies between the sea and the moors, but "northward, where it is narrowest, it may be only three miles across, but the moors are in some parts so wide that a man could scarcely pass over them in two weeks, though in other parts perhaps in six days." Ingram's translation of Ohthere's account.

and they took the "path paved with stones" which led straight from the low ridge to the "glittering hall." As they walked

> Hard and riveted by hand,
> Beamed the battle byrnie.   Braced with rings, the sheer sword
> Sang upon their shirts of war[1]   when aforward to the hall,
> In their grisly war-gear,   ganging on they came.
> Then they set, sea-wearied,   broadly-shapen shields,
> Targets wondrous hard,   'gainst the wall of Heorot!
> And they bowed above the bench,   and their byrnies rattled,
> War-array of Æthelings!   Up arose the spears,
> Weapons of sea rovers,   stood up all together,
> Gray above, a grove of ash.   *Beowulf*, l. 321.

Outside the hall a warrior on guard asks them of their ancestry and their coming.

> From what land do ye bear   your gold-flakèd shields,
> Gray-coloured sarks   and grinning-masked helms
> And a heap of host-shafts?   Of Hrothgar I am
> Voice-man and servant.   Ne'er saw I strangers—
> So many of men—   of a mightier mood.
> I ween that in war-pride   and not in outlawry,
> But for high-heartedness,   Hrothgar ye sought.
>   *Beowulf*, l. 333.

Beowulf tells his tale, and Wulfgar, "who knew the usage of the court," bids them wait without while he brings their errand to Hrothgar. Hrothgar sits on the high seat in the hall with his earls around him, old and bald-headed, and declares (and it is characteristic of the great noble throughout this tale to know the lineage of all who are also noble) that he knew Beowulf's father and mother, and Beowulf himself when he was a boy. He knew also his war deeds, and that he has the strength of thirty men in his grip. Wulfgar summons the strangers in, "the king," he says, "knows

---

[1] This is otherwise translated—"The bright ringed-iron rang on their war-shirts," that is, the iron rings of which the byrnie was made, rattled as they moved; but we have had this before, and though repetition is frequent in Anglo-Saxon poetry we need not select a repetition when the words may bear another meaning.

their kinship, but they must go into the hall armed only with helm and swords and war-shirts; their shields and spears must be left outside;" such was the custom of the court. They left the benches then that were set against the outside of the hall on either side of the door, and entered. Beowulf saw before him a hall,[1] differing somewhat in arrangement from that of his lord Hygelac. At home among the Geats there was no dais. But here, as in the later Icelandic halls, Beowulf saw Hrothgar enthroned on a high seat at the east end of the hall. This seat is sacred. It has a supernatural quality. Grendel, the fiend, cannot approach it (line 926).

His queen, Wealhtheow, sat with him, and his daughter Freaware, and their women. At the foot of the king's "gift stool," as his seat is called, sat Hunferth [2] the speaker, perhaps the jester, the boon companion of the king. The other tables ran at right angles to the dais nearly the whole length of the hall, and were covered with boar's flesh and venison and cups of ale and mead. On these benches sat the thegns of Hrothgar, and among them his sons, between whom Beowulf is afterwards seated. In the midst, on the many-coloured floor, paved perhaps with variegated stones, were the long hearths in which the fires were piled, and in the roof were openings through which the smoke escaped. The walls and supporting shafts were orna-

---

[1] Both halls are of a simple construction in comparison with the elaborate and much later Icelandic hall, such as we find in the Njal Saga. In Heorot the beds are laid with their heads against the main wall, and the place they occupy is the place of the tables and benches. In a great Icelandic hall the beds are in the aisles on either side of the body of the hall, but here the hall is without aisles.

[2] *Unferth* is perhaps the best spelling of the name. He is the bitter-tongued, the envious, the fierce-tempered in his cups. His position and character resemble closely those of Conan in the Finn Legend.

mented with gilding and walrus bone and were hung
with shields and spears, and with tapestries.

> Gold-varied gleamed
> Woven webs on the walls.
> *Beowulf*, l. 994.

This was the aspect of the hall within, and the customs
that prevailed in it are now presented to us. When
Beowulf had told of his wish to fight with Grendel,
and Hrothgar had taken his offer with joy, seats are
found for him and his companions, and the song and
feast begin again. A thegn bore round the enchased
ale-cup and poured out the pure drink. Danes and
Geats, a goodly company, sat together.

> And the Scôp, from time to time
> Chanted clear in Heorot.   There was cheer of heroes.
> *Beowulf*, l. 496.

When the song was over, Hunferth, drunk and jealous,
challenges Beowulf concerning a swimming match he
had with Breca, his rival. Hunferth declares that
Beowulf was beaten. The answer is triumphant
and laughter fills the hall. Then rose Wealhtheow,
the queen, in her golden ornaments, and greeted
the guests. But first she brought the full cup to her
husband and bade him be blithe at the beer-drinking;
and the victory-famed king took the cup with joy.
Then the great queen, peace-bringer to nations, and
followed by Freaware her daughter, went round
the hall to each of the warriors, gave a bracelet
now to one, now to another, and last of all bore the
cup to Beowulf and greeted him, and the fierce hero
took the cup from her hands and said—

"This was my thought when I shipped on the sea;
sat down in my boat with a band of my men, that I
would fully work out the will of your folk, or fall on
the field of slaughter, fast in the grips of the foe. Earl-

like will I fulfil the daring deed, or abide my end-day in this mead-hall." The proud words pleased the queen, and she went to sit beside her lord. And now night had come and the mists, and under its shadow-helm creatures came stalking, wan under the clouds. The king stood up, and his thegns; each man greeted the other. Hrothgar gave over the hall to Beowulf and went to his dwelling outside where the queen awaited him. Then the benches and tables were removed. Beowulf stripped off his armour, gave it in charge to one of his thegns, and laid down with naked hands, his cheek upon his pillow. Around him many a snell seaman stooped to his hall-rest.

Grendel now comes before us, and the main action of the first part of the story—the fight of Beowulf with him. I gather together all the things said of him in the poem. He is a grim and giant demon, of the old Eoten race, of so great strength that Beowulf, who has the power of thirty men, scarcely overcomes him. His fearful head is so huge that four men carry it with difficulty. The doors of the hall burst open with the smiting of his hand, and the hall cracks and groans with the dreadful force he puts forth in battle. His whoop in pain rings through the house. The nails of his hands are like iron, monstrous claws, and it seems he wore a kind of glove, large and strange, made fast with wonderful bands, wrought by curious skill with devil's craft and out of dragon-hides.[1] Finally, he is spelled against all weapons. Like many an Iceland troll, no sword can bite his skin; he must be fought with naked hands.

---

[1] This glove business (line 2085) is probably a Christian interpolation. No heathen Englishman would have written of devils' crafts; and the glove which is said to "hang down" is probably a kind of pouch.

He is the fiend of the moor, the quaking bog and morass. Lonely and terrible he goes, a mighty mark-stepper who holds the fen and its fastness! Perhaps the gnomic verse which tells of the Thyrs, the giant, is written with Grendel in the writer's mind—*Þyrs sceal on fenne gewunian, ana innan lande.* "The giant shall dwell in the fen, alone in the land." "In Evernight Grendel kept the misty moors." Darkness is his native land, and helmèd night. There is no joy where he is. He is called the dark death-shadow. The Christian editor brings him from Cain, with other dreadful creatures—eotens and elfs and orks and the giants (with a classical reminiscence) who fought with God. In all this he is the impersonation of the superstitious dread which men felt when they looked from their island of reclaimed land over the surrounding moors and saw the strange shapings of the cloud upon them as evening fell, and heard through the mist the roaring of the sea. Then, as men sat by the fire, dreadful tales were told, tales of those who were lost in marsh or pool, in the tempest and the snow—slain by the evil will of the ghostly dwellers in the wastes.[1] It was the same horror of the desolate lands which created in Scotland the kelpie in the black pool, the river demons of Tweed and Till, and the misshapen monsters that rose out of the sea.

For Grendel was not only the demon of the mist and moor, but also of the sea. The trackless moors in *Beowulf* ran right up to the cliffs, and the actual dwelling of Grendel and his mother is in a cave, the

---

[1] He seems to be the master and bringer of the mist, and we might illustrate this connection of his evil will with the stormy and misleading powers of nature by the power which Dante gives the Devil over mist and rain. "Quel mal voler," who
    Mosse il fume e il vento
    Per la virtù, che sua natura diede.

entrance to which is under the sea, and their companions are sea-monsters. The Mere, that is, the sea-hollow where they haunt, is called the mere of the nickers, and a full account of it and its scenery is elsewhere given. The only point to be made here is that these sea-wolves, as they are called, represent not only the ghastliness of the deadly fen, but the ghastliness of the deadly sea-gulfs among the cliffs, deep, narrow-entranced clefts filled with boiling waves, which invariably collect ghostly legend round their solitudes.

The character of this man-beast is like his shape. He is said to be greedy of blood, fierce, ravenous, furious, joyless, firm in hatred of men, pleased with evil; and he is, like evil, restless. The moment night comes he roams incessantly. It adds a special touch of horror to him that, when he had emptied Heorot by his harryings, he spends the dark nights of winter in the hall. Only at night can he appear. He is the creature of the winter and the sunless gloom, like the Icelandic Trolls who, at the touch of the sun, burst asunder, or change into stone. He abhors the pleasant noise of men, and chiefly the song and the harp, like those giants who hated agriculture and the sound of church bells. It is this which leads him to attack the hall, and when he attacks there is so much of the savageness of a wild beast in his work that some have supposed that he represents the furious bear of the North. He laughs as he sees his victims, springs on them and tears them limb from limb, breaking the bones, drinking the blood, and devouring them, head and hands and feet and all. Those he does not eat in the hall he carries away to the moor and consumes them alone, unpityingly. On the first night he invaded Heorot, he slew thirty men, but after a night or two, the warriors did not sleep in the hall for twelve years, but outside in their houses, into which he does not seem to be able to enter. Now and then, however, men, with the valour of drink in them, slept in the hall, and in the morning the mad fury of the monster is plain enough. The "benches are covered with blood, the hall afloat with gore." With all this, he has, when he meets his match, the blind fear of the wild beast, terror driving him to cry out for the darkness of the morasses whence he came; terror the Icelandic story does not give to Glam.

The description of his onset when Beowulf and his thegns wait for him in the hall is full of power. " In the wan night came the shadow-ganger stalking, while the warriors slept—all save one." Beowulf, awake in wrath, abided the battle. Then, for the poet repeats what he has said already, gathering himself together for the great event, beginning a new song—

> 711. From the moorland came, under misty hills,
> Grendel ganging on ! Wrath of God he bore ;
> Neath the clouds he strode.

He smote the door with his palms, and it fell inwards. Ireful, the bale-bringer trod over the fair-paved coloured floor. Loathsome light, like flame, stood in his eyes. He saw the heroes sleeping in the hall, and his heart laughed. He thought how he would glut his hunger. He seized a thegn and rent him to pieces. Then he laid hands on Beowulf and knew that at last he had met his match. Fear got hold of him, he strove to flee back into his native darkness. But Beowulf remembered his evening boast, and his fingers cracked as he gripped the monster. The hall sounded with the struggle; its walls cried aloud. It was wonder it did not fall to the ground. Were it not bound so fast with well-smithied bands of iron, it would have perished. Dreadful was the noise as the wrestlers wrought from bench to bench; dire terror stood over the North Danes who heard from the wall (from their houses outside) the whoop of Grendel, his awful song. The thegns of Beowulf join the fight, draw their old swords, but Grendel's flesh is charmed.

At last the grip of Beowulf dragged out Grendel's arm from the shoulder, the sinews were torn apart, the bone burst, and the monster, streaming forth blood, fled away doomed to the ocean-cave under the slopes of the fen. He reaches it and dies.

When the morning dawns Beowulf has hung the arm and claw of Grendel on the cross-beam above the king's seat in the hall; and many come to see them. Then the awaking of the hamlet is described. The men, riding, follow over the moor the blood-stained track of Grendel's flight until they reach the cliffs and the deep cleft in them where the waves are seething, and this is what they saw: "There the foaming sea was weltering with blood. The fearful upleaping of the waves, all mingled with ulcerous gore, boiled with blood of the sword. The death-doomed had dyed it when in his despair, he had laid down his life in the lair of the fen, his heathenish heart. There Hel[1] took him away." Then the old men and their young comrades come back from their glad course, proudly riding on their horses. They set the games on foot. They rode races on their yellow steeds where the paths seemed fair to them. A famed Ætheling, a king's thegn mindful of songs, who many old-time sagas remembered, framed a tale well bound together. We see him, as

---

[1] This exactly expresses the personality and the business of the dark goddess Hel. If the line be Christian, the personality of Hel seems a remnant of the old belief.

I think the passage means, pacing the meadows, musing how he will throw into words his song of praise of Beowulf when the feast begins, and he thinks, that he may weave it well, of the ancient song of Sigemund which it was his wont to sing. As the morning light grew stronger many more go to the high hall to see the wonder of Grendel's hand; and with them at last the king arrives.

> From his bridal-bower   did the Ward of hoards of gold
> Mighty, march in glory;   mickle was his troop.
> Known by worth he was,   and, with him, his Queen,
> With a many of her maids   measured down the meadow-path.
> *Beowulf*, l. 921.

Heorot is now cleansed, a great feast is appointed, and we again see the customs of the hall. It is filled in the afternoon with kinsmen and friends, and Hrothgar, in requital of Grendel's overthrow, gives to Beowulf a golden ensign, a helm, a coat of mail, and the great treasure of a sword. Also eight steeds are led into the hall for him and displayed, and on one of them lies the saddle itself of Hrothgar, his war-seat in battle, wrought with embroidery and gems. A sword, an heirloom, is given to each of Beowulf's thegns, and blood money paid for Hondscio, that one of them whom Grendel had torn in pieces. So was fulfilled the great duty which fell to the lot of kings the free giving of gifts.

After this, while the feast goes on, the minstrel sings the saga of Finn and his sons, of Hengest, Hnaef and Hildeburh. When the song is over the servants pour forth the wine, and Wealhtheow came forth from the women's chamber, going under her golden crown, and offered the wine-cup to her lord, wishing him joy on the cleansing of Heorot, and on his desire to call Beowulf his son. Then she turned to Beowulf, bringing him also the cup, and with the cup gave him a byrnie and armlets and a jewelled collar, well known all over the north, as fine as the Brosings' collar that Hama wore, and had wrested from Eormanric.[1] "Use this collar, dear Beowulf!" cries the queen.

When Beowulf, on his return home, recalls that festal day, he recalls it with that grave and imaginative humanity, equally touched with fatalism and tenderness, which is one of his chief qualities. "Dark and true and tender is the North" exactly marks his soul. "There was song and social glee," he says to Hygelac, "when we were at the feast that evening," and he sketches King Hrothgar, and his singing, and the old man's memories.

> There was song and social glee,   and the Scylding gray,
> Asking after many (tales),   told of ancient times.
> Whiles, the Beast of war   waked the harp's delight,
> Greeted the glee-wood ;   now he told a tale
> Sooth and sorrowful :   then a story strange
> Did the king big-hearted   sing aright from end to end.
> Then again began   that gray-headed warrior,
> All upbound with eld,   for the battle strength to mourn
> That he had when young ;   and his heart within him swelled
> Now that old in winters   on it all he thought.
> So the livelong day   lingered we within,
> And delight in hall we seized   till the dark came on.[2]
>   *Beowulf*, l. 2105.

---

[1] "This necklace is the Brisinga-men — the costly necklace of Freyja, which she won from the dwarfs and which was stolen from her by Loki, as is told in the Edda. Like the ἱμάς of Aphrodite it awakened desire. As Here wears it, so the Norse goddess wears it. As Freyja has an inaccessible chamber, so also has Here, one which was wrought for her by Hephaistos. When Freyja breathes deep with anger, the Brising necklace starts from her breast. When Thor, to get his hammer back, dresses up in Freyja's garments, he puts on the Brisinga-men. The jewel is then so closely woven up with the myth of Freyja that from its mention here in *Beowulf* we may safely infer the familiarity of the English with the worship and story of Freyja." This is Kemble's view, but I have my doubts of it all. I think the old singers of *Beowulf* knew little or nothing about these matters.

[2] It is not an uninteresting illustration of this passage to quote the following

And now that night had come and Hrothgar had gone and Beowulf with him to sleep outside, the hall, as in times before Grendel had wasted it, was prepared for the sleeping of the earls of Hrothgar. They bared the bench-floor, beds and bolsters were laid over it. At their heads, hanging on the wall, they set their disks of war, their glittering shield-woods. On the shelf, over each warrior, it was easy to see the high-crested helm and the war-shirt of rings and the stout spear. This was their use at night—that they were often thus ready for war, at home, as in the host, whenever their Man-lord might have need of them: an apt and ready folk they were!

While the warriors sleep, another part of the tale begins — the story of the mother of Grendel, of her vengeance for her son, and of her slaying in the sea-cavern by Beowulf. She, like her son, is a spirit of Elsewhere, foreign to human nature, greedy and raging, restless, a death ghost, a scathe of man, a huge mark-stalker, a creature of the mirk and mist. She swims the sea like a sea-monster, clutches to Beowulf in its depths; a sea-wolf (*brim-wylf*), a sea-woman (*merewif*), (*grund-wyrgen*), a wolf of the sea-bottom. Her hands are armed with claws, and grim is her grasp. No common weapon can bite her flesh, only a sword, by eotens made long since; but her blood is so venomous (she is an *aeltren ellorgaest*) that even this

---

from an account which Priscus gives of a banquet to which Attila invited him (448 A.D.). The singing habits are the same—nay, the very feelings: "When evening came on, torches were lighted, and two barbarians coming in and standing opposite to Attila recited songs previously composed, in which they sang of his victories and his warlike virtues. The banqueters gazed earnestly on the minstrels: some were delighted with the poems; others, remembering past conflicts, felt their souls stirred within them; while the old were melted into tears by the thought that their bodies were grown weak through age and their hot hearts compelled into repose."—*Dynasty of Theodosius*, Hodgkin, p. 180.

magic-tempered blade melts away with it, like ice in the sun. No good thing belongs to her save her fierce sorrow for her son's death and her desire to avenge it. In the dead of night she bursts into the hall now reoccupied by the thegns, seizes on Æschere, Hrothgar's right-hand man in war, and bears him away to her cave. She, like her son, rent the body limb from limb. The head of Æschere was found lying on the cliff.[1] Beowulf had slept outside Heorot, but at dawn he is summoned, and loud is the king's outburst of grief when Beowulf asks him if he had a quiet night. "Ask not thou after happiness; sorrow is new again to the Dane's people. Dead is Æschere, Yrmenlaf's elder brother; my *rune-wit*, my rede-giver, my shoulder-to-shoulder man, when we in war warded our heads, when the foot warriors rushed together, and the boars (the chiefs) crashed in the onset. Such should an earl be!" He tells the tale of the night, describes the place where Grendel's mother lives. "Seek it if thou darest!" he cries; "I will pay thee with old treasures, with rings of gold." The reply of Beowulf is couched in his grave, half-reproving, fatalistic way. Life is nothing, high deeds and

---

[1] That this story of Grendel's mother was originally a separate lay from the first seems to be suggested by the fact that the monsters are described over again, and many new details added, such as would be inserted by a new singer who wished to enhance and adorn the original tale. The details of the scenery are so particular, and seem so much derived from personal observation, that it has often occurred to me that in this second part we have the original myth (with the Grendel-mother addition), actually localised by the new poet in the scenery that surrounded the town where his tribe lived. If that should be true, and if it also should be true that the fight of Beowulf with Grendel's mother was a later addition to the first story, it makes the first story very old. The scenery in the second part is continental — that is, it was described before the Angles left their native land. The first story would then belong to a time long previous to that departure. This is a possible but a doubtful inference. It might be said that, though the first story belonged to the Angles on the continent, the second was added in England or recast in England, and the scenery drawn from English scenery, as Mr. Haigh suggests. But I remember no such place as that described on the coasts of Yorkshire or Northumberland.

courage are all, and the vengeance for a friend. "Sorrow not, wise man"—but I have quoted the passage before—"Not in earth's breast, nor deep in the sea, nor in the mountain holt, nor in the abyss of ocean, go where she will, shall Grendel's kin escape from me."

They mount their horses then and ride to the cliffs, to the dwelling of the fiends. It is this dwelling we must now discuss. It seems to be conceived by many as a deep morass in the midst of the moor, overhung by trees. But this is a careless reading of the text. It is a sea-mere, a sea-pool. Æschere's head is found on its edge, and its edge is the sea-cliff (*holm-clif*). In its waters are sea-dragons that seek the sea; the nickers lie there on the sloping rocks of the ness, monsters that at mid-day go out into the open sea, and voyage on the sail-road. The one of these who is killed swims in the *holm* (in the sea). Beowulf, before he plunges, arms himself to mingle in the depths of the sea, to seek the welter of the sea—the *mere-grundas*, the *sund-gebland*. It is the ocean surge (the *brim-wylm*) which receives him as he plunges. The beasts who attack him are sea-beasts (*sac-dcor monig*). Grendel's mother is the sea-wolf (*brim-wylf*). It is a sea-headland where Beowulf's thegns sit and watch for his return; the booty he brings back, the sword-hilt and Grendel's head, is sea-booty (*sac-lac*). When they all return, they return from the sea-cliff (*holm-clif*).

There is not a trace in all this of a deep pool in the moor, of a morass. We are on the sea-nesses, looking down into a sea-hole, and it is not difficult, from the indications given, to sketch the place with some accuracy. Indeed, so clearly is it drawn that I believe the describer had seen the very spot. In a verse of the poem it is said to be well known (line 2135), and a much greater amount of trouble is taken with this piece of natural description than is usual in early English poetry. It completes our vision of the scenery round Heorot. It tells about the range of cliffs up to the very edge of which extends the moor. It is the first in the long series of natural descriptions which have made English poetry celebrated for more than a thousand years, and the supernatural element in it is the product of that work of the imagination on Nature, and that transference of human passion to Nature, of which modern English poetry is so full. Hrothgar describes the place—

> Where they ward; wolf-haunted slopes,
> Fearful is the marish-path,
> 'Neath the Nesses' mist,
> Under earth[1] its flood is,
> But the measure of a mile
> Over it (outreaching),
> Held by roots the holt is fast,
> There an evil wonder
> In the flood a fire!
> None alive is wise enough
> If the heather-stepper,
> If the strong-horned stag
> Put to flight from far—
> Secret in its gloom the land-windy headlands (o'er the sea);
> where the mountain stream,
> nither makes its way,
> nor afar from here it is,
> where the mere is set.
> hang the rustling trees :[2]
> and o'er-helms the water!
> every night a man may see—
> Of the sons of men
> that abyss to know.
> harried by the hounds,
> seek out this holt-wood,—
> sooner will he flee his soul,

---

[1] "Under the earth" means that the stream had worn itself a deep channel far below the surface of the moor. Through this it flows till it reaches the cliff over the stony lip of which it leaps in a waterfall.

[2] *Hrimge* is Walker's reading, and means "rime-clad or decayed." But I do not see the meaning. It was not winter when Beowulf came. Nor can it mean withered, brittle boughs, for the stream and the sea-mists would make the foliage of these trees plentiful, and withered boughs would not hang down or cover the waters with a helmet. So I have taken the reading *hrinde — hrinende* (rustling or roaring), O. N. *hrina*, "to resound" which is the reading of the MS. In the Blickling Homilies, *hrimge hearwa* occurs, but I do not see that the phrase there forces us to adopt it here. There is no reason for the trees decaying in the circumstances described, but a good deal of reason in the leaping water and the dreadful storms for their roaring or rustling.

> Yield his life-breath on the bank— ere he will therein
> Seek to hide his head. Not unhaunted is the place!
> Thence the wylming of the waves whirlèd is on high,
> Wan[1] towards the clouds, when the wind is stirring
> Wicked weathers up; till the lift is waxing dark,
> And the welkin weeps.
>
> *Beowulf*, l. 1357.

What we see then is this. At a certain point in the cliff face, between two jutting nesses, there is a deep sea-gorge, with a narrow entrance from the sea. The waves are driven into it, boil and welter in the confined space, and are whirled on high. At the landward base of the cliffs, the rocks slope downwards, and on these rocks, as we see afterwards, the nickers (pictured from the great seals and walruses) are lying, whose habit it is—and the phrase points to an observation of real animals intruded into the tale—to sleep in the morning stretched out on the ness-slopes, and at midday to get ready "for a sorrow-bringing expedition into the open sea, into the sail-road." At the land end of the sea-gorge the cliff rises and forms the neck between the two lateral nesses, and the moor, coming down to the neck, has been worn away into a deep channel by the working of a mountain stream. All along this hollow channel the descending stream has made trees grow, but when the torrent comes to the edge of the cliff— "a ledge of gray stone,"—it leaps over in a waterfall into the weltering waves below. Over this waterfall the trees, fast-rooted, hang down and darken the pool underneath. They rustle in the wind that comes up from below, and the vapours from the spray of the

---

[1] *Wonn*, translated *wan* above, means *dark* or *black* in Anglo-Saxon. It is an epithet of the raven or of night. The modern meaning of the word is *pale, colourless*; and "the word," as Skeat says, "has thus suffered a remarkable change. The sense, however, was probably *dead* or *colourless* which is applicable to black and pallid alike" (*Etymological Dictionary*. W. W. Skeat). Whenever I use the word in this book, it has its Anglo-Saxon meaning of *black*.

waterfall and the sea-tumble underneath mingle with the inland mists driven seaward from the moor.

I have seen such places on the coasts of Cornwall and the north-west of Ireland. I have no doubt that there are many such among the fiords of Norway and Sweden. Legends always collect round them, and the touches of fire on the flood, of land animals not daring to take shelter in them,—it is plain there was a path to the sea-level by which Beowulf and the thegns descend, —of their being the dwelling-places of the "worm-kind, wild sea-beasts, strange wave-swimmers with battle tusks, mere-women, sea-wolves, wolves of the abyss, of the sea," and the rest, might be paralleled again and again.

When Hrothgar and Beowulf and their attendant thegns mount their horses and ride to this place, additional touches of description make us realise that we are on the cliffs, and make the scenery more clear. They pass along "steep overhanging clefts by narrow roads, above precipitous cliffs and nicker houses"—that is, by paths on the side of the cliff, a precipice below them, and at their base shelving rocks, where again the great sea-beasts are said to be asleep. At last they reach the sea-hollow, where the water is tossed in waves. They descend to the rocks, and find the head of Æschere, cast down by the mere-wife ere she plunged to find her dwelling. The water is troubled and bloody, under the overhanging joyless wood. They blow on the horn an eager war-music, and the sound rouses from their sleep to a fierce anger the strange sea-dragons tumbling in the wave. The lord of the Geats shoots one with an arrow, and slays him; he is stabbed with boar-spears, and drawn with sharp hooks on to the rocks—it is a walrus-hunt,—and the men

gaze on the grisly guest, the wondrous wave-swimmer.
The picture is extraordinarily vivid.

Then Beowulf armed himself before he plunged,
and Hunferth, honouring him whom he had mocked,
gave him a well-known sword, "Hrunting by name,
one of the old treasures of the world, its iron edge
hardened with the sweat, that is, the blood of war,
damasked as it was forged with distilled venom of
twigs, and never had it deceived any man in battle."
"Remember!" cried Beowulf, "O son of Healfdene,
what we have spoken of before; if for thy need I lose my
life, that thou wert to be in a father's stead to me. Be
guardian of my hand-comrades, send the treasures thou
hast given me to Hygelac, that he may know, when he
see the gold, that I found a good giver of rings, and
let Hunferth"—so magnanimous is Beowulf—"have
the curious sword thou gavest me. I will work fame
with Hrunting, or let Death take me." Then the
ocean surge received him, and it seemed a day's space
ere he reached the bottom. "It was a day's space,"
says the poem, but the phrase must be metaphorical,
for he plunges in at morning, and at the ninth hour
(line 1600) he comes again to land, having fought his
fight and finished it.

Grendel's mother saw him, and grasped him in her
dreadful claws; and the tusked sea-beasts attacked
him, but the sea-wolf bore him upwards from the
bottom into her ocean-hall, a cave where the water
was not.[1] There was firelight in the roofed cavern

---

[1] This cave under the sea seems to be another of those natural phenomena of which the writer had personal knowledge (line 2135), and which was introduced by him into the mythical tale to give it a local colour. There are many places of this kind. Their entrance is under the lowest level of the tide. The diver plunges, and rising through the water, finds himself in a high arched cavern, with a sloping beach of sand, up which the water flows to the level of the tide. But

brightly shining; and Beowulf struck at the merewoman. The ringed blade sang a greedy war-song on her head. But the war-beam would not bite—for the first time—into the flesh of its foe, and the hero flung it, angry, on the floor, and trusted to his grip alone. The sea-wolf seized him in her fierce grasp, and, as he stumbled, overthrew him, sat on his breast, and drew her short sword, the seax, broad and brown-edged, and stabbed at his heart. But his war-sark, the battle net, lent help to him, and withstood the blow. He leaped to his feet and looking round him, saw among the arms hanging on the wall a sword, hallowed by victory, an old sword of the eotens, doughty of edges, greater than another could wield in the war-play, a pride of warriors. He seized the gold-charmed hilt and smote at her neck therewith.

beyond the level of the tide the cavern, covered with fine dry sand, extends inland under the rocks, lit and aired by crevices in the roof which penetrate to the outer surface of the cliff. It is in such a cave, "whose only portal was the keyless wave," that the lovers in Byron's *Island* take refuge, and Byron found the original in Mariner's account of the Tonga Islands. It is such a cave in one of the islands of the Fiord that Miss Martineau describes as the shelter of Rolf in her story of *Feats on the Fiord*, and I might give many more instances of this trick of Nature. The probability is that a cave of this kind was known to the people who composed the lay of Beowulf's battle with Grendel's mother; and the waves, in such a place as the poem describes, would be likely to hollow out a cavern of this fashion. They have begun to do so, for instance, at Boscastle in Cornwall. All the statements in the account confirm this conjecture. Beowulf and Grendel's dam, close embraced, dive *upwards* into the cave. When they get in they are in "a sea hall where the water is not." On the walls of the cave are hung weapons; there is a rocky couch in it, and treasures lying about; and the light is conducted on the dry sand, under a lofty roof. There is firelight, but I think, when we look at all that is said of this light, the writer meant that the light was like fire, and that in reality he thought of the pale daylight that filtered through the rocks above. "He saw firelight, a brilliant beam brightly shining," that is the first statement, and it is a touch which belongs to the story of Grettir's attack on the Giant in the cave under the force. Then when he looks round after he has slain the sea-wolf, he sees by the light Grendel lying dead on a rocky couch and the light is thus described "A glancing light gleamed, a light stood within, even as from heaven serenely shines the candle of the firmament." This seems to mean daylight. But even had they firelight, it would not change my contention. We have here a cavern of which kind many known examples exist, and such a cavern was, I think, known to the poet. It marks especially the sea-nature of the Grendel-kin.

The brand gripped on her throat, broke the bone-rings, pierced through her body; she fell on the floor. The blade was bloody, Beowulf rejoiced in his work. A light, a beam streamed into the cave, and was in it as when from heaven brightly shines the candle of the firmament. Again he looked round, and lifted his weapon, and there by the wall lay Grendel, dead, weary of war. The body sprang far away when the hero smote off its head.[1] All the blood streamed into the water; and the thegns of Hrothgar, sitting on the shore, and it was near the ninth hour, saw that the waves were mingled with blood. "We shall not see him again," they said, and took their way back to Heorot. But Beowulf's own thegns remain, sick in their mind, wishing, not hoping, to see their dear lord again. While they waited, the giant's sword blade melted in Beowulf's hand, by reason of the "battle sweat of the icicles of war" (the blood droppings from its edge), so poisonous was the gore of the two monsters—melted, "likest to ice when the Father looses the band of frost, when he unwinds the ropes of the flood," and Beowulf took the hilt and Hrunting and Grendel's head, as he dived up through the cleansed seas, rejoicing in his sea-booty. The brave band were glad to see the seaman's Helm, and loosed his armour, and measured back the path to Heorot. Proudly they marched, and four men bore on spears the giant head of Grendel, entered Heorot, and flung it by the hair at the feet of Hrothgar and his queen. "So, son of Healfdene, we have brought thee this sea-spoil, which here thou beholdest." Then the tale of the fight was told, and the golden hilt of the

---

[1] *This* sword, then, could divide the charmed flesh of Grendel, being a magic sword. The fact that these monsters keep their own bane in their own dwelling, puts us in mind of many analogous examples in Folk-Tales.

Eoten sword given to the king.[1] He wondered as he saw it, for there on the guard of pure gold was written the origin of a combat in ancient times, and

> Rightly graven there, in the runic signs,
> It was set and said for (what King) the sword,
> At the first was forged. Finest it of steels;
> And with spotted snakes was the hilt entwined.
> *Beowulf*, l. 1695.

Then Hrothgar tells of King Heremod, who slaughtered his people, and gave no gifts. Not so will he act. "Go, honoured in war, to thy seat. There shall be many treasures common to us both, when morning comes." When the feast was over, "swart was the night-helm, dark o'er the warriors. The great-hearted rested till the black raven, blithe-hearted, welcomed the joy of Heaven." The sun arose; "brightly it came, o'er the shadows sliding." Then Beowulf and Hrothgar took leave of each other and declared a firm alliance of Scylding and Geat, "after old custom doing all things. Hrothgar kissed and wept over Beowulf, and love of the hero glowed in his blood. Long was his gift-giving praised among men."

So Beowulf departed, and marching over the grassy plain, found beyond the ridge his ship anchored to the beach, and the warden of the coast on guard. To him the hero gave a sword, with gold wires round the hilt of it, and for that gift the warrior was ever after more honoured at the mead. In the hollow bosom of the ship, under the mast, the treasures, arms, and horses were stowed away, and the next day the adventurers

---

[1] "It went to the noblest of the world kings of the two seas, of those who in Scedenig treasure divided," line 1685. This supports the theory, I think, of the continental origin of this lay. *Scedenig* is the O. N. Scán-ey, the southernmost part of the Scandinavian peninsula and the whole of the Danish kingdom.

landed on their own coast, where Hygelac dwelt near
the sea-wall in a noble hall. The customs in that hall
are much the same as those in Heorot. There does
not seem, however, to be any dais at the east end of
the building. The king sits in the middle of the long
bench on the south side, and Beowulf opposite him on
the northern side. In this hall the queen, Hygd, does
not sit with the king, as Wealhtheow among the
Danes appears to do when the supper begins. Hygd
comes in during the feast and bears the mead-cup round.
Beowulf is then called on for his tale. He tells it
from the beginning, and orders the treasures given him
by Hrothgar to be brought into the hall. He gives
everything away except one horse and the sword. The
gray coat of mail he bestows on his lord Hygelac,
crying, "Use it well," and four of the eight horses
Hrothgar had given him. Three more of the horses,
slender and of bright saddles, he gives to Hygd, and
above all, the great and glorious collar, like the Brising
collar, which Hygelac loses afterwards when he is
slain in Friesland. Hygelac is not backward in return
of gifts. He gives to Beowulf a sword enriched
with gold, seven thousand in money, a country seat, the
dignity of a prince.[1] It is now, then, that Beowulf,
when he is thirty years old, seems to have attained
a settled position — heritable land, a home and its
rights. With this interchange of gifts the first part
of the poem closes.

 The second part of the poem of *Beowulf* opens
fifty years later, and is the tale of Beowulf's fight with
the Fire-Drake, and of his death and burial. The

---

[1] *Brego-stol*, "a throne," hence "rule." When Hygd, after Hygelac's death, offers Beowulf the kingly power, it is *brego-stol* which she offers him.

history of those fifty years is soon told. On his return from his slaying of Grendel he had been Hygelac's faithful thegn. Always on foot, and in the front, in the clashings of battle, and also in peace, he had never failed his lord. But most of all he was true comrade in the last fight, when Hygelac fell in combat with the Frisians and the Hugs. He could not save his king, but he avenged him on Daeghrefn, the champion of the Hugs, and in the same way as he slew Grendel. "I slew him!" cries Beowulf, "not with the sword, but in battle I grasped the throbbing of his heart, and broke his bone-house." Nor was he wounded himself, but, carrying off thirty war-harnesses,[1] went down to the sea, unpursued, so great was the terror of him, and swam (*i.e.* sailed) home with his old swimming skill over the seal's bath, to bring the news to Hygd, the wife of Hygelac. And Hygd, thinking her son Heardred too young for so many enmities, offered the throne to Beowulf. But the hero refused, faithful to his master's son, and brought him up and loved him and maintained him. But in vain, for Heardred fell, murdered by Eanmund. Beowulf then became king, and when he was settled, remembered vengeance and slew Eadgils, the brother of Eanmund, slayer of Heardred.

Noble, valorous, unconquered, he had outlived every enmity and every conflict, and dwelt, worshipped by his people, at peace, until when he was near his eightieth year the dragon came to spoil his folk. This was his final weird. We hear how the fate arose. One of his thegns found the secret barrow

---

[1] This touch illustrates the way in which additions were made to a folk-tale. Beowulf has the strength of thirty men in the original tale. Here, then, the new inventor makes him carry off thirty coats of mail.

where the dragon's hoard was hidden, and stole a gold cup while the monster slept.

The account given of the building of this barrow and the hiding of the treasures in it is very romantic, and is either a legend used by the writer or is invented entirely by him. The lament of the prince reads like a separate piece of poetry which has been inserted by the singer. Portions of it resemble the fragment of the *Ruined Burg*, and the poetical quality of this little lyric, which might be quite isolated from the rest of the poem, is as good as that of the Ruin. As wild and desolate too as the scenery in which it is placed, is the short story which leads up to the lament of the prince. Three hundred years ago, in Hygelac's land, this prince dwelt with his nobles. A great war, a life-bane, took away his folk, and of all, none at last was left but he. "Mourning his friends," he wandered to and fro alone, "and wished for delay of death," even then, that he might enjoy the precious treasures, the last legacy of a noble race. But when he felt death at hand, he brought together all the costly things, gold cups and rings, treasured jewels, helms and swords, a golden banner, great dishes and old giants' work, and hid them in a huge mound, low by the headland near the moving of the waves, and sung over them his lament—

"Hold thou here, O Earth, now the heroes could not,
Hold the wealth of earls! Lo, within thee long ago
Warriors good had gotten it. Ghastly was the life-bane
And the battle-death that bore every bairn away.
All my men, mine own, who made leaving of this life!
They have seen their joy in hall! . . . .
   None is left the sword to bear,
Or the cup to carry, chased with flakes of gold,
Costly cup for drinking. All the chiefs have gone elsewhere.
Now the hardened helm, high-adorned with gold.

> Of its platings shall be plundered !   Sleeping are the polishers,
> Those once bound to brighten   battle-masks (for war),
> So alike the battle-sark   that abode on field, (stricken)
> O'er the brattling of the boards.   biting of the swords,
> Crumbles, now the chiefs are dead !   And the coat of ringèd mail
> May far and wide no longer   fare with princes to the field
> At the side of heroes.   Silent is the joy of harp,
> Gone the glee-wood's mirth ;   nevermore the goodly hawk
> Hovers through the hall ;   the swift horse no more
> Beats with hoof the Burh-stead.   Bale of battle ruinous
> Many souls of men   sent away, afar."
> So, in spirit sad,   in his sorrow he lamented,
> All alone when all were gone—   Thus unhappy, did he weep
> In the day and night,   till the Surge of Death
> On his heart laid hold.   *Beowulf*, ll. 2247. etc.

This is the hoard over which the dragon watches. The Worm and the place are both accurately described, and it is fitting that we should collect what is said of both, first of the worm, and then of the place. This dragon story is not, like that of Grendel, unique. There are a multitude of parallels to it in the Folk-Tales, and the most famous of these is the story in the Volsunga Saga. But the drake in *Beowulf* is not the huge earth-worm like Fafnir. That beast is found in our poem at line 887. He is there the guard of the hoard, and lives, like our present dragon, under a hoary rock, a wondrous spotted worm ; and when he is slain, his own heat melts him away ; like the Chimaera, nothing of him is left. He, like the Volsunga Fafnir, is wingless, for it seems that men who became dragons had, as dragons, no wings.

The Fire-Drake here is the true dragon, our old Romance acquaintance, whose breath is fire, whose wings are strong (the wings mark the dragon proper), and who has feet and claws in front. At least it appears as if in the fight he threw his forefeet around Beowulf's neck. But he is also scaleless, naked, and Beowulf's sword and knife pierce his flesh, though the

sword breaks on the bones of his head. Like many
another dragon in Folk-Tales, he is a seeker, a finder,
and a keeper of hidden treasures, of which he is proud,
and which he guards with jealous covetousness. He
lies round them in a cave, as Fafnir, like a Python, lay
coiled over his hoard. So constant was this habit
among the dragons, that gold is called Worms' bed;
Fafnir's couch, Worms' bed-fire. Even in India, the
cobras, especially their king, are guardians of treasure. Three hundred years before Beowulf met the
drake, that beast—so old is he (and great age is a
characteristic of the dragons),—flying by night, and
wrapt in his own fiery breath, had found the ancient
hoard. All day he watches it now in the hollow of the
barrow under the hill, or sleeps around it. Probably
he was not yet long enough to quite encompass it,
since the gold cup is stolen from him, and there is
evidence in the poem that the thief got in between his
head and his tail (ll. 2289-2290), and I have somewhere
else seen a folk-tale in which this element of the
dragon story appears, and where, owing to this gap,
the hoard is robbed by a peasant. He is, however,
fifty feet in length. He moves on the earth, hunts his
foe by scent, smells round his cave; hunts also by
sight, and finds the footsteps of the robber near the
cavern. He is once called the Earth-Drake, a name
I have not elsewhere seen. But the air is also his
proper element. He flies in it, and is called the wide-
flier, the deadly lift-flier, the war-flier. But it is always
by night that he flies. He is the old foe who comes
out in the twilight; before day dawns he returns to his
cave. In this he is quite unlike those dragons who
sun their gold in fine weather. But our dragon is
wholly of the night. It is said of him: " Who, all on

fire, seeks to the mountains, naked, full of hate, flying through the night enfolded in flame; whom the earth-dwellers gazed at from far," and it is a fine touch of description. Fire, then, as well as earth and air, is in his power. Fire is his very nature; he goes forth with burning, winged with flame. Fire is his weapon; when he is robbed, he longs to take vengeance by fire, but he must wait till nightfall. Then he rushes from the cave, and rising in the air, spits forth gleeds, and the hate he feels intensifies the glow. When he comes forth to fight, he breathes hot and venomous fire, the hot sweat of battle; it wells from his breast. His breath of fire enwraps him, so that he seems embroidered with gouts of flame. The steam of his breathing is like the hot gore of battle; earth resounds as he moves over it. In the crisis of the fight he gathers in his breath till his breast swells, and pours a welter of flame on Beowulf, flinging it far and wide. Finally, he can make himself into a bow, or like a ring; he rolls along in curves when he comes out of his lair. Like so many dragons then, splendour and pliability mark him; and "glitter, gold and fire," as Grimm says of other worms, gather round his presentation. Moreover, he lives close to the desolate and hoar heath that runs inland from his cavern, and the wild heath is the constant companion of the northern and gold-guarding dragons. A dragon is called a heath-worm. The "fani-gold" is gold of the fen in the heath where dragons lie. It is on the "glistening heath" that Fafnir has his den, and the *hæðen* gold of *Beowulf* may mean gold of the heath as well as heathen gold. This then is the image of the great beast, whom the hero, like Hercules, Apis, Jason, Sigmund, Sigurd, Frotho, and a hundred others, lays to sleep; by whose breath he dies, like Thor by the breath of the Midgard serpent.[1]

The poet not only describes the beast, he enables us to place him. The scenery and his refuge may be conceived with clearness from many indications in the poem. The Nesses rise one after another along the coast, with dips of land beneath them. The loftiest of these is called Hrones-naes the Whale's Ness; next to it is Earna-naes the Sea-Eagles' Ness.[2] The cliff-face descends between these in a scoop, and the meadowy space between the two Nesses is walled in on either side by their lateral rocks. On the top of one of these ridges is a grove of trees. Close to these trees, on the edge of the rock wall, and looking over to the opposite rocks where the worm has his shelter, Beowulf sits before he goes down to the meadow below to fight the dragon; on the same ridge his thegns watch the old king contending with the beast, and into the wood behind, all of them, save Wiglaf, fly in fear. It

---

[1] There is another picture of a dragon in Anglo-Saxon literature which I may as well insert here for the sake of comparison. It is in the Fifty-Second Riddle of Cynewulf. The beast he conceives has two resemblances to the *Beowulf* dragon. He is a swift flier in the air, and a guardian of treasure. But a new touch is added by Cynewulf. This dragon dives into the waves and disturbs the sea. Like the dragon of *Beowulf*, he has paws with which he walks the earth. These are the four wondrous beings with which the riddle begins—

> Four beings I saw, strange was their fashion,
> Travelling together: their foot-tracks were black,
> Very swart was their spoor.

Then, the riddle changes from plural to singular, from the feet of the dragon to the dragon himself—

> Swifter than the swallows, swimming quickly in the air!
> In the deep, he dived, dashed it into foam,
> Like a fighting warrior; then he showed the ways
> O'er flaked heaps of gold, to all the four beings.

"Dashed it to foam" is, literally, behaved himself stormily in it, and the last lines mean that the dragon led his four feet to the place where the gold lay, each piece of it piled in a heap, overlapping the other like plates of iron on a stitched coat of mail.

[2] It is suggested that the name may be connected with Rán, the giant goddess of the sea, the daughter of Ægir—Ran's Naes; but with Earna-naes immediately following, the unmythological explanation is plainly right.

is on this side also that Beowulf, with his back to the cliff below, is driven to bay by the dragon. On the other side, but higher up the dell, nearer to the edge of the sea-cliff, whence the raging of the waves may be heard, the great barrow stands, built by the prince over the treasures and bodies of his tribe. Near it is the cave, entered into by a rocky arch, within which are the treasures and the lair of the worm. A stream breaks out of the mouth of the cave, and flows down the slope of the meadow, to lose itself in the gray heath and moor-land. This is the place, and when the dragon is slain, his carcase is pushed over the cliff to fall on the beach below, while Beowulf's body is borne upwards for burial to the point of Hrones-naes.

It was from this hidden and lonely dell that the dragon, when he awoke and found he was robbed, went forth at night for vengeance, vomiting gleeds. The palace hall was devoured by the flame. It was the "greatest of sorrows—the sacred gift-stool of the Geats was destroyed." But the fire of battle did not blaze less hot in Beowulf than of old, and he said he would alone, not with a host, go forth in his old age to meet the worm. So he let an iron shield be made, for a forest-wood—a wooden shield—would be burned up by the breath of fire; and with thirteen men (the thirteenth is the thief of the cup who alone knows the way) went to the ness opposite the cave and sat thereon, and Wyrd was very nigh him. Like an Indian chief, he sang his death-song, recounting his life, and deeds of war. "I all remember, since I was seven years old." He bids his thegns farewell, takes his shield and war-mail, not naked now as he strove with Grendel, because he has to fight with fire. "Not one foot will I fly the Ward of the hill; but at the rock-wall it shall be as

Wyrd wills, Wyrd the measurer of each man's life. Wait ye on the hill, clad in your byrnies. Then the fierce champion, brave under helm, beneath the stone cliffs bore on his mail-sark." And he saw, by the rock-wall, an arch of stone standing and a stream from under it break from the mountain; the flood of that burn was hot with battle-fire, for it was aflame with the breath of the Fire-Drake. Enraged, the king shouted; stark of heart, his cry was like a storm. " His shout, clear sounding in battle, entered in under the gray stone. Then the hoard-ward knew the voice of a man." And first rolled forth the monster's fiery breath—hot sweat of battle, and the earth roared. The lord of the Geats upraised his shield, standing with his back against the steep rock, and the worm, rolling in curves and burning, moved forth to the fight. Beowulf swung up his hand and smote the grisly head with his sword, but the brown edge slid off on the bone, bit too feebly on it, for Wyrd did not permit him victory, and in a moment the king was wrapt in whirling fire. Again they met, and the fire was worse than before, nor was there any who helped the hero. All of his thegns, looking on, fled to the wood in terror—all save one. Wiglaf alone, whose breast welled with sorrows as he looked, Wiglaf, Weohstan's son, one of the Waegmundings, kinsman of Beowulf, remembered the land, the folk-rights Beowulf had given him, and seized the fallow shield, and gripped his ancient sword (Onela had given it him, a giant's sword it was), and cried to his companions—" We promised, drinking mead in the hall with our lord, that we would repay him with help in need. Dearer far it is to me that flame should clasp me along with my gold-giver than that we should bear home our shields in safety."

Then through the deadly reek he waded, and stood beside the king. "Well-loved Beowulf!" he cried, "as long since in thy youth thou saidst thy Honour should never fail, so now strong in deeds, ward thy life. I will stand by thee." Wiglaf's shield was soon burnt up, but he fought on under Beowulf's iron targe. The king smote hard again, but Naegling, Beowulf's sword, snapped asunder, an old gray brand, that never before had failed in battle,[1] at which the Drake rushed on and clasped the hero round the throat, and the king's life-blood bubbled forth in waves. Now Wiglaf struck lower, and his sword dived into the dragon so that the fire abated. Then Beowulf drew his deadly knife, bitter and battle-sharp, the seax that he wore on his byrnie, and cut in twain the worm through the middle. Thus the battle ended.

But in the poisonous grapple the king had got his death wound. It began to burn and swell and the venom boiled in his breast. So he sat down, wisely thinking, and looked on the giant's work, and how the stone arches of the cave were fast on the pillars, while Wiglaf washed his wounds and unloosed his helm. And then he spoke, and the whole scene has a dim

---

[1] There is a curious passage introduced here by some late editor. Naegling, which may mean Nailer, the sword which drives like a nail into the foe—or perhaps with jewelled nails in the hilt (Nagelring, in the Wilkina saga, is the best sword in the world, and is a part of the ancient story of Angerboda)—breaks, the writer says, because the hand that swayed it was too strong for the sword. This is absurd, for Beowulf had fought with it all his life. But the intrusion of the detail here is done by some one who had heard of the legendary Offa and of his fight.

The legend goes that Offa, getting ready for his island duel at Fifeldor in defence of his blind father Wermund, broke all the swords that were given him when he waved them in the air—so mighty was his strength. At last Wermund reminded him of a magic sword that long since he had hidden in the earth. So bitten with rust and worms and thin was Skrep, for that was the sword's name, that Offa feared to break it and forbore to fight with it in the battle. At last, angry, he raised it and struck, and Wermund was saved from despair by hearing the hiss with which Skrep cut his enemy in half, from helm to thigh.

likeness in it to the death of Arthur, as human, as pathetic—

"Now to some son of mine I would give this War-weed, had it so been granted to me that an heir, sprung from my loins, should come after me. Fifty of winters I held my sway over this people; nor was there one folk-king of them all, of all who sat on their lands around me, who durst greet me with their war-friends, to press on me with the terror of war. I tarried at home on the hour of my fate; I held my own fitly; I sought out no feuds; I swore not many oaths and kept them not; so may I for all this, though sick with deadly wounds, have comfort, since the Master of men is not bound to charge me with murder-bale of kinsmen when out of my body life takes its flight." It is an English death, and in the same temper many an English soldier has passed away. Nor is his desire to see the treasure less natural to our nation, less characteristic. "Now hasten, Wiglaf beloved," he adds, "and view the hoard beneath the hoary rock; bring it here that I may see the ancient wealth, the bright and cunningly-set gems, so that I may, all the easier, after the sight of it, give up my life and my peopleship that I have held so long."

Wiglaf hurries to the cave, and he beheld marvels there; glittering gold lying in the den of the worm, vessels of old time, pitchers and cups, plates and precious swords and helmets, eaten through and worn with rust, curiously wire-enwoven armlets, a sword iron-edged, and, greatest of wonders, an all-golden banner at rest, high over the hoard, curious handiwork woven with magic songs, and from it shone so mystic a light that Wiglaf saw by its gleaming all things in the cave. Then he loaded himself with the treasure and came forth to find Beowulf bleeding away his life, sprinkled him again with water, showed him the treasure to cheer him, until the last words of the old king, gazing sadly on the golden store, broke from his breast. "I thank the Glory-king for these treasures that here I stare on, for that I, ere I die, have won them for my people, have paid my own old life for them. But do thou supply the need of my folk; I may no longer be here."

> "Bid the battle-famed   build a barrow up,
> Clear to see when Bale is burnt,   on the cliff above the surge;
> Which may for my folk,   for remembering of me,
> Lift its head on high   on the Hrones-ness;
> That sea-sailing men,   soon in days to be,
> Call it "Beowulf's Barrow,"   who, their barks afoam,
> From afar are driving   o'er the ocean mists."
> *Beowulf*, l. 2802.

Then he did off from his neck the golden ring and gave it to Wiglaf, also his gold-wrought helm and collar and byrnie. "Use them well," he said, "thou art the last left of our kindred, of the Waegmundings. Wyrd swept them all away, each at the fated hour; earls in their strength. I must go after them." This was the last word of the old man, the "last of the thoughts of his heart." And as Wiglaf sat there mourning, the thegns who had been untrue to their lord, and fled when they should have helped, came stealing down from the holt where they had refuged, and, ashamed, gazed at Wiglaf and their king. Wearied he sat, near his lord's shoulders, and reproached them bitterly; and the deep disgrace it was for an English warrior to fail through cowardice in the duties of comradeship is nowhere better set forth than in the following speech—

"This, in sooth, one may say, who has a mind to speak the truth, that the Man-lord who gave fair things to you, the bright weeds of war in which here ye stand; when at the ale-bench he allotted helm and byrnie to the sitters in hall (as a war-leader to his thegns, whom far off or near, the trustiest of men he was able to find) — has utterly wasted these weeds of the battle. When War met him, the king of the folk had no cause to boast of his comrades in arms. . . . Too few of those who should ward him pressed round their Lord when the stress of fight came upon him."

> "Now shall getting gems, giving too of swords,
> And the pleasure of a home, and possession of the land,
> Be no more to kin of yours; and each man of that kindred
> Must bereft of land-right roam, when the lords shall hear
> From afar (of all your fear), of your flight (to-day),
> Of your deep disgrace. Death is better far
> For whatever warrior than a life of shame!"
>
> *Beowulf*, l. 2864.

I have translated this passage for its historic value. It equals the passage in Tacitus which describes the tie of chief to companion and companion to chief among the Germans, and which recounts the shame that fell on those who survived their lord.

The news of the death of the king is now carried to the host who waited on the sea-edge the issue of the fight. The messenger describes what he has seen, and then (relating in an episode, which I have elsewhere spoken of, the blood-feud between themselves and the Sweons) predicts that the Sweons will come and harry them now that Beowulf is dead. There are treasures where he lies, but none shall wear them in memory of the dead, neither warrior nor maiden fair; and with the word he thinks again of the fates of war that overhung them because "the leader of their battle has ceased from laughter, from sport and singing joy."

Therefore shall the maidens, sad of mood, of gold bereft, not once, but often, tread an alien land.

> Therefore shall the spear,
> Many a one, now morning-cold, be by fingers met around,
> Lifted in the hands (of ghosts); and the Harp shall never more
> With its clanging wake the warriors, but the Raven wan,
> Fiercely-eager o'er the fated, shall be full of talking,
> To the earn shall say how it sped him at the gorging,
> When he with the wolf on the war-stead robbed the slain.
> *Beowulf*, l. 3021.

This is a finer use than usual of the common poetic attendants of a battle, the wolf, the eagle, and the raven. The three are here like three Valkyrie, talking of all that they have done; and I have elsewhere said that the wild note that fills the passage is repeated centuries after in the ballad of the *Two Ravens*.

Then all the host rose and went, weeping, to see the king where he lay, under the Ness of the Sea-Eagle, and the poet (whose work is here not a little spoiled by later insertions) paints the scene so that we see it with our eyes. They found the giver of rings dead, outstretched upon the meadow, and Naegling, his sword, broken by his side, and the Fire-Drake, scorched with his own gleeds, fifty feet of him, on the fire-blackened and blood-stained ground. They saw the rocky arch above the cave, and the stream that rushed from it, and Wiglaf, seated on a stone in that grassy place, near his dear lord, and the shamed cowards standing by, and, in the midst of all, shining as if in mockery, golden cups and bowls scattered on the grass, rings and jewels, "swords that had lain a thousand winters, it seemed, in the lap of earth, so rusty, eaten through" were they; and above them, as fitted a dead hero, as was the honour of Scyld when he died, the golden banner glistened.

Add to this the picture of the host descending into the hollow between the cliffs, and gathering round their king, and we see the whole as the poet meant us to behold it. Wiglaf tells them how bravely the battle was fought; how impossible it was to hold back the prince from dying for his folk; how he had seen the cave and the golden things and borne them forth to Beowulf while he was yet alive. "He bade me greet you, and prayed you to make a high barrow for him on the cliff. Let the bier be made ready, and I will show you the wonders of the hoard." Seven went with him, and one bore a lighted torch. Little was left in the cave, but they bore it forth, laded a wain with the wrought gold, heaved the dragon over the cliff, and carried the hoar-headed warrior to the point of Hrones-naes.

<pre>
                              Now the gleed shall fret—
And the wannish flame wax high   on the War-strength of the warriors,
Him who oft awaited   iron showers in the fight,
When the storm of arrows,   sent a-flying from the strings,
Shot above the shield wall,   and the shaft its service,
Fledged with feathers, did,   following on the barb.
                                  Beowulf, l. 3114.
</pre>

So cried Wiglaf in his pride and sorrow; and they burned their king, as I have told at the beginning; and then they made his barrow and sang his death-song.

<pre>
Then the Weder-folk   worked upon that place,
On the hanging cliff, a howe   that was high and broad,
By the farers on the waves   far and wide to be descried;
And within a ten of days   they uptimbered there
Of the Battle-fierce the beacon;   and the best of Brands [1]
With a wall they wrought around,   as most worthily (his men),
All the men of wisest mind,   might imagine it.
</pre>

---

[1] *Bronda betost.* I do not think I can allege any authority for translating *Brond* here as a title of Beowulf. But the O. N. *Brand-r* a sword, often means a warrior, as the German *Degen* does. And we use the term "a good sword" for a good fighter. I have let the translation remain, but otherwise it would be "the best, the most famous of Burnings."

Then they did into the barrow   armlets and bright gems,
And the precious things of price,   all that from the hoard
The high-hearted men   late had heaved away;
Let the earth hold fast   of the earls the treasure,
Gold within the grit-wall;   where it now abideth,
Of as little use to men   as of old it was.
Then about the barrow   rode the Beasts of battle,
Twelve in all were they,   bairns of Æthelings,
Who would speak their sadness,   tell their sorrow for their king.

So with groaning sorrowed   all the Geät folk,
All his hearth-companions,   for their house-lord's overthrow;
Quoth they that he was,   of the world-kings all,
Of all men, the mildest,   and to men the kindest,
To his people gentlest,   and of praise the keenest.
                                        Beowulf, l. 3157.

With these words of pathetic farewell *Beowulf* closes; and I think that this carefully-wrought conclusion, and this retrospective summary of the hero's character, go far to prove, however many ballads and lays may have been used by the writer, that the poem was composed as a whole, with one aim, by one poet.

CHAPTER IV

THE EPISODES OF "BEOWULF," AND THE "FIGHT AT FINNSBURG"

THE episodes in the poem of *Beowulf* are sufficiently important to deserve separate treatment. One of them is connected with the *Fight at Finnsburg*, a distinct fragment of heathen English poetry; and this fragment is included in this chapter. Another, the first episode, is the story of Scyld and his burial, but this belongs so plainly to the mythical elements in the poem that I reserve it for the chapter on those elements.

I begin, therefore, with the second episode which is that of Beowulf's swimming match with Breca. On the evening of his arrival at Hrothgar's court, Beowulf is mocked by the jealousy of Hunferth, who is the king's feast-companion. "Art thou that Beowulf who strove with Breca in swimming, risking your lives in the deep water, when winter's flood weltered with great billows? Seven nights ye strove, and he conquered thee in swimming." Beowulf answered, full of wrath, that Hunferth was a liar, and that the victory was his, not Breca's. He describes his adventure, his battle with the sea-monsters, his coming to the land.[1] The interest

---

[1] There are those, of whom Laistner is the most minute, who turn the whole of this Breca and Beowulf story into a Nature myth. "Beowulf, who is a wind hero" (the cloud-cleanser, for Laistner makes Beowa = der Feger, and Wolf = Nebel), "is in this story of Breca, the spring-wind. Breca is *der Brecker*, who rules over the Brondings, that is, the sons of the flaming brand, and is himself a son of

of the story lies in this — that even if the story be mythical, it is coloured by the sea-life of our ancestors or of their northern kindred. Many were the young men in the ancient days who challenged one another to go forth in winter time upon the sea to fight with whales and great seals and the walrus.[1] Five nights Beowulf and Breca

Beanstan who stands for *Bohnstein*, the sun. His swimming wager with Beowulf through the wintry sea, in the teeth of the icy northern storm, means 'the sun and the wind fight with the winter.'" This is the most interesting of the mythical explanations of the story. There are many others, but they are easily imagined and easily invented.

[1] I may as well introduce here in a note two verses and a half of Anglo-Saxon poetry, which belong to that early time when Christianity and Heathendom were still somewhat interwoven. They are supposed to be of the eighth century, and they refer to some whale or walrus hunt on the sea-coast. The lines seem apart from the English type of poetry, and I should conjecture that they were carved much later by some Englishman who had been roving with the Northmen, and who, perhaps by way of the Mediterranean, came to France, and left his casket behind him. This inference is suggested by the history of the lines.

They are cut in runes on the side of a casket made of whale or walrus bone, and they record the closing event of the hunt. On another of its sides is the rude carving of a scene (as Bugge has shown) out of the Weland saga. A woman, Beadohild, comes to Weland; the body of her murdered brother lies at her feet, and another man, Egil, Weland's brother, catches birds that Weland may make his feather-garment for his flight. Over his head *Egili* may be traced, written in runes. The casket was found, as well as conflicting evidence will allow us to judge, in the sacristy of a church at Clermont-Ferrand in Auvergne. Thence it came into possession of a family in Auzon, Haute-Loire, and was used as a work-basket. The silver bands were removed from it, and it fell into pieces. In this state it was bought at Paris from an antiquarian dealer by Franks, who gave it to the British Museum. The next thing to say is that the maker not only knew the Weland saga, but was also a Christian, for on the side opposite the scene from the saga is carved the birth of Christ, and the worship of the Magi. In runic writing near the three men the word Magi is cut. Stephens identified the carving on the top and the sides of the casket as the Taking of Jerusalem, the Beheading of John the Baptist, and the Suckling of Romulus and Remus by the Wolf. It is plain that these identifications are disputable. If the Latin wolf-story be really represented, it suits my conjecture that the writer was a Northumbrian who went with a Viking to the Mediterranean. One side, long lost, has now, I am told, been found, and is said to represent part of the Siegfried story.

Here are the lines, with my translation—

        Hronaes ban
  Fiscflodu ahof on ferg(enbyrig);
  Warþ gasric grorn, þaer he on greut giswom.
        [This] bone of the whale
  Up-heaved the fish-floods to a fortress of waters;
  Sore the sea wailed, when he swam o'er the shingle.

The lines have been translated in many different fashions; and we owe to kept together, not swimming, but sailing in open boats (to swim the seas is to sail the seas), then storm drove them asunder when they were near the land—some indented coast where the sea-beasts had their haunt. "Flood drove us apart," said Beowulf, and the whole description breathes of the Northern seas—

> Wallowing waters, coldest of weathers,
> Night waning wan; while wind from the North,
> Battling-grim, blew on us; rough were the billows.
> *Beowulf*, l. 546.

A great sea-beast attacks him, he is drawn out of the boat into the sea, and plunges to the bottom with the foe; but he stabs him to the heart, and rises again amidst the herd. It is plain the fight takes

---

Mr. Sweet the explanation of *gasric* by *garsecg*, which makes the last line clear. But he makes *fiseflodu* the subject and *ban* the object. "The fish-flood lifted the whale's bones on to the mainland." Wülker has shown, as I think, the impossibility of this translation. *Flodu* is a neuter plural, and must be the object after *ahof* and *ban* the subject. The whale's bone he takes to mean the whole whale, and translates "the whale heaved up the fish-floods." *Ferg-(enbyrig)* has also its difficulty; and Sweet translates it by "the mainland"; but, again, Wülker seems right when he translates it *wasserburg, meeresburg*. *Fergen, firgen,* frequently means "water, the sea," and *fergen byrig* would be "a sea like a fortress." Wülker does not, however, ask himself what the writer of the runes *saw* when he was writing them, nor is there any need for the harsh taking by him of the bone of the whale for the whole body of the whale. The story told in the lines, and I presume that it is the story told by the hunter of how he got the ivory of the casket, seems to be something like this—

The bone of the whale is the ivory jaw and teeth of the Sperm whale, a portion of which is here made into a casket. It is this, set in his mighty head, which lifts the sea in front of him as he rushes through it, into a piled-up heap of waters which, indeed, driven before him into a wide curve, would closely resemble the half circle of the outwork of a fortress; and many a time the whale-men have seen the animal carrying the sea in front of him in this fashion. Or, our casket-maker—and this explanation gives more meaning to the *fergenbyrig)* —may have seen the whale broach head foremost into the air, bearing up with him, as it were, a castle of water, a mountainous burg of sea. Then he tells the rest of the story of his piece of ivory. The hunters drove the great beast shoreward, or of itself it got entangled in the shallows and reefs, and there it died on the shingle pierced with lances; but before it died all the shallow waters of ocean, lashed by its struggles, wailed and mourned.

If this be a true explanation, it is the rapid record of the hunt in which this very piece of ivory was secured; and it tells first of how the whale behaved in deep ocean, and then how it died in the shallows. Perhaps, for the sake of the vividness of the picture, and of seizing this bit of our fathers' sea-life clearly, this note is not too long. See Note at the end of this volume.

place near to the land, for the dead are lying on the sea-strand in the morning, "put to sleep by swords." Beowulf slays nine of the nickers, "so that never again they shall hinder the journey of those that fare upon the sea." Then the sun arose—

> From eastward came light,
> Bright beacon of God; the billows grew still;
> So that now I could see the sea-nesses (shine),
> The windy rock-walls! Wyrd often delivers
> An earl yet undoomed, if his daring avail.   l. 569.

"Then the flood bore me up to the land of the Fins, worn with my voyage."

Whether this adventure actually belonged to Beowulf or got into his story from some other quarter, makes little matter. Breca, who is in the tale a young fellow, is afterwards chief of the Brondings, a tribe mentioned in *Widsith*. The story seems legendary, not mythical; and the return of Breca to his home reads like a piece of Homer. When the sea had upborne him on the land of the Heathoraemas it is said, "Thence he sought his sweet home-land, beloved of his folk, the land of the Brondings, his fair city of peace, where he kept his people, his citadel, his treasure. So, in good sooth, did the son of Beanstan fulfil against thee (Beowulf) all the pledge that he had made." Some history lies at least in the names, and removes the tale from the region of pure myth. Moreover, this nicker story, and the description of the nickers that lie and sleep on the reefs around the sea-hole where Grendel lived, render it, I think, probable that the walrus and the greater seals lived in prehistoric times on the coasts of Norway and Sweden, and that out of them were created by the popular imagination the sea-monsters of mythology and legend.

The third episode is introduced in the description of the bard who, in the morning after Grendel's death, strives to compose with art a tale of Beowulf's exploit, so that he may sing it in the evening. Apparently he kindles himself up to this creative endeavour by reciting the saga of Sigemund the Waelsing. What we hear of it in *Beowulf* is quite different from the Norse or the German versions, and is probably the oldest literary form of the saga. It is not Sigurd or Siegfried the son of Sigmund, who destroys the worm (not here as yet named Fafnir), but Sigmund himself; and the bard at Hrothgar's court looked back on the story as an old one. He told what he "had heard men say of Sigemund's noble deeds, of much that was unknown, of the battles of the Waelsing, of the feuds and the crime, of his far journeys of which men knew nothing certainly, save Fitela (the Sinfiötli of the Edda), who was with him; for ever they were true comrades in all battles, and very many of the race of the eotens had they slain with swords. But to Sigemund came no little fame, and after his death it lasted, since the hero had slain the worm, the watcher of the hoard. He, going under the gray stone, alone had dared the dreadful deed. Fitela was not with him. Yet his sword drove through the wondrous worm, so that the noble iron stood fast in the wall of rock. There lay the dragon dead. The offspring of Waels enjoyed the hoard of rings. At his own will he bore into the breast of the ship the glittering treasures. The worm (so I read the meaning) melted in his own heat. Of wanderers he was the most widely famed among all people by deeds of strength; a shelter of warriors. For that in old time he had honour."

This is all that is said in *Beowulf* about the Volsunga Saga.[1] Whether the episode be as old, or older than the rest of the poem, cannot be said for certain, but it is worth while to put it clearly forth, so famous is the story; and the rude simplicity of the tale, undeveloped as yet into the two personages of Sigmund and Sigurd, makes for its antiquity. It pleases me to think that it is in English literature we possess the first sketch of that mighty saga which has for so many centuries engaged all the arts, and at last in the hands of Wagner the art of music.

The fourth episode is the story of Finn king of Friesland over-lord of Jutland[2] and of his sons, in battle with Hnaef and Hengest his lieutenant, and of the events which followed. It is sung at the feast in Heorot after the death of Grendel. That it was a well-known and popular lay is plain, not only because the bard sings but a portion of it, as if the rest were well known to his hearers, but also because we possess a fragment of another poem on the same subject, written also in English by another

---

[1] I have wondered if the phrase used about the treasure hid in the dragon's cave in lines 3069, 3072 may not be a late intrusion into the story from the Volsunga Saga, and related to the curse which attended on the hoard of the Niblungs.

[2] I follow Grein in the arrangement of this story; but it has been explained in many other ways. It is questioned whether this fragment relates the first battle with Finn (as in the story told above), or whether it is an account of the second battle in which vengeance is taken on Finn. It is questioned *who* is besieged in Finnsburg—Finn himself or his enemy? And it is questioned whether this fragment is part of a larger poem, or the lay of a single battle? Various have been the answers to these questions and the ingenuity of the theories is such that the main question—of what kind is the poetry?—somewhat disappears.

There was no doubt a Finn saga sung all over the coasts of the Northern Sea, with many stories built into it, and some of these may have been, in variant forms, carried on into later sagas. I do not think that this English fragment is a part of this larger saga, but that it is a separate lay, of which we have lost the beginning and the end.

hand. Curiously enough this other fragment, which has been entitled the *Fight at Finnsburg*, supplies us with a part of the tale which is wanting in *Beowulf*; and I shall speak of it before I come to the related episode in *Beowulf*.

It seems that Finn, king of the North Frisians and of the Eotenas, *i.e.* of the Jutes, son of Folcwalda, was married to Hildeburh, daughter of Hoce the Dane and sister of Hnaef. Finn, angry with or jealous of the Danes, invited Hnaef to come and stay with him as guest (much as Ætla invites the Niblungs) with the intention of slaughtering him. Hnaef comes with sixty men, and his right-hand man was Hengest. They are lodged in a great hall in Finnsburg—Finn's town in Jutland,—and at night, when all are asleep, Finn and his men surround the hall with fire and sword. It is at this point that the *Fight at Finnsburg* begins.

This fragment of fifty lines which, for the sake of form, I speak of here and not separately, is probably much of the same date as the early lays of Beowulf. It was discovered by Dr. George Hickes on the cover of a MS. of Homilies in the library at Lambeth Palace, and published by him in his *Thesaurus Linguarum Septentrionalium*. The leaf itself has been lost. We have only the copy Hickes made of it. It is a happy fortune which has selected so vigorous and picturesque an episode for preservation. The shout of Hnaef, aroused from sleep by the cry of the besiegers, his call to his comrades, the fierce and rapid speech of the warriors to one another, the challenges, the delight in war, have almost an Homeric manner, and we ought to have some pride when we think that verse of this direct and passionate character was written by men of our own race so many years ago.

Hnaef[1] had leaped to his feet "young and warlike," at the noise of the foe outside, and cried aloud—

    This no eastward dawning is,   nor is here a dragon flying,
    Nor of this high hall   are the horns a burning.

    But they rush upon us here;—   Now the ravens sing,[2]
    Growling is the gray-wolf,   grim the war-wood rattles,
    Shield to shaft is answering.   Shining now the moon is,
    Full the welkin under;   now the woeful deeds arise,
    Which will into making put   all this malice of the folk!
    But do ye awaken now,   men of war of mine,
    Have your hands a-ready,   think on hero-deeds.
    Fight ye in the front,   be of fiery mood.
    .   .   .   .   Then did many a thegn
    Rise, begemmed with gold,   girt him with his sword.

    And two lordly warriors   went to guard the doors,
    Sigeferth and Eaha,   and their swords they drew.
    At the other gates up-stood   Ordlaf and Guthlaf,
    And Hengest himself.   He strode upon their track.

Garulf and Guthhere, two other warriors, urge each other on, and a fierce hero cried aloud, "Who held the door?" And the answer came such as Ulysses might have given in his hall to Antilochus.

---

[1] Wülker thinks that this young fellow is Hengest and not Hnaef. In his opinion (and he follows others) the fight in this fragment is to be introduced between lines 1145, 1146 in *Beowulf*. Hnaef has already fallen, and it is Hengest who speaks. See for the rest of this view page 315 in the *Grundriss*.

[2] *Fugelas singað, gylleð græghama*, is often translated, "the birds sing, the cricket chirps," but the phrase seems to have no meaning. I think that Hnaef is declaring that war and fighting is come upon them, and he uses the well-known images of the bird and the beast of battle to tell his folk what is at hand. The *fugelas*, the "birds," would then mean the ravens whose song went with the hosts to war, and *gylleð græghama* would then be "the gray wolf (him of the gray cloke) is howling." Others, however, make *græghama* mean the "gray war shirt," and *gylleð* "is ringing," and this seems adopted by the best scholars. If so, I certainly would not retain the translation of *fugelas* as "birds," but take it metaphorically, and translate it "arrows" or "spears." Both, when flying through the air, are spoken of by the Anglo-Saxons as "adders of the battle," and I see no reason why they should not be called "birds." As to the spears singing, yelling through the air, that is a common phrase in ancient folk-poetry.

Sigeferth's my name, quoth he,   I'm the Secga's lord,
Widely known, a wanderer;   many woes I bore,
Battles hard to bear!   Here is banned to thee
Whatsoever thou thyself   will'st to seek on me.[1]

Then was at the wall   wail of deadly battle,
Then the boat-shaped shield   must the bone-helm break
In the hands of heroes.   All the house-floor rang again;
Till amid the fight   headlong fell Garulf—
He the earliest of all   of these earth indwellers,
Son of Guthlaf—   good men many fell about him.
High the heap of corses;[2]   hovered there the raven,
Swart and sallow-brown;   shone the gleam of swords,
As if all Finns-Burh   were with fire aflame.
Never heard I that more nobly   sixty heroes brave
Better bore themselves   in the battle-strife of men.
Never since did swains of war   better pay for sweetened mead
Than his house-carles then   paid to Hnaef their due.
Five of days they fought   and there fell of them,
Of his war men, none;   but well they held the doors.

The few lines which follow seem to tell that their chief was at last wounded to the death. He said that his byrnie was broken, and his helm cloven, and he gave over the command to another. But no name is here mentioned, and we should not have known what happened were it not for the singer in Hrothgar's hall. He has taken up the story at the very point where the fragment of the *Fight at Finnsburg* drops it. We hear that it was Hnaef who was slain, and that Hengest, succeeding him, fought on until nearly all the men of Finn were slain, and among them Finn's sons by Hildeburh.

It is a tragic position, such as is frequent in these Northern stories, and the woman dominates it. Hilde-

---

[1] This is a very doubtful translation, but I suggest it, and mean by it "The fate, whatever it may be, which thou thinkest to inflict on me, will be your own. You would slay me, I will slay you; that is determined for you." But it may be better to translate it more simply and literally "I have borne many woes, hard battles, which are again decreed here; which thou wilt seek with me."

[2] This is a guess at the meaning. There are a number of different readings.

burh has lost her brother Hnaef at her husband's hands, and she has lost her sons who had fought against her brother. Peace is made between Hengest and Finn, pledges and blood-money taken; but the central point of passion in the singer's song is the grief of Hildeburh and the burning on one pyre of her brother's body with that of her son. No man could believe that this peace would last; too much of grief, anger, and brooding revenge is contained in the things done.

Hengest went with Finn to Friesland and spent the winter with him and Hildeburh. He remembered his land, but the "ocean rolled in storm, and the waves were locked with ice," and he could not go. But when the winter was gone and the bosom of earth was fair, he "thought more of vengeance than of voyaging," and stayed on to slake his wrath. Finn knew it; and Hengest fell by the hand of Hunlafing.[1] Nor did the feud end there, for Guthlaf and Oslaf took up the quarrels of their dead chieftains Hnaef and Hengest, and gathering a host sailed away to Friesland. In turn, they attacked Finn in his hall, stormed it, and brought death-bringing sword-bale to him. All his high Burg was covered with the dead, and the Scylding Danes loaded their ships with his plunder. Moreover, they took Hildeburh (who, we may imagine, had wrought against her husband), and bore the royal woman back over the sea-road to the Danes, to her own people. It is but the outline of a story, but it is of that quality in the events which is capable of fresh development as singer after singer took up the theme. The situations are passionate, and the events; and

---

[1] This passage, lines 1143-1145, is otherwise explained. See Earle's note on the passage. *Deeds of Beowulf.* Clarendon Press.

every singer could refit them as he pleased and create new ones. It is a pity they did not get hold of it in Iceland, where they might have given it the form it so lamentably lacks at present.

Another story, the story of Heremod (not, I think, the mythic Heremod), was also in vogue when *Beowulf* grew into a poem, and was evidently used to point the moral of the duties of a king; a stock example of a bad chieftain. The tale is used in this fashion twice in *Beowulf*, and enables us to see one of the ways in which the bards filled up their subject when they sang. Heremod's shame is contrasted with the glory of Sigemund, and with the prudence, patience, generosity, and gentleness of Beowulf as a chieftain. But his wickedness caused him to be remembered, and he illustrates that type of man among the Northerns, of which there are examples in the Icelandic sagas, whom power and pride destroy through the indulgence of passion. Heremod slew all his servants till he was left alone in a joyless life; he gave no rings to men, and when his strength was decayed, he was betrayed to his foes.

The next episode is that of Thrytho, the wicked woman, as Heremod was the wicked king. She is contrasted (and her story is brought in for that purpose) with Hygd, the queen of Hygelac, young, wise, well-trained, and generous. No one dared look Thrytho in the eyes, save only her husband, and whoever did, paid for his courage, for she had him slain. She seems also to have compassed the death of her husband. But afterwards, driven by her father's counsel from her country, the mythic Offa married her and tamed her. But she was happy to be tamed, for great love held her for this prince of heroes. As a violent woman stained with crime, she stands alone in *Beowulf*.[1]

The women of *Beowulf* are of the fine Northern type; trusted and loved by their husbands and by the nobles and people; generous, gentle, and holding their place with dignity. They serve the heroes in hall with the mead, not as servants, but as doing honour to their friends. They, like the king, bestow gifts. At the king's death they are regents while their sons are young, and can dispose of the kingdom, as Hygd attempts to do. Wealhtheow is lady of the feast, and when Beowulf comes to her husband's help, is mindful of courtesies, and welcomes him. Her heart is pleased when the hero boasts of his prowess. When he has conquered Grendel, she is the first to speak to him at the feast. But she does all in order. First she speaks to her husband, then to his nephew Hrothulf, and claims the kindness of Hrothulf for her sons. Her motherhood is foremost in her heart. When she sees Beowulf sitting between her boys, she gives him a jewelled collar, and begs his friendly counsel for them. Her last words make clear that she is obeyed like her lord, and sketch in a moment the Teutonic tie of king to thegn, of people to their king.

> Here is every earl   to the other true,
> Mild of mood he is, true man to his lord,
> All the thegns at one, ever eager are the people
> Do as I demand of you, warriors drinking here!
> *Beowulf*, l. 1228.

---

[1] Two accounts seem to be given of her, one after another: two forms perhaps of the original saga. One represents her as a termagant even after her marriage, the other as mild and gentle after her union with Offa. The other explanation which gives her two different husbands and makes the whole story one, is given above in the text. Suchier finds parallels to the story in many other sagas. Thrytho has herself been compared with the historical Cyneþrið, the Drida of Matthew of Paris; and it is probable that this tale of Drida slipped into the legend of the Mercian Offa from the saga of Offa the Angle.

The other women are Hildeburh and Freaware.
Of the first enough has been said in the Finn story
to make us feel her character; of the second Beowulf
speaks when he gives an account of his doings to
Hygelac.

Nothing is said of her personally, but Beowulf's
talk about her sets before us another episode intruded into the poem. It contains a position of
affairs which we might easily match in the Icelandic
stories.[1] There has been a desperate battle between
Hrothgar the Dane Freaware's father, and Froda,
King of the Heathobeardnas, in which Froda is
slain. To appease the feud, Hrothgar gives his
daughter to wife to Ingeld son of Froda, and it is
owing to this custom of putting an end to wars by
means of a marriage that women have in Northern
poetry the name of "peace-weavers." Beowulf has
not much hope that this peace will last, and the reason
he gives illustrates the way a quarrel broke out again
among our forefathers. "What will happen," he asks,
"when Freaware, the Danish princess, comes into the
hall of the Heathobeardnas, and they remember the
slaughter of their folk that the Danes had made?
What will happen when they see with her a son of the
Danes wearing the sword of Froda?" The answer
he gives has all the character of an extract from a
separate saga inserted in this place.

The Prince of the Heathobeardnas and his people
will take it ill, when Freaware steps into the hall, that
the Danish prince who attends on her (one of her

---

[1] This episode of Freaware and Ingeld the son of Froda may be compared
with the saga of Ingellus in Saxo Grammaticus. That saga is worked up out of
old Northern lays, and we have here a part of one of these. "When Withergyld
was slain" is otherwise translated "where the indemnity, or the vengeance,
failed." The phrase is on the next page.

brothers, of whom seven sagas were written) should boast himself there of the spoils of the Heathobeardnas. On him gleams the heirloom of the old hero, his hard and ring-decked sword, a treasure of the Heathobeardnas. Then at the beer-drinking a gray spear-warrior will see the jewelled hilt, and remember him of the spear-death of Froda who carried it of old. Wrath will be in his soul; he will turn to Ingeld, the young chieftain at his side, and stir his war-fury with this word—

Canst thou not, my friend,   know at sight this sword,
Which indeed thy father   into fighting bore,
Underneath his hosting-helm,   in his latest hour?
Dear that iron was,   where the Dane-folk murdered him!
Theirs was then the war-field,   when Withergyld lay low,
After heroes' slaughter!   Keen the Scyldings are!
Now of these same slaughterers   here the son of one,
Prideful of his spoils,   paces through the hall,
Yelps in triumph of the slaying,   bears with him the treasured sword
That thyself of right   should'st alone possess.

Beowulf, l. 2047.

Thus with bitter words he stirs up Ingeld, till the Lady's thegn, for that his father slew Froda, sleeps blood-stained after the biting of the bill, having paid the forfeit of his life; but the slayer escapes, knowing well the land. Then the sword-oaths on either side will be broken, both by Danes and by Heathobeardnas. Deadly hate will boil in Ingeld — though he has caused the death of the boasting Dane—and the love he had for Freaware will become cooler through the waves of care. Therefore, ends Beowulf, put no trust in that alliance![1]

---

[1] There is an allusion to this same story of Ingeld and Freaware and Hrothgar in the *Widsith*; and Beowulf's prediction (put, after the event, into his mouth to show his wisdom) was fulfilled. Ingeld *did* go to war with Hrothgar his father-in-law, to avenge his father's death. The warriors of the Heathobeardnas came sailing into the same fiord that Beowulf sailed into when he came to Heorot,

It is a vivid picture, and, as we read it, a whole troop of similar motives come flying to its side out of the Icelandic tales.

The other episodes are the death of Hygelac, the earlier events of Beowulf's life, the earlier wars of the Geats. Of these I have already given an account in the story of Beowulf's life. The manners of our forefathers, as the tale represents them, now remain to be noticed.

Of the customs of the men and women from whom we have descended, and of their types of character much has been told in the poem and in the episodes. We have seen them as kings and queens, and there is a certain grave stateliness about their bearing and speech, and about the ceremony with which they are approached. They are respected by, and they respect, their followers. Rank is duly observed, and it is fitting that kings and nobles know the rank, the ancestry and the renown of other kings and nobles in other countries. The tie that knits the thegns — the comrades in war and feast — to the king and to each other is kept unbroken, and is the first of the duties of life. The breaking of it through cowardice or untruth is attended with mortal disgrace, with outlawry it may be, and brings dishonour on the families of the cowards. Extreme courtesy is the rule, rudeness such as Hunferth's the exception; and jealousy and drink, combined with a character which is itself violent even to slaying of his kinsmen, are carefully

---

landed, stormed over the hill, and attacked Hrothgar in his hall. But the king, though old, was still dreadful. Hrothulf, his nephew, whom we hear of in the poem, was faithful, and they stood bravely to their arms for the homestead. The Heathobeardnas were pushed back to the sea, and Ingeld was slain. The lines from *Widsith* tell us the story. "Hrothwulf and Hrothgar hewed down at Heorot the host of the Heathobeardnas. There they bowed the point of the sword of Ingeld."

VOL. I   H

assigned as the causes of this rudeness. Hospitality and frank generosity, lavish gifts and their interchange are also rigorous duties of life. If they drink hard, we have seen that they also sing well. Poets are always at their feasts, and the playing of the harp; and singing and harp-playing are not only in the hands of professionals, if I may use the word. Every warrior is supposed to be capable of these arts. As to the hard-drinking, it has been, if we look into these Anglo-Saxon poems, much exaggerated. It does not seem that they drank as hard as the gentlemen of the eighteenth century in the British Isles. Frequently we find passages, not only here in these early poems, but afterwards, where the man who gets drunk is looked on with scorn and reproof. All this is very different from the traditional image of our English ancestors, which is still painted of them by some of our own writers, and by our neighbours over the channel. In Taine's *History of English Literature* his sketch of the early English folk is ridiculous. One would think that the ancestors of the French were less greedy, less drunken, less brutal, less vicious than those of the English; that they were more dignified, more loyal, of better manners, and of better laws, than the Teutonic folk. The contrary was the case; and as to literature, the forefathers of the French had none which time has considered worthy to last.

There is, in conclusion, a word to say upon the literary merit of *Beowulf*, and on the Christian elements in the poem. The first of these Christian elements is the sense of a fairer, softer world than that in which the Northern warriors lived. I shall draw attention to this change hereafter, but here is an instance of it. After the description of Heorot among its desolate moors the Christian poet writes—"*He* said, who could tell the tale of the creation of men from old,[1] that the Almighty had wrought the earth, the glorious-glancing plain that water girts around: and in victorious power set the gleam of sun and moon to give light to dwellers in the land, and adorned the fields of earth with branched and leafy trees." The lines seem to have a softer movement than the other *Beowulf* verses, and above all, that sought-out pleasure in natural beauty which does not belong to the pagan, but does eminently belong to the Christian poetry of the English before the Conquest.

Another Christian passage derives all the demons, eotens, elves, and dreadful sea-beasts from the race of Cain. The folly of sacrificing to the heathen gods is spoken of; but a kind of excuse is made for this, as if the writer were sorry for his forefathers. "They knew not the Lord God." In another passage, with curious forgetfulness of this previous statement, Hrothgar is made to give thanks to God for the death of Grendel, and Beowulf's work is done in the strength of God. "The King of Glory works wonder on wonder; let thanks to him be quickly given. Now hath a hero, through the might of God, done that which all our wisdom could not do. Lo, whatever woman brought forth this son may say that the eternal Creator was gracious to her child-bearing."

---

[1] It seems to me (and perhaps others have without my knowledge thought the same) that this Christian piece may be from Caedmon. It reads like a quotation, "He who could the creation of men from old relate, said—" and the lines which I have translated above might be part of the three leaves missing in the MS. of the *Genesis* after the 168th line. Those missing pages would contain the account of the creation of the sun and moon and of the clothing of the earth with grass and trees. The *Beowulf* lines are 92-97.

As to the Wyrd, God has either made it, or He can avert it, or He is identified with it; all these ideas are expressed. Then there is the sermon of Hrothgar to Beowulf after the victory over Grendel. It is couched in the manner of the gnomic verses. God is director of the fates of men, and they are many. A few are sketched, and the fate of the man of mighty race who comes to a prosperous kingdom is chosen. He is happy, till a portion of pride enters into his soul—pride which in all early English poetry is the chief overthrower of the life of man—and the passage where the slayer of the soul lodges the bitter arrow, the deadly sin of pride, in the heart of the man is a good example of homiletic English verse, and its metaphor constantly occurs in Anglo-Saxon poetry.

The only other point is the belief in immortality, of which the early Teutonic pagans had but a dim vision, for the Valhalla seems to have been a post-Christian conception. The poet uses of the death of Hrethel and others common phrases like those we find in the *Anglo-Saxon Chronicle*: "He gave up human joy and chose the light of God" or "he chose the everlasting gain." Wherever these phrases occur, they spoil the natural impression of the poem, and we owe some thanks to the poet that he was merciful, and thought too well of his original story to do much of this kind of work.

When we think of the whole poem as it appeals to us in its unity, and ask ourselves what poetic standard it reaches, we must confess that it is not one of the great poems of the world. If we think of the date at which it was composed, the English have a right to be very proud of it, for it stands alone. There may have been others as good in the vernacular languages of Europe, but time has not chosen to preserve them, and this which it has preserved has a certain distinction in the fact that the story is unique, and the Grendel myth in it stands alone.

It has been called an epic, but it has no continuous self-evolution. It has, rather, two narratives concerning two remarkable events in a hero's life, each of which might be considered apart. It is narrative, then, rather than epic, but it has an epic quality in this—that the purification of the hero—the development of his character to perfection—is the main motive of the tale. When he appears again after fifty years of silence, he has the same moral dignity, the same equal and heroic heart in age that he had in youth. But we find him in a nobler position. He is not now the isolated hero; he has become the father of his people, the image of a great and worthy king. And at the last he dies for the sake of his folk, and leaves an immortal name. He knows, as he goes forth to the dragon, that Wyrd will now conquer his body, but she shall not conquer his soul. The moral triumph is attained, and fate, not Beowulf, is really conquered in the contest. This is the purification of the hero, and it is the ever-recurring theme of many a splendid poem. The subject, standing thus at the head of English literature, has silently handed down a great tradition of which our poets have not been unworthy. Nor have they been unworthy of the character-drawing which is so excellent in this poem. The unity of Beowulf's character gives to a broken-up poem some unity of design. There is also a force, a clear outline, a distinctiveness of portraiture in the other characters, which foretell that special excellence in English poetry — an excellence which has made its drama perhaps the most varied in the world.

It is another excellence of *Beowulf* that, when we leave out the repetitions which the oral condition of the poem created and excuses, it gets along. It is rapid, and it is direct. The dialogue is short, and says forcibly what it has to say; but it says it without much imagination, with scarcely one of those touches which mingle earth and heaven, or which go home to the depths of the human heart. But in many places it is imaginative by its direct vision of the thing or the situation which is described, and by the short and clear presentation of it. A certain amount also of imagination collects round the monsters of the moor and sea, but that is rather in the myth itself and in our own imagination of these wastes of nature than in the poetry, though I do not deny it altogether to the verse. Then, again, the poem is lamentably destitute of form. Each of the lays used had no doubt its own natural form, which we should find good if we could isolate them one from another. But the poet did not understand how to shape them afresh or to interweave them well. The Grendel part is much better done than the Dragon part; indeed, there are portions of this last story in the poem which seem to have been broken on the wheel.

But when all is said, we feel that we have scarcely a right to estimate the poem in this critical fashion unless we could have heard it delivered. To judge it in our study is like judging an altar-piece far away from the town and the associations for which it was originally painted. If we want to feel whether *Beowulf* is good poetry or not, let us place ourselves in the hall as evening draws on, when the benches are filled with

warriors and seamen, and the chief sits in the high
seat, and the fires flame in the midst, and the cup goes
round—and then hear the Shaper strike the harp.
With gesture, with the beat of his voice and of the
hand upon his instrument at each alliterative word
of the saga, he sings of the great fight with Grendel
or the dragon, of Hrothgar's giving, of the sea-voyage,
to men who had themselves fought against desperate
odds, to sailors who knew the storms, to the fierce
rovers of the deep, to great ealdormen who ruled
their freemen, to thegns who followed their kings
to battle and would die rather than break the bond
of comradeship. Then as we image this, and read
the accented verse, sharply falling and rising with
the excitement of the thing recorded, we understand
how good the work is, how fitted for its time and place,
how national, how full of noble pleasure.

CHAPTER V

THE MYTHICAL ELEMENTS IN "BEOWULF"

Now that we have gone through the *Beowulf* and its episodes, we are in a better position to consider certain elements in it which belong to literature, and to those myths which are the mothers of poetry. The historical and geographical questions are apart from my subject, nor do they belong to our England; but the question of the cycles of song which we trace in the poem, of the myths of Beowulf and Grendel, of Scyld and the Dragon, belongs to literature and to English literature.

As to the cycles of song, we have in the *Beowulf* evidence of heroic sagas which are contemporary with the supposed historical life of the hero, that is, with the sixth century; and evidence also in it of still earlier cycles. The first saga-cycle includes the songs sung concerning the earlier deeds of Beowulf before he became king. I do not mean the Grendel story, which was taken into the legend of Beowulf after the lay of his death, but the lays to which the hero himself alludes when he is dying. Then it is also plain that there was a lay which concerned the deeds of Hygelac, and especially his death in the sixth century. If Hrothgar too was an historical personage, and we may well believe it, his doings at Heorot, his feuds and battles were sung; and the mention of him and his quarrel with Ingeld in the poem of *Widsith* makes this very probable. We also understand from the accounts of the fates of Hrethel and his sons that there were a number of lays about treaties, feuds, and wars among the Swedes, Danes, Geats, Frisians, and others, which have no record except in the pages of *Beowulf*, but to which allusions are made in later sagas. Far-famed heroes like Ecgtheow, Ongentheow, Froda, pass us by, noble phantoms, the likeness of a kingly crown upon them, and are seen no more. The whole cycle of these lays is probably contemporary with those songs sung among the Goths of which Jordanes tells—the *barbara et antiquissima carmina* which Eginhard in the ninth century says were collected by command of Charles the Great, but which have unfortunately been lost.

Beowulf suggests to us the existence of a still earlier cycle. The poets at the court of Hrothgar sing not only of heroes of their own time, but of men and women who have passed away, who have already become legendary. They chant the deeds of Finn and Hnaef and Hildeburh and Hengest, of Heremod and Healfdene, of Hoce; and the mention of these names, outside of *Beowulf*, in the poems of *Widsith* and the *Fight of Finnsburg* confirms the conjecture that there was a whole cycle of lays which preceded *Beowulf* and dealt with these partly mythical, partly historical personages. Another legendary hero whom we touch in the later part of *Beowulf* is Offa, and the stories connected with him have already become lays. A yet older lay is that of Sigemund and Fitela, and we are told in *Beowulf* that the story was already ancient in the days of Hrothgar. If Sigemund be Siegfried, and Siegfried, as Vigfusson thinks, Arminius, we reach back, but only through the name, to the first century. But we seem to be able to go even farther back to a still earlier cycle, to personages who are not legendary, but mythic. We come on Ing, the first king of the East Danes, the divine root of the Ynglings as well as of the Scyldings, of the Angles as well as of the Danes, and Ing is, some say, the same as Sceaf. We hear of Weland, the semi-divine smith, whose name is mossed with gray antiquity. Most important of all, we have in the legend of Scyld with which the poem opens, and whose tale is the same as Sceaf's—the story of the divine founder of the Teutonic tribes north of the Elbe, the earliest ancestor-god our fathers worshipped. These tales, these allusions belong to a distant cycle of lays, and may have been sung in centuries long anterior to our poem. In this point of view then, that of age, and suggestions of a still greater age, the interest of *Beowulf* is extraordinarily great. Embedded in it we find lay after lay, like fossil after fossil—each of which testifies to a different stratum of song.

The next question has regard to myths and mythical elements. There are commentators who seem to make the whole poem and all the personages in it mythical. This is to go too far in an easy path, and to forget the slow upbuilding, I do not say of the poem as we have it, but of the subject. A common nature-myth no doubt runs through the whole of it. An historical myth of great antiquity, the myth of Scyld or Sceaf, appears in its introduction. Added to these mythical, there are legendary elements, which have had either a root in some actual historical event, or have been connected with some hero who actually fought and ruled, and whose deeds, passing through legend, became part of the folklore of the nations; and the half-mythic, half-real animals of the sea in the story, belong, I think, to this folk-tale element. Added once more to this, there are historical elements like the battle of Hygelac with the Frisians.[1] Thus myth, legend, the folk-tale and a little history are conglomerated in the poem. These various elements do not exist separately, or at least it is very rarely that they do so. For the most part they interpenetrate one another. This is the case in the lay of the prince who sang his death-song and hid his treasure; who died after all his people had perished, and whose treasure the dragon found and guarded. A possible bit of history, a folk-tale, and a dragon myth mingle in that lay.

Again, to leave out many others, we come across elements which belong to commonly extended folk-tales in the story of Beowulf's youth. It is stated that he was not esteemed when he was young, and then appeared suddenly, to the surprise of all, as a great warrior. This is also told of the legendary Offa, son of Wermund, and stole afterwards into the tale of Offa of Mercia. Now it is one of the well-known characteristics of the heroes of the folk-tales—a characteristic handed down perhaps from some nature-myth —that their early years are obscure, and their person despised, that they are slothful or have some bodily defect, and that all in a moment, when their brothers

---

[1] Hygelac became in after days a legendary person. He is identified with Hugleik of the Heimskringla, and with a certain Huglacus Magnus, of whom an account is given in a MS. of the tenth century, where he has become a mythic personage, and where the enormous strength of Beowulf seems to have been added to him.

have failed, they suddenly shoot into power and intelligence. The very nursery tales, the flotsam and jetsam of the folk-tales, are full of the dull boy who rises, like the sun freeing itself from clouds, into the sudden and bold adventurer.

We get nearer to myth in the nickers of the poem, but there is a mixture of natural fact in the description of them. These great sea-beasts who attend on Grendel's dam, and guard, like the herds of Proteus, her sea-cave, may be partly mythical—images of the monstrous fury of the waves, of the lower powers of the wintry sea. We are told that their name is afterwards mixed up with Hnikarr (who is Woden in his relation to the sea), and with the Nix, the water demon, in his various forms. But when we touch them in the poem, we are with regard to them on the borderland between fact and myth, for at times they are scarcely to be distinguished from the tusked seals, and they are hunted by Hrothgar's men in much the same way as the Esquimaux to this day hunt the walrus. When they are also mentioned in the story of Beowulf's swimming match with Breca, they are half-mythical and half-actual sea-beasts, just like the story itself, which is myth, legend, and fact all rolled together.

These are not pure myths, but there are three things in the poem to which we may give that name— the story of Scyld, the contention of Beowulf with Grendel and the dragon, and the representation of Grendel and his dam.

The first of these is the story of Scyld. It is the introduction to the whole poem, and is followed by his burial, of which I have already written. Here is the passage—

> See now—of the Spear-Danes we have in stories heard,
> All the fame of our folk kings in the far-off days;
> How the doughty nobles did mighty deeds of war.
> Oft has Scyld, the son of Scef, from the Scathers' host,
> From the multitude of tribes, taken their mead-benches!
> Awe-inspiring was that earl, since when erst he was
> Found in his forlornness. Comfort did he find for that!
>
> *Beowulf*, ll. 1-7.

How he was forlorn is explained later on in the account of his burial when his subjects recall how he came as a child to their shores. "They laid him," it is said, "in the ship's bosom, with no less of costly treasures on his breast than those had done, who at his beginning had sent him forth of old, alone, an infant, over the ocean waves." Who *those* were, none knew. He had come in a boat, drifting to the shores of Scania, and when he is launched by his people into the sea after his death, and the poem says "That none knew who took up that lading," it refers to the mysterious *Those* who had sent him forth.

The next lines mark what the God-given child did for Scedeland—

> He up-waxed beneath the welkin, in his worthy glories grew,
> Till that every one, of the folk abiding round
> O'er the pathway of the whale, had to pay him tribute,
> Had to give him service. That was a good king. ll. 8-11.

Of him was born Beowulf (that is the Beaw of the Anglo-Saxon genealogists, not our Beowulf, who was a Geat, not a Dane), "the son of Scyld in Scedeland." Then Scyld died at his appointed time, and was buried.

This is our ancestral myth, the story of the first culture-hero of the North, "the patriarch," as Rydberg calls him, "of the royal families of Sweden, Denmark, Angeln, Saxland, and England. We might say that Sceaf (the Scyld of the poem) belongs especially to England, for it is only in England that this myth has been preserved. It is told, not only in *Beowulf*, but by four English chroniclers, who add details not given in *Beowulf*—Æthelweard, William of Malmesbury, Simeon of Durham, and Matthew of Westminster. The myth lasted then in the popular voice till the time of Henry II., and Rydberg says, with that certainty of a theorist which awakens doubt, that "a close examination shows that these chroniclers, with the *Beowulf* poem, have their information from three different sources, which again have a common origin in a heathen myth." They describe the boat drawing near the Scanian land, and a little boy asleep in it, with his head on a sheaf of corn, and around him treasures and tools, swords and coats of mail. The boat is richly adorned, and moves without sail or oar. The people draw it ashore, take up the boy with gladness, make him their king, and call him Scef or Sceaf, because he came to them with a sheaf of grain. This Sceaf is the same as the Scyid of *Beowulf*, or, as Scyld in the poem is the son of Sceaf (Earle translates *Scyld Scefing*, Scyld of the sheaf), the story of the father is there attributed to the son. Though the tale exists only in these English sources, yet the name Scef or Sceaf is elsewhere found in Northern Saga, and according to statements which may be traced to a Scef Saga, Denmark, Angeln, the north of Saxland, Götaland, and Svealand were ruled by him. "Legend derives from him," says Rydberg, "the dynasty of Upsala." *Beowulf*, as we have seen, brings all the royal family of Denmark from Scyld, the son of Sceaf, who in the Formanna sögur is called the god of the Scanians. Matthew of Westminster says that he ruled in Angeln, and the *Anglo-Saxon Chronicle*, in the complete genealogy of Wessex, traces back to

Sceaf the origin of the West-Saxon kings. He is also, if we may believe Rydberg,[1] the same as Skelfir, in the Icelandic Sagas, who is the progenitor of the Skjoldings and the Ynglings, and is further identified with Heimdal, the Vana god, who, under the name of Rig, lived among men for a time, and did for them the same good deeds that Sceaf did for Scania. He is then, it seems, the mythical hero from whom the tribes round the mouth of Elbe, and north of it in Denmark, South Sweden and the islands derive their origin and their civilisation. His story is the myth of the man who first taught them agriculture, and this is signified by the sheaf which is his pillow in the boat, and by his very name. The lines in *Beowulf* continue the sketch of him as the "culture-hero." When he waxed to man's estate he became, we hear, the king, established law and government, and first welded together from one centre the scattered tribes into a people. "All the folk abiding round had to give him service."

The question as to the place where he set up his kingdom, and whence he spread his cultivating influence, also belongs to the myth, and may belong to the larger question—Whence, in distant prehistoric times, came the Teutonic Aryans? The old Teutonic myth declares that out of Ash and Embla, two trees, the gods made the first human pair. These trees were found upon the seashore, as if they had drifted thither out of the great Ocean. We may infer then that there was a tradition that on some place on the sea-coast the

---

[1] Rydberg, *Teutonic Mythology*, pp. 87-95. When we have made every allowance for a certain fancifulness, and for the bias which a well-loved theory creates, this book is a real contribution to Northern mythology, and the myth of one original ancestor hero of the Danes, the English, the Saxons, and others, is rendered extremely probable.

Northern race stepped into history. The myth of Sceaf, in all its forms, tells the same tale; and the very region is named. The coast to which he comes from the sea is the coast of Southern Scandinavia. It is in Scedeland, we hear from *Beowulf*, that this dawn of Northern culture begins. "Scef," writes Æthelweard, "cum uno dromone advectus est in insula oceani quae dicitur Scani." William of Malmesbury and Matthew of Westminster bring him to the same place. When he grows up, he is, however, especially linked to Angeln. In the tale William of Malmesbury heard, Sceaf reigns, in a town which was then called Slaswich, but now Haithaby. Æthelweard tells the same tale — " Anglia Vetus sita est inter Saxones et Giotos, habens oppidum capitale quod sermone Saxonico Sleswic nuncupatur, secundum vero Danos, Haithaby." According then to the English tradition, Sceaf is our origin; the maker of the old England realm, the root of the English stem, and probably the divine race-hero and then the tribal deity whom the Angles worshipped when they came to Britain. It is in Sceaf then, as I dare to conjecture, and not in Woden, that we English find our earliest origin. He, veiled in the mists of ancient myth, may be our most ancient forefather, our ancestral god. The traditions of English chroniclers enshrine the story, and the ancient lay, of which we here speak, used as the introduction to *Beowulf*, tells of him — under the name of his son Scyld — of his advent to the land whence our fathers came, of his glory, his death, and his romantic burial.

This ancestor-worship was part of the ancient religion of the Angles. The founders of their tribes, the heroes who taught them agriculture and organised war, who had wrought many peoples into one nation, were supposed to be still alive in the hills and barrows where they had been buried, and to have a continual interest in their folk. In process of time they became more and more divine, and the mysterious passage of Scyld after his death into the unknown seas, and his reception by unknown beings, may symbolise his gradual rise from the hero into the semi-divine personage.

Behind these ancestor-deities were greater Beings, objects of a more solemn worship; and I venture to think that in early times the English had very few of these gods, and that their conceptions of them were of great simplicity. They worshipped a personification of the Heaven, whom they may afterwards have called Woden, and who lived, not in the shielded hall of Valhalla, but in the watch-tower of a mountain fort in the sky. They worshipped Earth, the wife of Heaven, the great Mother of all. They worshipped their Son, whom after-ages called Thor or Thunder, "the farmer's friend," the god of the work done on the soil of the earth, the glorious summer who fights with the wintry giants and with the monsters who make the blight and the fog—a personification of the beneficent and renewing powers of nature. This is the Trinity which includes, as I permit myself to think, all the great gods reverenced by our English forefathers. The complicated mythology which in after times the Norsemen made, partly out of old heathen and partly out of Christian elements, and which we are accustomed to impute to our forefathers' religion, was, it seems to me, at first unknown to them. If we would realise what the English thought of religion when they came to our island, we must clear our minds of these late conceptions, and think only of the Heaven and the Earth, and the Summer; of the Father and Mother of all things and of their Son, who *may* have been called - for we do not know whether they were or not —by the English equivalents of Woden, and Frigg, and Thor.[1] As time went on, new forms of these old thoughts produced new deities. We have instances of these in the two goddesses named by Baeda—Rheda (Hrede) and Eostra (Eastre), nature-deities, both of them probably personifications of the glory and brightness of the summer. Rheda, according to Grimm, is the shining and renownful goddess; Eostra the radiant being of the dawn, of the upspringing light. It was the worship of this latter goddess, and not of Balder, that the Christian priests found so deeply rooted among the English people that they adopted her name into Christianity, and transferred it, with all the thoughts that belonged to her myth, to the day of the resurrection of Jesus. They could not afford to lose all the emotions which belonged to the conquest of the Winter by the Summer.[2]

In opposition to, and beneath these beneficent powers, were the personifications of the destroying and harmful powers of nature, of the deep abyss of darkness, of the winter, the frost and storms, of the deadly vapours of the moorland and the fen, of the angry and overwhelming waves of the sea—the creatures of the dark, the giants, the ogresses, the fierce elves of the wood, the furious wives that rode the winds and the waves, who afterwards rose into goddesses

---

[1] I have placed a note at the end of this volume on the relation of Woden to Sceaf, and on the question as to whether the Angles gave the name of Woden to their highest God.

[2] Rhedmonath a dea illorum Rheda, cui in illo sacrificabant, nominatur . . . Antiqui Anglorum populi, gens mea . . . apud eos Aprilis Esturmonath, quondam a dea illorum, quae Eostra vocabatur . . . nomen habuit: a cujus nomine nunc paschale tempus cognominant, consueto antiquae observationis vocabulo gaudia novae solennitatis vocantes. Baeda, *De temporum ratione*, cap. 13.

or sank into witches—the demons of sea and land and sky. These could scarcely be called objects of worship, but objects of fear who were hated by the strong, and propitiated by the weak. Wells, stones, trees, hills, and a multitude of other things in nature received veneration, and finally behind them all rested, it seems, the Wyrd, the Fate-Goddess, who ruled the destinies of men, who tended to become in men's minds supreme even over the highest gods. This was the simple, rude, primeval religion of the early tribes who came over to England, and their sacrifices and feasts were probably imageless.

The early nature-worship contained in this religion is particularly enshrined in the second myth of which we have here to speak,—the myth of Beowulf; not of the quasi-historic hero of the poem, but of his namesake the son of Scyld, whom the Anglo-Saxon genealogies call Beaw and who is usually styled Beowa. His mythical deeds, as I have previously explained, were transferred in process of time to the hero of the poem, and we may therefore consider them in that connection. Beowulf, in his youth, overcomes Grendel and his dam, and in his old age, the dragon. In the latter strife he dies himself.

Both contests are, at least partly, two different forms (modified by local elements) of the same original nature-myth of the Sun overcoming the Night, of the Night overcoming the Sun. Among the Northern tribes who had only two seasons, this daily contest was extended to the yearly recurring battle between Winter and Summer; between the frost and storm-giants who destroyed men and the labours of men, and the bright beings who, coming in the summer, brought life and fruitfulness and peace to men. Varied modifications of this, arising from peculiar features of the scenery and climate in which the inheritors of the general myth lived, were continuously made. Grendel and his mother, when we consider them as mythical, represent not so much the fierce winter powers, as the winter powers on the sea-coast, the demoniac welter and destroying strength of the stormy sea; and along with that, the horror and the pestilence of the moors beyond the fringe of inhabited land which extended between the sea and the moor; the malarious fogs which brought death and disease to men and vegetation, the blinding mist, the overwhelming and destroying rains and hail and snow to which the moorland seemed to give birth. Beowulf would then symbolise the Summer who puts an end to these terrors, the strong bringer of light and fruitfulness, the saviour of men. The dragon story is another form of the same root-thought, and we need not particularise it too much. Some have, with great nicety, made Grendel represent the wild sea of the spring equinox, and the dragon the storms of October and November, in fighting against which the summer dies. But when the myth first arose there was none of this complex thinking. It was a kind of childish story about summer and winter, about storms and calm, such as might arise to-day in Greenland.

The general statement is, then, that the whole tale of Beowulf and Grendel and the dragon had its far-off origin in the myth of the Summer conquering the Winter. But there are special elements in the myth of Grendel and Beowulf which make this general statement inadequate. The Grendel story seems to me the acorn of the whole poem, the aboriginal, primeval matter. The theory which some have started, that the dragon story was the earliest, and that Grendel was grafted upon it, appears to be wanting in the sensitive instinct for what is old. The dragon tale *is* the ancient myth of the serpent Darkness attacking the Light, but it is that myth in a somewhat modern shape, degraded into one of its thousandfold forms in the Folk-Tales, and centuries later than a grim, gray-haired creation like that of Grendel. It is, however, uplifted to a higher level in the poem, though still further modernised, by being moralised. The composer of *Beowulf* intended, I think, and this seems also Professor Earle's view, to represent under the destroying fires of the dragon, the evil forces which injure just government and noble kingship, and which are overthrown by the self-sacrifice of Beowulf for his people. The dragon myth in *Beowulf* seems to be a modern form of the ancient myth, and to have been made more modern by an ethical direction.

It is very different with Grendel. His story is the antique matter of the poem, and it is, as it stands, unique. It received no further circulation, and it awakens great curiosity. The name itself of the monster is a puzzle. Grimm connects it with the Anglo-Saxon *grindel* (a bolt or bar), a word found in various forms among the Teutonic languages. It carries with it the notion of the bolts and bars of hell, and hence of a fiend. He compares it to the German *höllriegel* (a hell-bar), hence the devil or the devil's own; and he compares Grendel, thus derived, with Loki, whose name he links to *lukan*, to shut up. This is somewhat far-fetched, and a much simpler etymology has been suggested. Ettmüller was the first, I think, to connect the name with *grindan*, to grind, to crush to pieces, to utterly destroy. Grendel is then the tearer, the destroyer, and if we bind him up as a water-spirit with the stormy sea, this derivation well expresses the crushing and battering force of the waves that grind the rocks, break up the ships, and rend the seamen. But I suspect that the name belongs to the most ancient forms of the Teutonic tongue—to a language as old as the hills—such as was spoken in the Stone Age to which I should like to refer the myth of Grendel. It may have come to the Teutons through the Celts; and indeed the only resemblances to it I have been able to find are Celtic.

With regard to the conception and story of Grendel and his mother, there are two questions to ask. First, Is there anything like it in the myths of other countries? and secondly, Is there anything that resembles it in after-story?

As to the first question, there are general resemblances in many demoniac and robber forms, in the Rakshasas of India, and other oriental persons who are cannibals, and in all the ogres of the Folk-Tales. Polyphemus, too, lives in a cave by the sea, and devours men. The story of Cacus may be compared. But these have no closeness to the subject-matter of Grendel. We come nearer to it when we think of the giants of the Northern imagination, the eotens who dwell, like Grendel, in the wild wastes, who afterwards become the hill-folk; the trolls who live in the crags and caves, but who are also conceived, in the earlier and simpler way, as the huge indwellers of the dark caves under the overhanging cliffs which run back from the beach of the great ocean which clasps the Earth. Grendel may be a local personification of one of these giants, with traits added to him derived from the scenery of the place where the story first upgrew, and I daresay something of this conception entered into him. But there is more in him. He belongs not only to the sea, but to the moor and the marsh, and those who have made him the personification of the plague of the poisonous fen, and Beowulf the healthy storm wind that disperses the deadly vapour, have something to say for themselves. But to confine the conception of Grendel to this, and to leave out the sea, is to be too fond of a single idea. He is a mixture of many things, the last result of a number of rude folk-ideas. The nearest parallel to him which I have been able to find is a Celtic myth, and it seems to be of the same great age which I impute to Grendel. In it also the thoughts of the sea and the moor are combined, not of the moor itself, but of the mists and waters of the moor. For Grendel is essentially a water-demon.

In the mythic history of Ireland, the Fomori disturb Partholon and his people under the leadership of a *giant and his mother*. The Fomori are monsters, one-handed, one-footed. Their name is derived from *fomuirib* (under seas), and they are water-demons who are hostile to men, who pay unwelcome visits to the land, who, dwelling in the seas, have power over the ocean and lakes, who are also mythic representations of the mists and baleful fogs, the cold and stormy winds that injure the farmer's work. The Welsh have also a Mallt y Nos, the Night Mallt, a she-demon associated with the cold malarious fogs on marshy lands at night. Now these Fomori, demons like Grendel of the sea and mist, but also, like him, semi-human, are fought with by Nuada of the Silver Hand, and conquered, as Grendel is by Beowulf; and this battle is, of course, as that of Beowulf also, made by the mythologists into the dispersion of the mists by the sun, and the stilling of the winter storms and sea by the triumphant summer sun.[1] It is curious that in the Beowulf myth Grendel loses his arm, but in the Irish myth that Nuada, the conqueror of the Fomori loses his hand; like Tyr, when in the Norse tale he binds the Fenri wolf. The hand business is thus reversed.

I have also found in Curtins' *Myths and Folk-Lore of Ireland* an independent parallel to the rending away of Grendel's arm. It is in the *Tale of the Seven Brothers and the King of France* (p. 270). The King of France loses his children, and asks Finn to help him. He sails over the sea, and one of the seven brethren with him is *Strong*. They hear that when a child is born to France, a hand comes down the chimney and takes the child away. On their arrival a child is born, and at the dead of night the hand descends and gropes for the child. "Strong caught the hand, and it drew him nearly to the top of the chimney. Then he pulled it down to the ashes, again it drew him up." All night this struggle continued, and every stone in the castle of the King of France was trembling in its place from the strife. But at break of day Strong tore from its shoulder the arm with the hand, and there was peace. Then they go to find the other three children, and find them drawing water to cool the shoulder of MacMulcan, from whom the arm has been torn. They deliver the children, and MacMulcan, who has a sister, pursues them. They saw the sea raging after them. "That is MacMulcan," says Wise, another of the

---

[1] For all this I refer my readers to the *Hibbert Lectures* of 1886, by John Rhys, Professor of Celtic at Oxford, pp. 592, 603, 610.

seven brothers. This dæmonic sea-fiend drags the ship down, and they are only saved by Strong making a flail out of MacMulcan, and thrashing the head off his body on the ship; and the sea is filled with blood. This is a curious parallel. Strong is of course the same as Strongback in the common folk-tale; but nevertheless he suits with Beowulf's mighty strength. The sailing over the sea is like Beowulf's voyage. The trembling of the house in the strife is like the shaking of Heorot. The rent arm is, of course, a similar incident. By itself it might only be a coincidence, but what follows is remarkable. MacMulcan is, like Grendel, a creature of the sea, is identical in the tale with the raging sea. His head is struck off, and the sea, as in *Beowulf*, is filled with blood. He has a sister, like Grendel's dam, a female demon. I wonder if the Grendel tale may not be a Celtic story, which in very ancient times became Teutonic. These are the only similitudes to Grendel of sufficient importance I have been able to recover, and they point to the myth of Grendel being, as I maintain, of a primeval age, of the age of the giant rather than of the hero myths; that is, it existed before the myth of Beowa, which was afterwards bound up with it. The deadly influences of nature were probably impersonated before the beneficent influences.

It was necessary, since so much has been made of it, to discuss this story from the point of view of the Nature-mythologists; but I think that we may wander far, and with great vagueness, in that direction. I am much more disposed to refer the whole story of Grendel to such a tale as may have arisen all over the North in the remoter days of history. In very early times a general tale might have grown up of the struggle of the first Teutonic settlers with the aboriginals who lived in caves in the unknown lands, and whose size would be magnified by superstitious dread. There are stories of this kind in Iceland, of wights who lived in deep and gloomy caverns. There is a cave-dweller's tale (edited by G. Vigfusson), and the cave-wight in it, whose burning eyes are like two full moons, chants monstrously and in a big voice a song which is supposed to be a death-song over the cave-kin of the country.[1] No doubt if such a story was used in a heroic tale like *Beowulf*, myths of nature would be mixed up in it, and it would be handled as poets handle folk-tales. It would lose the simple form, the naturalness of narrative, and take heroic proportions with a semi-divine element mingled up with it. Now if such a conjecture were hereafter to be rendered probable, we might find that the story as it stands in the Grettis Saga would be one of the representatives of this quasi-historical source of the Grendel story.

As to the after existence of the story, that fortunately lies plain before us. The first time that any one who knew the Beowulf poem read the Grettis Saga, he recognised his old acquaintance under another form, and said to himself that the story of Grendel had been brought over to Iceland from Scandinavia or England, or that the same thoughts out of which the Grendel story grew took a similar form in similar circumstances of climate, in a land incessantly covered with dark and dangerous mists. The point of difference is that Glam, who represents Grendel, has nothing to do with seas and waters, nor is he a primeval demon. He is only the embodied ghost of a thrall

---

[1] Grettis Saga, Magnusson and Morris, Notes, p. 277.

into whom the demon nature of the Haunter he has slain has entered. The semi-divine element is altogether gone out of him. But the fight of Grettir with him is very similar to the fight of Beowulf with Grendel. Farther on in the tale is another parallel. Grettir overcomes a giant who lives in a cave underneath the waterfalls. This second tale seems to have grown out of the fight of Beowulf with Grendel's dam, and is connected not with the sea, but with the turbulent waters of the earth. I content myself with quoting from Morris and Magnusson's translation the passages out of the saga which was probably written down in the thirteenth century.

It is told in the story that the valley where Thorhall fed his sheep was so haunted that his shepherds were evilly entreated, and none at last could be got to tend the outlying folds. But in the end he found a herd—Glam by name—"huge and uncouth, with gray and glaring eyes and hair that was wolf-gray, who was minded to do the work." This is a description which recalls Grendel, and the things afterwards told of his ways are also in tune with the monster. Folk cannot abide him; he is a loather of church song, and his whoop is as big as his body. Moreover, he is pagan at heart. "The ways of men," he says, "were better when they were heathen." He goes forth to the hills on Christmas Eve and, like Grendel, into the heavy weather—thick mirk, roaring wind, and driving snow. The haunter meets him, and next day he is found dead, blue as hell and as great as a neat—a thing of loathing. But he begins a new life and haunts in his turn instead of the haunter, slaying those who meet him, riding the house roofs at night, a dreadful scather of men, and worse in winter (here the old myth creeps in) than in summer.

Thorgaut, a tall strong man, says that he will serve Thorhall the farmer, and strive with Glam. But on Christmas Eve he is slain, and Glam waxes mightier now and slaughters the cattle and the neat-herds at the farm, till all men, save the farmer and his wife, flee from the place; and it was feared that the whole valley would be laid waste. News of this is brought to Grettir as news of Grendel is brought to Beowulf, and he has like Beowulf the strength of many men. So he comes to Thorhall-stead and says that he will have a sight of the thrall and lies down at night in the hall waiting for Glam, and the hall was all broken and wrecked, as Heorot was after the strife. Then there is a great battle which is like the battle between Beowulf and Grendel. "Light burned in the hall through the night, and when the third part of the night was passed, Grettir heard huge din without, and then one went up upon the houses and rode the hall and drave his heels against the thatch so that every rafter cracked again. That went on long, and then he came down from the house and went to the door; and as the door opened, Grettir saw that the thrall stretched in his head which seemed to him monstrously big and wondrous thick cut.

"Glam fared slowly when he came into the door and stretched himself high up under the roof, and turned looking along the hall, and laid his arms on the tie-beam and glared inwards over the place. The farmer would not let himself be heard, for he deemed he had had enough in hearing himself what had gone on outside. Grettir lay quiet, and moved no whit; then Glam saw that some bundle lay on the seat, and therewith he stalked up the hall and gripped at the wrapper wondrous hard; but Grettir set his foot against the beam, and moved in no wise; Glam pulled again much harder, but still the wrapper moved not at all; the third time he pulled with both hands so hard that he drew Grettir upright from the seat; and now they tore the wrapper asunder between them.

"Glam gazed at the rag he held in his hand, and wondered much who might pull so hard against him; and therewithal Grettir ran under his hands and gripped him round the middle, and bent back his spine as hard as he might, and his mind it was that Glam should shrink thereat; but the thrall lay so hard on Grettir's arms that he shrank all aback because of Glam's strength.

"Then Grettir bore back before him into sundry seats; but the seat beams were driven out of place, and all was broken that was before them. Glam was fain to get out, but Grettir set his foot against all things that he might; nathless Glam got him dragged from out the hall; there had they a wondrous hard wrestling, because the thrall had a mind to bring him out of the house; but Grettir saw that ill as it was to deal with Glam within doors, yet worse would it be without, therefore he struggled with all his might and main against going out-a-doors.

"Now Glam gathered up his strength and knit Grettir towards him when they came to the outer door; but when Grettir saw that he might not set his feet against that, all of a sudden in one rush he drave his hardest against the thrall's breast, and spurned both feet against the half-sunken stone that stood in the threshold of the door; for this the thrall was not ready, for he had been tugging to draw Grettir to him, therefore he reeled aback and spun out against the door, so that his shoulders caught the upper door-case and the roof burst asunder, both rafters and frozen thatch, and therewith he fell open-armed aback out of the house and Grettir over him.

"Bright moonlight was there without, and the drift was broken, now drawn over the moon, now driven from off her; and, even as Glam fell, a cloud was driven from the moon and Glam glared up against her. And Grettir himself says that by that sight only was he dismayed amidst all that he ever saw.

"Then his soul sank within him so, from all these things, both from weariness, and because he had seen Glam turn his eyes so horribly, that he might not draw the short-sword, and lay wellnigh 'twixt home and hell. But herein was there more fiendish craft in Glam than in most other ghosts, that he spake now in this wise—

"Exceeding eagerly hast thou wrought to meet me, Grettir, but no wonder will it be deemed, though thou gettest no good hap of me; and this must I tell thee, that thou hast got half the strength and manhood which was thy lot if thou hadst not met me: now I may not take from thee the strength which thou hast got before this; but that may I rule, that thou shalt never be mightier than now thou art; and nathless art thou mighty enow, and that shall many an one learn. Hitherto hast thou earned fame by thy deeds, but henceforth will wrongs and manslayings fall on thee, and the most part of thy doings will turn to thy woe and ill-hap; an outlaw shalt thou be made, and ever shall it be thy lot to dwell alone abroad; therefore this weird I lay on thee, ever in those days to see these eyes with thine eyes, and thou wilt find it hard to be alone—and that shall drag thee unto death."

"Now when the thrall had thus said, the astoniment fell from Grettir that had lain on him, and therewith he drew the short-sword and hewed the head from Glam, and laid it at his thigh."

The next parallel to *Beowulf* in the Grettis Saga is still more remarkable. The parts of Grendel and his dam are reversed. It is the Troll-wife who goes forth to a certain house to slay and cut men to pieces and to carry them off to her cave under the force. It is the man-giant who stays at home in the cave. The creatures are water dwellers and are mixed up with the powers of water like Grendel and his mother. The cave where they dwell and the firelight in it are like the cave and the fire in the ancient poem. The battle with the giant in it is as like the battle with Grendel's dam as the previous battle of Grettir with the Troll-wife is like that of Beowulf with Grendel. The Troll-wife dies of the loss of her arm as Grendel dies of the same loss. The tearing, rending and battering down of the house belong to the idea of Grendel. When Grettir comes to the edge of the waterfall and plunges into the boiling wave and dives under the waterfall to reach the cave while the priest sits waiting above, we recall Beowulf coming to the edge of the Ness and diving into the welter of water and up into the cave, while the thegns sit waiting on the rocks above. When Grettir slays the giant and the waves of the force are stained with blood and the priest, believing Grettir dead, goes home, we remember the blood-stained sea and that the thegns of Hrothgar returned, thinking that Beowulf was dead. There is even a parallel in one of the words used. The giant fights with a glaive which cuts and thrusts, and the saga says that men called that weapon "heft-sax." Hrunting, the sword Hunferth lends to Beowulf, is called *hacftmece*, and the term occurs only this once in the whole of Anglo-Saxon literature. The question then arises, Did it slip from *Beowulf* into the Grettis Saga?

Here are the parts of the story necessary to quote. They are, as before, taken from Morris and Magnusson's translation.

Steinvor, the good wife of Sandheaps, has lost her good man and her house carle by a haunting. Blood was left in the house, about the outer door. Grettir heard the tale and says that he will abide the night in the house, and he lay down but did not take off his clothes. "When it drew towards midnight he heard great din without, and thereafter came into the hall a huge Troll-wife, with a trough in one hand and a chopper wondrous great in the other; she peered about when she came in and saw where Guest (this was Grettir's assumed name) lay, and ran at him, but he sprang up to meet her, and they fell a-wrestling terribly and struggled together for long in the hall. She was the stronger, but he gave back with craft, and all that was before them was broken, yea, the crosspanelling withal of the chamber. She dragged him through the door, and so into the outer doorway, and then he betook himself to struggling hard against her. She was fain to drag him from the house, but might not till they had broken away all the fittings of the outer door, and borne them out on their shoulders: then she laboured away with him down to the river, right down to the deep gulf.

"By then was Guest exceeding weary, yet must he

either gather his might together or be cast by her into the gulf. All night did they contend in such wise. . . . But now when they came to the gulf of the river, he gives the hag a swing round and therewith got his right hand free, and swiftly seized the short-sword that he was girt withal, and smote the Troll therewith on the shoulder and struck off her arm, and therewithal was he free, but she fell into the gulf and was carried down the force."

So ends the first fight, but, as in *Beowulf*, there is another underneath the waterfall. Grettir is sure that there is more to be known of these monsters, and he passes to the cliff, fifty feet above the whirlpool, and girt with the short-sword leaped off the cliff into the force.

"And Grettir dived under the force, and hard work it was because the whirlpool was strong, and he had to dive down to the bottom before he might come up under the force. But thereby was a rock jutting out, and thereon he gat; a great cave was under the force, and the river fell over it from the sheer rocks. He went up into the cave, and there was a great fire flaming from amidst of brands; and there he saw a giant sitting withal, marvellously great and dreadful to look on. But when Grettir came anigh, the giant leapt up and caught up a glaive and smote at the newcomer, for with that glaive might a man both cut and thrust; a wooden shaft it had, and that fashion of weapon men called then, heft-sax.

"Grettir hewed back against him with the short-sword, and smote the shaft so that he struck it asunder; then was the giant fain to stretch aback for a sword that hung up there in the cave; but therewithal Grettir smote him afore into the breast, and smote off wellnigh all the breast-bone and the belly, so that the bowels tumbled out of him and fell into the river, and were driven down along the stream; and as the priest sat by the rope, he saw certain fibres all covered with blood swept down the swirls of the stream; then he grew unsteady in his place and thought for sure that Grettir was dead, so he ran from the holding of the rope and gat him home. Thither he came in the evening and said, as one who knew it well, that Grettir was dead, and that great scathe was it of such a man.

"Now, of Grettir must it be told that he let little space go betwixt his blows or ever the giant was dead. Then he went up the cave, and kindled a light and espied the cave. The story tells not how much he got therein, but men deem that it must have been something great. But there he abode on into the night; and he found there the bones of two men, and bore them together in a bag; then he made off from the cave and swam to the rope and shook it, and thought that the priest would be there yet; but when he knew that the priest had gone home, then must he draw himself up by strength of hand, and thus he came up out on to the cliff."

The parallel is very close, and three suggestions may be made concerning it. Either the Beowulf Saga was known over Sweden and Norway, and its lays came from Norway or the Western Isles to Iceland with the first settlers; or some of the roving Icelanders had heard of the tale in England, and brought it back to Iceland in a broken fashion; or there was a tale older than *Beowulf* itself—a combination of a nature-myth and a folk-tale—which was common property of the Northmen, and out of which the Grendel story in

Beowulf, and the Glam and Troll story both grew independently of each other.

One more parallel suggested in the *Corpus Poeticum Boreale* (vol. ii. p. 503) remains to be noticed. "In the English poem of Eger and Grime in the Percy MS., there is the echo of the Beowulf story in the hand of Grey Steele, the monster knight of the moor; and that noble brand Egeking mentioned there, which King Fundus got from 'full far beyond the Greekes sea,' may be the last traditional descendant of the hefti-sax," Beowulf's *haeft-mece*. I do not see much in the sword-part of this parallel. The *haeft-mece* in *Beowulf* is not Beowulf's sword but Hunferth's, and though it is famous, it would scarcely become traditional, as it fails in the encounter with Grendel. The only really mythic sword in *Beowulf* is the ancient sword of the cave itself, and of that nothing is really left but the hilt. There are swords enough to get Egeking from without tracing it to a failure.

CHAPTER VI

WALDHERE

It is a curious question how it came to pass that the story of Beowulf and Grendel did not, like the other sagas of the North, become a part of the Norse-German cycle of romance. The story stops dead; we hear no more of it. The Goths or Jutes who dwelt in the north of Denmark and Southern Sweden possessed it. The Danes of the islands possessed it. It passed downwards to dwell among the Angles, and the story may have reached the sea-board Saxons who came to England. But it gets no farther. Why did it not pass into the hands of the Old Saxons? Why did it not become a part of Northern German legend? It does not do so; there is no trace of it. There is no evidence for the conjecture that it was one of the ancient songs to which the Franks listened.

I have sometimes thought that the Angles alone threw the myths and tales of it into lays, and that when the whole body of them emigrated to our island, they left the Continent naked of the tale. It would not have had time then to become a part of German saga. If the Danes had put it into verse, I do not understand why it was not carried into Northern Germany. I conjecture then that something broke the literary connection on the Continent, or that the story was developed only when the Angles got into Britain.

Again, if the Jutes or Saxons had it, why are there only vague traces of it in place names in our Southern England? I conjecture again that the stories were not shaped into verse by the Jutes.[1] Or it may be, since they were a small party of warriors and had so desperate a bit of fighting to do, that they would think, if they had the songs, more of slaughter and of plunder than of preserving poetry. But the Angles went *en masse*, with all their women and all their bards, and they would take their literature with them. It was they, I hold, who in our England worked on the lays before the Christian poet wove them together.

Again, if the lays existed in Southern Sweden and in the north of Denmark, what became of them there? It seems as if there also they died out, or existed, not in verse, but only as a folk-tale. It was perhaps in that form that they got into Norway and thence to Iceland, if we may explain in this way the similarities between the Beowulf story and the tales of Glam and the Troll-wife in the legend of Grettir. But the more likely conjecture is that these similarities arose from Icelandic rovers bringing back the story from England or the Isles. Had the story really been established, even as a folk-tale, I think we should have had some further trace of it in the Norse tales.

I am inclined then to come to the conclusion that the Angles alone retained the Beowulf lays, or alone made them into a poem. If this have any truth

---

[1] Unless, as I have before suggested, there were Jutish or Frisian settlers on the sea-board, south of the Forth, among whom the Angles, on their arrival, found the lays of *Beowulf* existing. Such a discovery, if we may with any probability imagine it—would be likely to awaken in the Angles a fresh interest in their own form of the *Beowulf* lays, and to increase the vogue of the lays.

in it, it isolates the poem with us. But if we may be proud of this, we may be humbled by another consideration. The Norse and Teutonic sagas were developed on the Continent and in Iceland into full romances, carefully worked and treated with art. There was enough of poetic power to do this work. But after the seventh or eighth century the story of Beowulf underwent no further development, and what we have of it is rudely wrought. Yet we must not blame the Northern Englishmen too much for this. There was not time to work further at the tale. The Danes destroyed the Northumbrian poetry, and when literature was revived in Wessex by Ælfred, southern Englishmen seem to have had little care for poetry of this kind, and little power of imaginative invention. *Beowulf* stands alone then, when it is looked at along with the carefully wrought tales of Sigurd or Theodric, like some crag of Plutonic rock, rugged and weather-worn, which rises among the later strata of a gentler age; the sole remnant of an ancient cycle of stories which have entirely perished.

When that ancient cycle was dying a new cycle had begun, and its tales grew by accretion for centuries in Germany and among the Norse folk, and have continued working in literature to the present day. It was not till quite lately that we had some proof that any of them had an influence on English literature or touched at all our country. Now, however, since 1860, we know that one at least of this new cycle of tales— one which belonged to the Theodric cycle and was embodied in the Vilkina saga—was domesticated in England; and if one of them, and one of the least important, is found in a Southern English dialect, it is of the highest probability that others were also written

down from the songs of wandering bards. But, if
they existed, they have all perished. No land was
ever more ravaged by successive wars than the land of
ancient English literature. Scarcely a shred of romantic
manuscript survives; so thorough in destruction were
pagan Dane and Christian monk, were the years of
ignorance, of long neglect, of the tyranny of Latin, of
the harrying of the monasteries by war and by reform,
of modern fires and modern damps.

 The discovery of almost every important extant
Anglo-Saxon poem has been of special interest. And
the discovery of the parchment leaves which tell
us that the English had examples before them of the
Norse-German cycle after the age of *Beowulf* does not
want the element of sensation. Professor Werlauff,
looking through a great mass of loose papers in the
National Library at Copenhagen, turned up two
vellum pages of a great age which had been used for
the binding of a book, and saw that they were covered
with Old English lines of verse, sixty-two lines in all.
How they came to Denmark no one could tell, but
it was conjectured that when Thorkelin searched England for Anglo-Saxon manuscripts and found *Beowulf*,
he picked up also these two pieces of parchment and
brought them with him to Copenhagen. Werlauff
handed them on to Stephens to edit, and the literary
exultation of this scholar at the discovery makes his
little book upon them pleasant reading.

 He found that the two sheets were not continuous
but different portions of the poem, and conjectured
that the whole of the story had been in manuscript.
We had proof, he held, that a poem belonging to
the Teutonic cycle and perhaps as long as *Beowulf*,
existed in English, and Stephens thought that the hand-

writing was as old as the ninth century and the poem as old as the eighth. As the fragment refers to the Weland and the Theodric sagas, it makes it probable that both these sagas were known in England—a probability which is confirmed by the *Deor* poem. Those who have written on the fragment in Germany, and chiefly Müllenhof, agree on the whole with these dates. Each sheet contains thirty-one lines from the story of Waldhere. The first is Hildeguthe's speech to Waldhere, urging him to the fight with Guthhere. The second is the interchange of words between Waldhere and Guthhere. There is not, therefore, a long interval between the two fragments we possess.

The personages mentioned in these two leaves are Ætla, Guthhere, Waldhere, Hildeguthe, and Hagena, and they told Stephens that he was in possession of an early version of the romance of Walther of Aquitaine. There are three forms, Müllenhof says, in which this saga of Walther has come down to us—a German form, a probably Frankish form, and a Polish form. The oldest of these is the German. The German form is not in existence, but we have a translation of it into Latin hexameters written in the tenth century by Ekkehard of St. Gall. Our fragments are probably an English translation from the original German version. The story, as Ekkehard tells it, is perhaps worth a sketch—

Attila[1] has invaded the Franks under Gibica's rule, and taken from them tribute, treasure, and a noble youth, Hagen, as a hostage. Marching on, he attacks the Burgundians and takes Hildegund, daughter of Hereric their king, as hostage. Lastly, he descends

---

[1] I use the better known form of the names in this account.

on the Aquitanians, and their king Ælfhere gives him his son Walther as hostage, and Walther is already affianced to Hildegund. These three then are brought up together and become personages in the court of Attila. Hildegund has the care of all the treasures, Walther is the leader of the Hunnish host, and Hagen, his nearest friend, is his war-comrade. At a certain time Hagen flees to the Franks to join his new liege, Gunther, and afterwards Walther and Hildegund also escape. They carry off treasure from the Huns whom Walther has made drunk; and both, mounted on Walther's war-horse, Lion, ride away till, on the fourteenth day, they reach the Rhine, not far from Worms. The ferryman tells the tale of the great horse, the warrior, the maiden, and the treasure chests, in the hall of Gunther, King of the Franks. Hagen breaks forth into joy: "This is my comrade Walther from the Huns." Gunther cries out also for joy: "This is the treasure of Gibica, I will have it"; and with Hagen and eleven warriors he pursues after Walther who has reached the forest of the Vosges. But Hagen is sorrowful, not wishing to fight with his friend, and he warns Gunther that if he had ever seen Walther in the wrath of battle, he would not think him so easy to despoil.

Now night has come, and in a pleasant cave, between two hills, and soft with green grass, Walther is slumbering, his head on his lady's lap, while she keeps watch; for Walther has known no sleep for fourteen days save when he leant upon his shield. In the dawn Hildegund sees a dust-cloud and wakens Walther. "Slay me," she cries, "lest I should belong to the Huns and not to thee!" But Walther knows the helm of Hagen, and laughing, says: "These are not Huns, but Niblung Franks" (*Franci nebulones*); and vows that the Franks shall not have a grain of the treasure. They parley, but in vain, and Hagen withdraws from the battle and sits down to look on from a neighbouring hill. Then the fight begins, and Walther, swording in a narrow place where only one can meet him, slays the eleven warriors, so that Gunther is left alone. Walther, watching from his vantage ground, sees Gunther fly to Hagen, and, after talk, these two kiss one another, and Walther fears that the kiss bodes no good. Nor, indeed, does it, for they have agreed to draw Walther from his hold and ambush him upon the way.

It is now again night, and Walther, having wept and prayed over the warriors he has slain, sleeps in a cave, and in the morning, taking horses and treasure, goes on his way. But when a mile was now measured, they hear the beating of horse hoofs, and see Gunther and Hagen riding down upon them. "Flee, flee!" cries Hildegund. "No," he answers; "if honour fail, shame waits on my last hour." Then he appeals to Hagen, for old friendship and love, as Cuchulainn appealed to Ferdia, not to fight with him; but Hagen has lost his nephew—"my tender, soft, bright flower"—in the battle, and he will have requital for his blood. So two meet with one, and Walther smites off Gunther's leg, and Hagen Walther's right hand, for Walther's sword has flown to pieces, so dire was the blow he gave to Hagen's helm. But a right hand lost is nothing to the great warrior, and driving the stump of his arm into the shield, he fights on with his half-sword in his left hand. And now enraged he strikes Hagen so fierce a stroke that his right eye is forced out and all his face laid open to the jaw. This is enough, and they sit down in full friendship again, renewing their bond of blood; joke over their wounds, and part—Hagen with Gunther for Worms; Walther and Hildegund and all the treasure for Aquitaine, where, after a glorious marriage and his father's death, he reigns triumphantly for thirty years.

This is the outline of a story which is told with a great deal of vigour, and with some feeling for natural scenery, that kind of soft woodland in which the romance writers delighted. It is greatly enlivened by dialogue, which rises sometimes into passion. There was evidently plenty of dialogue in the early saga, and all that we have in our English fragments is dialogue. The first of the two fragments, which I give here, is the speech by which Hildeguthe kindles Waldhere to the fight with Guthhere and the eleven warriors, and proves again, if we needed proof, with what eagerness the Teutonic women joined in the interests of war and felt for the honours of their lord. "Then did Hildeguthe courage him greatly—"

> "Truly of Weland the work ne'er deceiveth
> Any of men who Mimming[1] can wield,
> Hoary of edges! Oft failed in the war
> Man after man, blood-marbled, sword-wounded!—
>   Ætla's fore-fighter, let not thy force now
> Drop to-day downward; let droop not thy lordship!
> . . . . Now is the day
> Thou shalt have one thing or else another—

---

[1] Mimming (Mimungr) was the masterpiece of Weland, the most famous sword in the Northern world. It descended to Widia or Wudga, his son. This is the only mention of it in Old English, but we hear of it later on in the romance of *Horn Child*, a Middle English poem—

> Than sche lete forth bring
> A swerd hongand bi a ring;
> To Horn sche it bitaught.
> It is the make (mate) of Miming;
> Of all swerdes it is king.
> And Weland it wrought;
> Bitterfer the swerd hight.

But Mimming is originally the work of Mimir, the great smith, who was the master of Weland, and who is the same as Regin in the Volsunga saga. At least so Grimm declares.

> Or lose thy life, or long-lived dominion
> Make thine among men, Ælfhere's son!
> At no time, my Chief, do I chide thee with words;
> Since never I saw thee at the sword-playing—
> Through wretched fear of whatever warrior—
> Flee out of the fight, or in flight on the field,
> Or care for thy corse, though a crowd of the foe
> On thy breast-byrnie with bills were a-hewing;
> But to fight forward was ever thy seeking!
> O'er the mark was thy measure,[1] Meter of meeds!
> So I feared thou would'st fight, too fiercely by far,
> Around the camp-ramparts, in close set of war,
> With some other of heroes! Then honour thyself
> By thy great doings while good fortune rules!"

There are eight other lines, the allusions in which are obscure, but these are enough to show the writer's hand.

The second fragment is not so vigorous or so human. It is a portion of the dialogue between Guthhere and Waldhere, and its main interest is in the mention of names which belong to the cycle of Romance that collected round Theodric. As Weland's sword is spoken of in the previous passage, so here Widia, Weland's son, "the kinsman of Nithad," is spoken of as having rescued Theodric from great straits. It is plain that the poem was written when the Theodric saga was well established.

As to its date, the poem seems to be so antique in form that it is put back to the eighth century, and its German original belongs probably to the middle of the seventh. That was a time of copious production of lays among the Lombards; Vigfusson and Powell have unearthed from the record of Paul the Deacon, who died in 790, two close paraphrases of old Ælfwine lays which are contemporary

---

[1] "Thy measure o'er the mark," that is, I conjecture, "Thy place was beyond the front-line of the battle."

with the poems of Caedmon, if we take the probable date of them as between Paul and Ælfwine. Ælfwine Eadwineson is Alboin, King of the Lombards, who died in 572. They go on to say that "these songs" (assuming that Paul's prose was derived from songs, and assuming also their own date) "are the earliest remains of Teutonic epic poetry which we have any exact knowledge of." The first of these is certainly a brilliant example of the heroic lay; the second seems to me much more like a piece of monkish history. They will both be found at p. lii., etc., of the Introduction to the *Corpus Poeticum Boreale*. There are, perhaps, several other passages in Paul from poems of this early period.

One other vernacular fragment of song of an early time—belonging to the heroic cycle—is not English but German, yet is connected in manner and style with *Waldhere*. It is the ancient lay of Hadubrand and Hildebrand, and was found, as *Waldhere* was found, on a piece of parchment used in binding a book, in the monastery of Fulda. It is a MS., we are told, of the eighth century, and was probably sung as a lay in the seventh. The story is curiously like the story of Sohrab and Rustum, though we do not know the issue of the fight. Hildebrand challenges his son Hadubrand to single combat. Hildebrand asks of what parentage he is, and hears from Hadubrand enough to prove that he is his son whom he had left behind in Italy as a child of three years old when he fled years ago to the east from Odoacer. He declares his fatherhood, his son does not believe him—Hildebrand, he says, is long since dead. At this the father mourns the fate which is near him of falling by his son's hand; but, as he speaks, the war-fever seizes on him and the men fall to with spear and axe. We hear no more, but can well imagine that the story ends as Sohrab and Rustum ends. This is the only piece of German heroic verse [1] which can compete in age with those that we possess, and it is later, I believe, than the *Lament of Deor*, later certainly than the *Fight at Finnsburg* and the lays contained in *Beowulf*.

---

[1] The Weissenbrunner Prayer in alliterative High German verse belongs probably to the eighth century, but its only value is its age. In the ninth century we find a Low German poem, the *Heliand*, of which we shall have something to say in connection with the poems attributed to Caedmon. But these are plainly Christian; they do not intrude among the remnants which coming down originally out of heathen times are romantic, not religious.

CHAPTER VII

THE CONQUEST AND LITERATURE

THE *Fight at Finnsburg* and the lays from which our *Beowulf* was composed were, as it seems to me, sung among the English who dwelt in the north of Denmark and the south of Sweden, and whose tribal name was the Jutes or Goths. They were also sung among the other English who dwelt in the south of Denmark and who called themselves Angles. And I have conjectured that it was in this part of the English territory that they and *Widsith* were best preserved. The Angles, even in their seats on the Continent, seem to have shown the same desire to take care of literature which they afterwards had in Northumbria. I do not think, for reasons to which I have alluded, that the songs of *Beowulf* were much cared for, among the other English whom we know as Saxons, who dwelt in Hanover and Friesland, and who were the most southern of these three tribes whose common name was English, whose language was called English, but all of whom the Welsh and Irish called Saxons.[1] The Saxons also had, we may

---

[1] It is well, even at the risk of repetition, to mark out—and I refer my readers to York Powell's Primer of *Early England*—the unity of the English tribes in the continental England. It has more bearing on literary questions than at first sight appears.

be sure, their own lays, and if we could but discover Ælfred's Handbook, we should no doubt find some of them in it.

When the English came over they continued to make songs, to chant the daily chronicle of the conquest. This was their only literature, their only history; and though there is not much to tell of it, yet the imagination loves to dwell upon its fragments. In these rude chants begins the poetry of our island-England. The glory of a thousand years of song shines backward on its sources. During 147 years the poetry of England was altogether heathen. It was unbroken by a single Christian voice, save perhaps, as the battle joined, by the chanting in the distance of the British monks, which, when the English heard they declared to be the singing of spells and the singers wizards. On this account Æthelfrith, at the battle of Chester, slew the dark-robed creatures, one and all. "If they cry to their God against us," he said, "they fight against us, though they do not carry arms."

In the year 597 Augustine brought Christianity to England, and the warriors of Æthelberht listened to the praise of Christ instead of the praise of their war-god. But for many years after, the war-songs, the rude verses sung by the freemen in the village as they ploughed, the charms for fruitful earth, against wounds, against the elves, the chants of the gleemen round the moot-tree or in the ealdorman's hall continued to be heathen. When Caedmon produced the first Christian poems the people in Sussex were still heathen, and in many parts of Christian England heathendom retained a considerable power. No doubt, poems which we might call heathen, such for instance as the *Wanderer*, were composed after Caedmon, as

Christian poems were composed before him; but nevertheless the date of his death, 680 A.D., may be taken to mark most conveniently the final conquest of heathen by Christian poetry. It ends a period of 230 years, from 450 to 680. It is this period which we shall consider in this chapter, collecting together the Old English verse which belongs to the events of the invasion and the settlement; and touching on other matters which are likely to throw light on the growth of English literature.

The English tribes had, from the beginning of the fifth century, made some small and scattered settlements on the coasts of Roman Britain, but it was not till the year 449-450 that they came to stay. In that year, the story goes, a band of Jutes, under two war leaders, Hengest and Horsa, landed at Ebbsfleet, and landed to remain. No doubt, as they pushed the bows of their three long keels on to the shore of the Isle of Thanet, they shouted short staves of verse with so great a roaring that Gildas might well call them "whelps from the lair of the barbarian lioness." But we may be sure that the songs were louder when, in 455, their numbers swelled by new arrivals, the whole host, clashing their spears on their shields and singing hymns to their ancestral gods, crossed the inlet that divided Thanet from the mainland and set forth to ravage the country. Of a different character, and done by the Scôp of Hengest, would be the song that followed the fight at Aylesford; but it would be mixed with sorrow, for Horsa was slain in that battle, and some days after they piled up his barrow, facing it with flint stones, on the neighbouring hill. There also they chanted, as his thegns did around the grave of

Beowulf, the great deeds and character of their fallen leader.

Three entries in the *Chronicle* then record the various stages of the conquest of Kent; and the eighteen years which it took to accomplish, show how stout was the resistance of the Welsh, as the English called the Britons. The last is as follows 473 A.D.: " Now Hengest and Æsc his son fought with the Welsh and took countless booty, and the Welsh fled the English as it were fire." This reads as if part of it were taken from a battle-song. The exultation in the countless booty that the English found in the fat meadows of the Romney marshes, the metaphor of the flight, as from fire driven by the wind, bear with them the savour of the war-song. Some years afterwards, 477, a band of Saxons landed in the south near Chichester, and when fourteen years of warring had gone by, took Anderida, 491, the Roman fortress where Pevensey afterwards stood. This soon made complete the little kingdom, as it was afterwards called, of the South Saxons or Sussex; and the record in the *Chronicle* which celebrates the slaughter of all within Anderida may be derived from the song of victory. Henry of Huntingdon's account of the siege is full of details which have on the whole been accepted as historical, and it is conjectured that he had before him some ancient versings of the fight.

I have connected these first battles with verse and song that it may be clearly understood how large a part poetry played in the life of the English. To dwell further in this fashion upon the connection of battles with verse would be mere book-making. I am content if my readers will realise that not a single battle, or feast in the evening, or great ceremony, or vow over the cup to carry the conquest further, or entrance of a fleet into the Humber or the Forth, or burial of a leader, or settlement by the river-side, but was accompanied with poetry. Hengest and Æsc, Cerdic and Ida and Æthelfrith sang as they fought. England was conquered to the music of verse, and settled to the sound of the harp. She was not alone in that, but it is as well to record it in this connection.

In 514, to follow Mr. Green's account, another band of Saxons, under Cerdic and Cynric landed "for definite conquest" near the Itchen river and fought their way up to Winchester, and the fight there, and that which ensued at Charford in 519, were followed a year after by a victory of the Welsh at Mount Badon which kept quiet for a time the English advance and saved Amesbury from destruction: "Amesbury, choir of Ambrosius, probably *the* monastery of Britain—the centre from which flowed the blessings of civilisation and Christianity."[1] Thus, Cerdic having been in 519 created king—a new title among the English,—the first kingdom of Wessex, that is the land now called Hampshire, was established. So then, Kent, Sussex, and Hampshire—the south-east of Britain—were now conquered and settled by the English.

There are two things bound up with literature, to

---

[1] This is Dr. Guest's phrase. He identifies Mount Badon with Badbury in Dorsetshire, and Amesbury with the Caer-Caradoc of the Triads. But it must be remembered that Mr. Skene places his historical Arthur in the north, and identifies his twelve battles with sites in the country between and below the Forth and the Clyde ; and, as far as I am fit to judge, he appears to have proved his theory.— *Four Ancient Books of Wales*, vol. i. pp. 51-58. When two authorities, however, each so wise in his work, disagree in their conjectures, some may perhaps wish to choose that conjecture which pleases them best ; and whether Arthur fought in the north or the south, he fought with so great a fervour that we can bind up, without loss of sentiment, the historical with the mythical hero. But, after all, I fancy that Arthur was originally a mythic name, and was given by the Celts in southern and northern Britain and elsewhere, to any great chieftain who, among them, fought and conquered their foes.

say about this last conquest in Wessex. The first is that at the battle of Mount Badon we meet for the first time, if Dr. Guest and others be right, with the historical Arthur whose myth has so profoundly influenced the literature of Europe. If it was he who conquered the English at Mount Badon and gave the land peace for nearly thirty years from the invaders, and who preserved the monastery and learning of Amesbury, we have an additional pleasure in thinking of the conquest his story made in after years of the imagination of the English people. If he actually brought a comfortable calm after the "tempest of ruin" which fell upon the Britons, we feel as if the legend that he is to come again and restore a golden peace received a new touch of charm.[1]

---

[1] It is not unfitting, even at this early period of a history of English poetry, to pause at the name of Arthur. Who he was, whether he really existed otherwise than as a mythical personage, whether northern or southern Welsh obeyed his call in war, are questions with which literature has but little to do, and which history may not solve with certainty. What is certain is this, that no name (and I speak only of our own land) has had more power over English poetry than the name of Arthur, and no story has had more influence over the imagination of English poets. Like most of the great tales, his tale has a divine vitality of its own, growing like a tree, continually reclothing itself in new foliage and sending forth, from age to age, new branches, so sturdy, so prolific, that they seem like distinct trees. Yet Arthur is always the root-stock of them, and the life of the root seems inexhaustible. Again and again new poetic periods, new forms of song, have started from Arthur. It was his story that kindled Layamon who began, after the Conquest, imaginative English poetry; which also stirred in that original English poet, the author of the "Grene Knight," and of the "Pearl." Chaucer, when he got home to his own English work, could not refrain from Arthur. Spenser, desirous to couch the new-born Muse in the loveliest of cradles, found it in the tale of Arthur. "Girt with British and Armorick Knights," Arthur kindled the first epic fire in Milton. Wordsworth, when Man and Nature, hand in hand, passed for moments from his view, felt, along with Scott, the alluring charm of Arthur. Tennyson, beginning a new world of song, saw the hero and his knights and ladies when first he wrote, and in after years wrought the scattered Idylls of the King into our latest epic.

These are a few names out of many, but to what a vitality, to what a power do they not bear witness? I have said nothing of the influence the Welsh story has had on literature at large, nothing of its invasion of our land along with the Normans, of the Anglo-Norman poems, nothing of its fresh invasion of Wales from Armorica, nothing of the story of Geoffrey of Monmouth with which the historians were so indignant, of the work on it done by Walter Mapes, and the further work done on it by Malory, nor of the extraordinary impulse these three

The second thing is in relation to the view that Gildas, whose History and Epistle were written about 545-560, took of the invasion and the invaders. When he was writing, the greater part of the land, north and west of this conquered corner in the south-east, was Roman Britain. Its fertile valleys and river plains were covered with villas where the provincial had lived with his serfs; the land was richly tilled and fed great herds of cattle; but the hamlets were scarcely touched with Roman civilisation. The towns were filled with a mixed population of pure Welsh and Romanised Welsh, and were often two towns in one, the Roman town upon the river, the ancient British town under the mounded fortress on the hill, as, for example, was the case at Uriconium.[1] The arts, the literature, the laws of Rome prevailed in the towns side by side with the vernacular poetry of the Welsh, but this Roman element seems to have been almost dead at the time of the Conquest, at least in some of the towns. Bath, Gloucester, and Cirencester appear from the *Chronicle* to have been under the rule of Welsh kings. Christianity was established amongst them, but we see from Gildas how little influence it had over the lives of the priests and the Welsh princes of his time. His epistle is a protracted denunciation of a condition of society in which vice and crime ran riot. A few, however, remained who were worthy of the better past, " by whose worthy lives, a pattern to all men, our weakness is sustained." His one hope for the country

---

versions or enlargements of the tale had on literature. Let them be only mentioned here. Enough has been said to more than excuse a pause at Arthur's name. We meet it now in the sixth century. We have him with us in the nineteenth, and he has played the part of a living man right through the literature of thirteen hundred years in Wales and England.

[1] Guest, *Origines Celticae*, vol. ii. pp. 305, 306.

was in the restoration of the purer life that had been, and he calls on all men to repair the Church of God, to bring back learning to the monasteries and good manners to the land. The hope was not fulfilled. The whole of the old culture was annihilated by the English. Gildas saw a part of this hurricane of ruin with his own eyes, and as we look back to his days from ours, in which English literature is one of the great powers, it is strange to listen to his horror of the fierce and impious Saxons, wolves, dogs, whelps of the lioness, barbarians, bastards, robbers, and yet to think that in the loins of these ravaging English warriors were Caedmon and Ælfred, Baeda, and Dunstan. Nor is it less strange to read of his misery for the trampling out of Christianity by the hoofs of pagans who not so very long after produced the first extant Christian poem in any modern tongue, whose schools of learning under Christian bishops sent forth missionaries to the heathen, instructed Europe in learning by the voice of Baeda, and advised the great Charles on all points of education and religious practice by the mild wisdom of Alcuin. So strangely do the eyes of decaying culture mistake the days in which it lives; so important it was for the sake of the literature of the world that in one country at least the Roman literature should be expunged for a time in order that the fresh originality of the Teutonic mind should have the ground clear for its growth. When, having rooted itself, it came again, through Roman Christianity, into contact with Roman literature, it did not lose the freshness of its own stock. It assimilated, at least in the North, Latin thought into a living body of English poetry.

With the end of the time of quiet after 520—a

time which seems to have lasted about thirty years —the West Saxons under Cynric (552) opened from Winchester an attack on Old Sarum, and soon won our Wiltshire, Dorsetshire, and Berkshire. From Berkshire they went eastward and having made Surrey and the Four Towns their own, returned to Wiltshire, and thence, but now under Ceawlin as leader, drove their war-plough to Cirencester (Corinium), and thence through a country crowded with the villas and estates of the provincials till they met the three Welsh chieftains of Gloucester, Cirencester, and Bath, at Deorham, a village northward of Bath. There the West Saxons (577) "fought with the Brits and slew three kings, Commagil and Condidan and Farinmagil in the place which is called Deorham, and took from them three cities Gleawanceaster and Cyrenceaster and Bathanceaster." This battle gave them the whole valley of the Severn south of Arden and east of the river. Seven years after they made another inroad up the Severn valley, entered Shropshire and went up the river till they reached Uriconium (Wroxeter), and having destroyed that town pushed northward still towards Chester. They were met on the borders of our Cheshire by the Welsh at Fethanleag (Faddilay), three miles west of Nantwich, and Ceawlin, defeated there, "returned thence in wrath to his own country."

I have introduced this bit of history because the destructions of Bath and of Wroxeter are connected with our literature. The first is bound up with the poem of the *Ruined Burg*, and the second with a Welsh elegy which, independent of its enabling me to draw attention to the influence of Welsh on English verse, is almost a parallel to the *Ruined Burg*.

Bath, during the Roman period, ranked in importance with Gloucester. They were both excelled by Cirencester, and Cirencester was inferior only to York, London, and Colchester. The Roman remains, even now found in Bath, prove its wealth; and the public buildings of well-wrought stone, the temple to its local deity, the colonnade and porches over its hot springs, its wide forum and splendid baths, were still in existence when the city was sacked and burned by Ceawlin. There is no actual statement in the *Chronicle* that Bath was destroyed by Ceawlin, but it was not the habit of the English at this time to dwell in towns, and Bath remained for fully a century in a state of ruin. These are the ruins that the poem called the *Ruined Burg* describes, at least that was Leo's view, and is Professor Earle's. Whether the lines are written about a *city* or a *castle* has been questioned, but the phrases, "many mead-halls," "high the crowd of pinnacles,"—point to an extensive town.

The date of the poem is of course much later than the overthrow of Bath by Ceawlin, but it is bound up by imagination with that terrible day. The poet who wrote the lay placed his thought in the midst of the destruction of the town by the West Saxons, and pitied those who suffered it. "In the wide slaughter," he says, "they perished when came the days of bale." We see that many years of decay and the wasting of Nature had passed over the ruins, when the singer stood first amongst them and was moved by their desolation. They are "undereaten by old age." And we may guess the very time. It was in 676 that Osric, an under-king of the Hwiccas, founded a monastery among the ruins of Bath; and around it in later years grew up a new town which was raised into importance by Offa in 781. Some Scôp, during these years between 676 and 781, coming in a chieftain's train to visit the place, or some monk of the monastery, wandering among the ruins in a winter evening ("hoar-frost is on the mortar" he says) made these verses, verses which have been rashly extolled as the best which the Early English Muse has left us, but which, amid their conventional expressions, have still a fine quality—

Wondrous is its wall of stone   Weirds have shattered it!
Broken are the burg-steads!   Crumbled is the giants' work.
Fallen are the roof beams: ruined are the towers;
All undone the door-pierced towers;   frozen dew is on their plaster!
Shorn away and sunken down   are the sheltering battlements,
Undereaten of Old Age!   Earth is holding in its clutch
These, the power-wielding workers: all forworn are they, forlorn in death are they![1]
Hard the grip was of the ground,   while a hundred generations
Move away of men.   Long its wall abode
Through the rule that followed rule,   ruddy stained, and gray as goat,
Under storm-skies steady!   Steep the court that fell,
Still it falleth . . .   (skilful ancient work it was)!
Strong in rede, (the builder strengthened),   strong of heart, in chains he bound
All the wall-uprights with wires,   wondrous-wrought together!
Brilliant were the burg-steads,   burn-fed houses many;
High the heap of hornèd gables,   of the host a mickle sound,
Many were the mead-halls,   full of mirth of men,
Till the strong-willed Wyrd   whirled that all to change!
In a slaughter wide they fell,   woeful days of bale came on;
Famine-death fortook   fortitude from men;
All their battle bulwarks   bare foundations were!
Crumbled is the castle-keep;   those have cringed to earth
Who set up again the shrines![2]   So the halls are dreary,
And this courtyard's wide expanse![3]   From the raftered woodwork

---

[1] *Forworn* is put in for the sake of the assonance with *geleorene*, but of course I do not mean that *forweorone* has anything to do with *werian*. It means (from *weosan*) decayed, tottering, *decrepitus*. I have put a full stop at *geleorene*, which is not the ordinary reading.

[2] *Betend crungon—hergas to hrusan.* Many translations have been made of this obscure passage. B. and T. translate "The atoning bands sank to earth." I do not understand what they mean. Earle translates "Pitifully fell the armies to the earth." I take *betend(e)* to mean those who restored or kept up the shrines, and this, if it be a possible translation, has a clear meaning.

[3] *Teafor geapu.—Teafor* is often translated as an adjective, signifying *red*.

(See) the roof has shed its tiles ! To ruin sank the market-place,[1]
Broken up to barrows ;   many a brave man there,
Glad of yore, and gold-bright,   gloriously adorned,
Hot with wine and haughty,   in war-harness shone ;—
Saw upon his silver,   on set gems and treasure,
On his welfare and his wealth,   on his winsome jewels,
On this brightsome burg   of a broad dominion !—
There the stone-courts stood ;   hotly surged the stream,
With a widening whirling ;   and a wall enclosed it all,
With its bosom bright.   There the baths were set
Hot within their heart ;   fit [for health] it was !

" Then they let flow in over the hoary stone the streams of heated water. The waves filled the round and boiling mere.[2] That was a kingly thing."[3]

Leo, for example, takes the two words together and translates them *rote Lücken*. I have chosen to render *geapu* (the wide opening) as the wide expanse ; and *teafor* (which means " foundation place ") the courtyard of, or the open space surrounding, the fortress, a place where the foundations for new buildings might be made. *Teafor* is then taken to be a repetition of *geapu*. " The wide expanse, the foundation place is also dreary." After this I place a full stop, and the words that follow begin a separate piece of the description. But this may be too audacious, and would certainly be so, were not the whole passage so obscure.

[1] *Wong*, which means a plain or a flat meadow, may here, I conjecture, mean the forum, the open space in the midst of the town, with all its shops in ruin, and this meaning agrees with the lines that follow.

[2] It might well be called a mere ; when the central bath was found in 1755, sixteen feet below the surface, it was ninety feet long by sixty broad. " There is a city six (12) miles from Bristol, where the hot springs, circulating in channels artificially constructed, are collected into an arched reservoir to supply the warm baths which stand in the middle of the place, most delightful to see and beneficial to health. This city is called Bath from a word in the English tongue which signifies *bath*, because infirm people resort to it from all parts of England for the purpose of washing themselves in these health-bringing waters—and persons in health also assemble there to see the curious bubbling up of the warm springs." This is the account of Bath given in the *Acta Stephani*. It reads as if the writer had seen our poem, and is certainly since the Roman arrangement was probably rebuilt or repaired a confirmation of Earle's belief that the ruined burg was Bath.

[3] Wülker reads *þing huse*, which may mean, " That was a place where a king's Thing might assemble." I may as well, in passing from this poem, quote, as an illustration of it, Gildas' description of the attack of the English on a town. " All the columns " (he speaks of the assaults as if they were made on the temple of God) " were levelled with the ground by the frequent strokes of the battering ram, all the husbandmen routed, together with their bishops, priests, and people, whilst the sword gleamed, and the flames crackled around them on every side. Lamentable to behold, in the midst of the streets lay the tops of lofty towers, tumbled to the ground, stones of high walls, holy altars, fragments of human bodies, covered with livid clots of coagulated blood, looking as if they had been squeezed together in a press, and with no chance of being buried save in the ruins of the houses, or

The second literary interest connected with the West Saxon advance is the Welsh song on the destruction of Uriconium. That poem is an old *marwnad* or elegy, and was composed, it is generally thought, by Llywarch Hen, who lived, men say, in the sixth century.[1] It is "in the soldier's triplet, the oldest known form of Welsh versification, and its style is lyrical." It has, no doubt, suffered changes in the progress of time, but, if here we may follow Dr. Guest, it represents a poem contemporary with the fall of Uriconium, and written by one who knew the details of the fight and had seen the place. The poet paints himself as an eye-witness, as escaping with his family from the slaughter, and looking down from a hill upon the town in flames. We find ourselves, in its verse, listening to another type of poetry than the English, to a much more imaginative, to a much better shaped poetry—poetry which, entirely Celtic in tone, had perhaps been influenced by the Roman culture. If it was really contemporary with the destruction of Uriconium in 584, we may say that this Welsh piece, with others even earlier, is, with some lays in *Beowulf* and the fragment of Finnsburg, and, it may be, a few Irish fragments, the oldest extant modern poetry.

Kyndylan of Pengwern (Shrewsbury) is the hero whose death is lamented. He is slain defending Tren, the White Town, the capital of the district.

---

in the ravening bellies of wild beasts and birds."—This is Dr. Giles' translation, and he borrows in places from the old translation. The whole passage is obscure.

[1] Guest's text of the poem is from the Red Book of Herghest, a MS. of the fourteenth century; and his translation is "intended to be *literal*." He thinks that this soldier's triplet (*triban milwr*) "suggested the use of final rhyme to the Latinists of the third and fourth centuries who first introduced it, and most of whom were Celts by birth." Is it not possible, then, that the rhymes we find in Anglo-Saxon poetry may be derived from Celtic poetry?

Tren is identified by Dr. Guest as Uriconium, the town built, not of timber, but of hewn stone, after the Roman fashion. Five miles from it was the British stronghold in the woods along the Severn bank, near Pengwern. Twelve miles up the valley of the Tern there is a high and remarkable ridge of rocks called Hawkstone, in front of which there was a strong British fortress, which, if the ridge were then called the Hel or El, might take the name of *Eli*. From these two the poet describes the eagles of the foe[1] descending eager for the flesh of Kyndylan. "Pengwern's eagle with the gray-horn beak, Eli's eagle, screaming aloud," both sail down their several valleys eager for the blood of men. There is no finer image in early poetry, and it brings the fierceness of the contest before us with extraordinary vividness. Not far off from these two fortresses stood a little group of Celtic churches, which Guest identifies with Baschurch, a small town or village about seven miles north of Shrewsbury. There lay Kyndylan, carried thither when the flight was over.[2]

> Bassa's Churches! There rests to-night,
> There ends, there shrinks within himself,
> He, that was the Shelter in battle;
> .   .   .   Heart of the men of Argoet.

---

[1] As both Pengwern and Eli, according to Guest's conjecture, were British fortresses, the eagles coming from them and eager for the flesh of Kyndylan, show us that these fortresses had been seized by the English. But it is, perhaps, fanciful to make the eagles into the foe, and more simple to think that they only mean the birds of prey. It may be also fanciful of me to say that the allusions to the wild boar are allusions to the English. But I let it stand. Kyndylan, "whose heart is now cold as winter's ice," has died by the "thrust of a wild boar through his head." The English called their chiefs the wild boars and in the tenth stanza the term is used of the whole of the English host: "The wild boar will not give back to Kyndylan his father's town." If the original poem then be contemporary, the English in 584 were helmeted with the boar, or crested with the boar, as we find them in *Beowulf*.

[2] The translation is Dr. Guest's. It will be seen by those who will refer to his essay how largely I am here indebted to him (*Origines Celticae*, vol. ii. p. 290, etc.) Nothing can be more vivid and interesting than his discussion of the poem.

> Bassa's Churches are lovely to-night,
> Their clover hath made them so ;
> Ruddy are they : overflowing my heart !

Then he turns to describe Uriconium, its gracious site, its pastures and ploughed lands, now stained with blood, its lusty young warriors, its gray and grave warriors, all lost and overthrown ; and, though it is not English poetry, yet I quote a few of its stanzas because it is Welsh poetry concerning an English battle—

> The White Town in the bosom of the wood !
> There has ever been of its lustyhood,
> On the surface of the grass, the blood.
>
> The White Town in the country-side !
> Its lustyhood,—its gray thoughtfulness—[1]
> The blood under the feet of its warriors.
>
> The White Town in the Valley !
> Joyful its troop with the common spoil of battle ;
> Its people are they not gone ?
>
> The White Town between Tren and Trodwyd !
> More common was the broken shield
> Coming from battle than the evening ox.[2]
>
> The White Town between Tren and Traval !
> More common was the blood
> On the surface of the grass than the ploughed fallow !

I have drawn attention to this poem, and to the distinct quality of its poetry, that we may, by placing a Welsh poem into relation with the English, realise that the Welsh literature began even in the sixth century to affect the English south of the Dee. The Celtic imagination began to influence the Teutonic. The same thing may be said, and with greater propriety, of the Northumbrian English and the Celts, but while that is more or less understood, the necessary influence of the Welsh on English song along the marches from

---

[1] Its gray-headed seniors.   [2] Returning from pasture.

Chester to the Bristol Channel has not been sufficiently considered. I believe that this influence, when English literature again arose after the Conquest, was a very powerful one, but even now its elements must have begun to work. Both English and Welsh were singing folk; both chanted their battles; among both, the kings and nobles had bards; and the same kind of rewards—horses, lands, collars, and the rest—were given to the poets of both folk. When alliances were made between Welsh and English, the poets of each people must have met and sung together. When war was not going on, intercommunion of the two peoples would have been frequent along the march. Travelling singers would cross the border to and fro, going from village to village, from farm to farm. The literary men of England, not so very long after this time, corresponded with Welsh kings. Ealdhelm writes a letter to Geraint of Devon, in which he called him the glorious lord of the western realm.

As to the alliances, they began to be made shortly after this overthrow of the White Town. Ceawlin himself, its destroyer, was utterly overthrown in 591 by the Hwiccas in alliance with the Welsh. The house of Ælla, on the fall of Deira, took refuge, at least so it seems from Welsh tradition, with the King of Gwynedd, and Æthelfrith's fear that this alliance of the Deirans and the Welsh would be too much for him in Northumbria, was the cause of his desperate attack on Chester in 613.[1] In 631 Penda leagued himself with Cadwallon, King of Gwynedd, against Eadwine. These instances, which might be

---

[1] 607 is the date of the battle of Chester in the *Chronicle*, but the *Annales Cambriae* date it 613, and Dr. Guest thinks this is probably the true date.

multiplied, are enough ; they prove that there must have been intercommunion of the poetical work of both peoples. This is still plainer when we think that in the later wars, waged by the West Saxons against the Britons, the Welsh were not, as of old, exterminated, but were allowed to settle down after conquest among the English, and were acknowledged as citizens, as living under the king's peace. "They could hold," says Freeman, "landed property, their blood had its price, their oath its ascertained value."

Welsh settlers then, we may be sure, brought with them Welsh poetry. Even the unsubdued Welsh, during times of peace, lived with the English in much the same way as the English and Scots of the Borderland lived with one another—in the constant association of raiding and fighting, but at the same time with an occasional interchange of mirth, of singing, and now and then, it may be, of intermarriage. As time went on, this literary intercommunion would increase till the prohibition of the Welsh crossing the border was enforced. In fact all along the marches from Chester to the Bristol Channel, and along the eastern border of West Wales, there was enough motion to and fro of the life of both peoples to produce so much communion between their poetry as would arise from the singers of one people hearing the singers of the other. The English influence on the Welsh is inappreciable ; but the Welsh poetry, being of a higher imaginative type, would be certain to influence the English poetry. It is not unimportant even at this early time to notice that the first English poem of literary quality after the Conquest was made by Layamon, whose home was at Areley, in Shropshire, and whose subject was British ; that the "Pearl," the loveliest of Middle English poems, was probably written in Lancashire, and is full of Celtic colour; and that the first English lyrics—like "Sumer is ycomen in"—were, I believe, born upon the Welsh border of Mercia.

These things being said, there remains nothing more to be usefully written in this place concerning the interests of English literature in Southern England. It is true that, with the arrival of Augustine, Roman literature entered Kent with Christianity. But it was not English, and it was not till the year 669-671 that even Latin learning took root in Canterbury and spread over the West Saxon realm. The history of that belongs to another chapter.

We turn now to the Angles and their conquest of Middle and Northern England, and touch on the few points which in their wars are linked to literature, and as we have carried Southern England up to 670, so we carry this Engle history up to the same date. It is perhaps necessary to apologise for introducing an historical sketch into a history of literature, but it is better, I think, that my readers should have some image of the divisions of England in their mind's eye, and especially understand the original, certainly the literary, apartness —even though they were at root one people—of the Northumbrians and West Saxons. Moreover a great number of the right answers to literary problems depends on the history and geographical distribution of the peoples among whom the literature in question arises, and even minor matters or side issues of history enable us to guess with a greater probability the causes of literary movements. For example, the persistency of York as a city, and the long continuance of heathendom in Mercia—which belong to the story of the conquests of the Angles, have a remote but distinct bearing upon English literature in Northumbria.[1]

The Angles, then, the third tribe of the English on the Continent, were the last to leave for the shores of Britain. When they started we do not know, but it was probably early in the sixth century. Ship followed ship, during a period of years, for the shores of our island, till the whole of the Angles had left their original country. In that they were different from the two other English tribes. The greater part of the Jutes remained behind in the fifth century, and, mingled up with the Danes, came afterwards with them to England. As to the Saxons, it was only their overflow that entered Britain. But when the emigration of the Angles was over, their native land was left uninhabited. Their exodus was like that of the Israelites from Egypt. The women and children came away; the implements of farm and household were carried with them, their cattle also and their slaves. Not a hoof was left behind. The *Chronicle* says: "From Angle, which has *ever since remained a waste*, between the Jutes and Saxons, came the men of East Anglia, Middle Anglia, Mercia, and all Northumbria," and Baeda bears the same testimony. I cannot help thinking that this unity of the Angles had something to do with the rise of vernacular literature in the north rather than in the south of England.

Those nearest the seaboard left first, and they descended on the "last unconquered remnant of the Saxon shore"— the line of coast between the

---

[1] It will be plain that I have followed, in the historical part of this chapter, not any work of my own, but the work done by Mr. Green, Mr. Skene, Mr. York Powell, Professor Freeman, Dr. Guest and others, and I trust that no mistakes of mine may wrong these honoured names.

Orwell and the Wash. These, when they settled, called themselves the North folk and the South folk, and were probably two distinct bands from different parts of Engle. The country they seized came to be called East Anglia. Part of them, or a new band, pushed northward along the coast to the Fens about the Wash, then northward still, east of the Wolds, as far as the Humber, and these were called the Gyrwas, and the Lindiswara. Another expedition of the Angles, finding the coast of our Suffolk, Norfolk, and Lincoln occupied, landed on the flat of Holderness and fought until nearly the whole of our East Riding was in their hands. Pressing still farther through a fertile land, studded with villas and rich with cattle, they stormed York, marched on to Aldborough, and were then stopped in their westward progress by the great forest of Elmet. But they won the coast as far as the Tees. This was the land of Deira, and the whole British population were driven out of it to die in the woods and in the caves of the rocks in utter misery and starvation. The great Roman towns were sacked and ruined. The rich villas of the meadows of the Derwent were burnt to the ground. It was like the passage of the Chimaera over the hamlets of Lycia. Nevertheless, a hundred and fifty years later, the centre of European learning was at York, and the descendants of these ravishing and burning warriors civilised the coast and filled the river valleys with monasteries in which were born, cradled, and nurtured the arts and sciences of Northern and Midland England. It may be that York, the "city of the Cæsars," was not so absolutely ruined as the rest. It was almost too big to ruin. At any rate it did not long remain a desolation. Early in the seventh century it was again a city, and a royal city, the capital of Eadwine. If it be possible that any of the Roman learning was preserved during a milder conquest, the fact would be another reason for the quicker rise and longer continuance of English literature in Northumbria. Big towns cherish and preserve literature. Even when the Danes came to York, they came more to settle than to destroy, and whatever literature was saved in Northumbria from the Danish horror was saved at York.

While Deira was being made, another band of Angles had entered the broad estuary of the Forth, and landing on its southern bank—where they may have heard of their Frisian or Jutish cousins, whom a certain tradition brings there long before this time—fought their way westward as far as the future site of Edinburgh, and turning round it, marched still westward as far as the valley of the Clyde, and southward till they reached the Tweed. After this the Angles drove their way southward, across the Tweed, and it is here that we come on the first known date in their conquests. Ida, whom his foes called the Flame-bearer, began to rule in 547, and during the twelve years of his reign made his way into our Northumberland, seized on the basaltic rock of Bamborough seated like a couchant lion on that stormy shore, enclosed it with a hedge and then a wall; and from that fortress he and his descendants won the land westward to Cumberland and southward to the Tees. When this was accomplished men called the country from the Forth to the Tees and from the edge of Cumbria to the eastern coast, Bernicia. In 588 Bernicia and Deira became one kingdom under Æthelric, and the name of the whole from the Forth to the Humber was Northumbria. This is the kingdom which for reasons we can only conjecture became the home of original literature in England.

Meanwhile the Angles who had settled down in Lincolnshire, pushed inland no doubt by new arrivals from their fatherland, penetrated by the valley of the Trent to the place where Nottingham now sits on the river and then to our Leicester, and the settlement of Middle England began. The Gyrwas south of the Lindiswara in the Fen country, and other Angle bands fought their path southward and westward, and the shires (loosely speaking) of Huntingdon, Cambridge, and Northampton, were first their prey and then their place of rest. These became the South Engle.

While this was being done the West Engle, moving north of these conquests, passed through the upper part of the present shire of Nottingham into the Peak country of Derbyshire, and then wheeling to the south, and leaving the Middle English and the South English on their left, occupied the belt of country between the Middle English and the South English on one hand, and the borders of our Shropshire and Cheshire on the other, going as far south as the forest of Arden. Afterwards since they lived on the Marches nearest to the Welsh, they came to be called the Mercians. These conquests finished the work of the Engle in central Britain in the latter half of the sixth century.

There were now seven little kingdoms in England, but some years later Æthelfrith, king of Northumbria, (593-617) joined all these kingdoms under his one sway, with the exception of Kent then ruled by Æthelberht, and I must hereafter draw attention to this Northumbrian glory as one of the possible causes of native literature being more fully developed in Northumbria than elsewhere in England. He was a mighty man, and having first at Daegsastan (Dawston in Liddesdale) beaten so completely the Scots who invaded him, that they were for a long time forced into quiet, he went into the Welsh country in 613, fought a fierce battle near Chester, and seized the town, the surrounding lands, and the sea-coast at the mouth of the Dee. This conquest of his cut off Cumbria from North Wales, as the battle at Deorham had cut off West Wales from our South Wales. At two points then the English had reached the sea, at Chester and at our Bristol, and the Welsh were now split asunder into three kingdoms, the kingdom of Devon and Cornwall, the kingdom of our Wales, and the kingdom of Cumbria, which extended from the Ribble to the Clyde. Afterwards the western frontier of Mercia was drawn from the mouth of the Wye to the Dee, and the river Tone was made by Ine the frontier between Wessex and West Wales, but the conquest was now practically finished, and the English settled down to till the lands they had won.

With the Middle English and Mercians literature has up to this date nothing to do, nor indeed has Northumbria much to do with it. The only thing needful to remark is that the wars in and about Northumbria between the Angles and the Britons, and during the whole of the period of which we are writing, were, according to Mr. Skene, the source of a number of Welsh poems which we have, much altered, in manuscripts, the earliest of which are of the twelfth century; and that the Welsh and English were nearer to one another and more mingled in Northumbria than they were on the March or on the border of West Wales.¹ We have no trace of poetry among the English during the years of the conquest of Northumbria. But there are several instances during the wars between the battle of Chester in 613 and the overthrow of Penda in 655 which prove that the war-song was still going on.

The first belongs to the battle between Æthelfrith of Northumbria and Raedwald, king of the East Angles, in 617. A line of poetry from some old song is quoted by the chroniclers, Henry of Huntingdon, Roger of Wendover, and others—

> With the blood of Angles Idle's stream was foul,²

and the description given by Huntingdon, as well as by the rest, induces us to believe that they had before them some early English account of the battle in verse. The troops advance with fluttering standards, bristling spears,—phrases which are, however, more Latin than English. Æthelfrith rushes on the foe as if he had "found a prey." In 633 King Eadwine was slain by Cadwallon and Penda at Heathfield, and Henry of Huntingdon repeats the same phrase—one perhaps of the conventional phrases of Anglo-Saxon poetry— "The plain of Hethfeld reeked red from end to end with a river of the blood of Æthelings; a place of sudden woeful slaughter of the bravest warriors." In

---

[1] The Welsh, it is true, settled down with the English under Ine, and the same mixture took place when the Wessex frontier was pushed on as far as the Tamar; it is also true that when Offa extended the Mercian frontier the Welsh and the English settled down together in the new land which the English won and both these facts are of importance for our literary history; but the mixture between Welsh and English in the North was longer in time, more complete, and its frontier more extended than it was in Mercia and Wessex.

[2] It is probable that short historical records like this in poetry, as well as others in rude prose (such as the pre-Christian entries in the *Chronicle*), were written down in the runic characters which came to Britain with the English, and were preserved on oak, beech, alder, or birch frames, perhaps like those later "Bardic frames" from Wales, which Dr. Guest describes (*Origines Celticae*, vol. ii. p. 161).

634 Oswald, the most Christian king, met the forces of the leader of the Britons at Denises-burn, and another fragment of an old song tells us that "the corses of men of Cadwallon choked the Dennisburn." But Penda had his way at Maserfeld in 642, and slew Oswald; whence "it is said," writes Huntingdon, "the plain of Maserfeld was white with the bones of the Saints." At last, in 655, Penda the Strong was made weak by Oswiu, and the "earth was wet with his blood and the ground splashed with his brains." The battle was fought near the river Winwaed, which, swollen over its banks with excessive rain, destroyed, as they fled from the field, more of the heathen men than fell by the sword. So great was the deliverance (and we hear, as we read of it, the song of another deliverance of the same kind—" The river of Kishon swept them away, that ancient river, the river Kishon") —that it was celebrated in a battle song of which the Norman chroniclers retained three lines—

> At the Winwede was vengéd the war-death of Anna,
> The slaughter of kings—of Sigbert, of Ecgrice:
> The death of King Oswald, the death of King Edwin.

In 658 Cenwealh, the West Saxon king, fought a great battle at Pen in Dorsetshire against the Welsh, and the account of the Norman chronicler has it in the character of poetry. When the fight was joined the English yielded, but they feared flight more than death, and stood to their arms. "Then weary grew the Welsh, their strength melted away like snow; they fled from Pen even to Pedred, and cureless was the wound given there to the children of Brut." It seems doubtful if all of these have an origin in Anglo-Saxon songs, especially the last, which looks as if it had a Briton lay as its source. Yet the three lines concerning the flight at Winwaed are enough to prove that the Norman chroniclers had some English lays before them when they prepared their history.

This brings the remnants of English literature, seen, it is true, in mere flights of song, up to 670, which is about the date of the first Christian poem, of Caedmon's song of the Creation; and which is also the date of the true beginning of Latin literature in the south, at Canterbury. A more detailed account of the influences which in Northumbria preceded and influenced the beginning at Whitby of a vernacular poetry, is reserved to a later chapter. Meanwhile, of what kind was the life these warriors and settlers lived? What did they think as they went to war, and as they struck in battle? How did they feel when they settled down to agriculture, when they built their homesteads, and when they drank together in the hall? What kind was the scenery among which they lived? What did they think and feel concerning the sea on which they sailed, and the storms which roared upon their coasts? Have we any record in their literature of these matters? Does their literature disclose to us their character, their emotions, their thoughts in war, at home, and on the ocean? These are the questions which the following chapters will attempt to answer. Before they were land-dwellers they were warriors, and we will begin with war.

CHAPTER VIII

ARMOUR AND WAR IN POETRY

In the earliest poems of the English we have already seen something of their customs of war, and of the armour they used. War was one of their chief businesses, and being knit up with courage, self-sacrifice, scorn of death, contention against fate, faithful comradeship, rescue of the weak, defence of the kinsfolk and the land, the praise of women, the worship of the gods, glory after death, reverence for ancestors, romantic adventure and other ideal matters, became naturally one of the great subjects of song. Everything pertaining to it was clothed in imaginative dress. The body-armour, the weapons, and chiefly the sword, were glorified. The war-smiths, especially as forgers of the sword, were garmented with legend, and made into divine personages. Of these Weland is the type, husband of a swan maiden, and afterwards almost a god. Battle, as in Homer, was attended by immortal creatures,—among the Norsemen by the shield-women—the choosers of the slain—by evil and good spirits among the English, and by Wyrd herself, the mistress of them all. The meeting of the warriors in fight—the wielding of the sword, the darting and pushing of the spears, the shield wall as it drove its way into the mass of the foe, the shower of arrows, the challenges of the warriors as they fought, the crashing and shouting, the way the armour behaved under the blows, were one and all adorned with metaphor; and every poet, while using the terms that had become conventional and which the guests in the hall expected, strove to add something of his own, or to express in a new fashion the well-known forms of description. Then, around the battle, and following it, like minor beings of fate and slaughter, were the birds and beasts that prey upon the slain—the eagles of the woods and of the sea, the kite and the hawk of the rocks, the raven, the carrion crow, the wolf, and the hill fox. These, screaming, croaking, howling, sang the "horrid song" of death, and their omens often foretold the issue of the fight.

An English warrior went into battle with a boar-crested helmet, and a round linden shield, with a byrnie of ring mail (or in the case of the poorer sort a cloth or leather coat, often covered with flakes of iron or horn), with two javelins or a single ashen spear some eight or ten feet long, with a long two-edged sword naked or held in an ornamental scabbard and a great knob at the head of the hilt. In his belt was a short, heavy, one-edged sword, or rather a long knife, called the seax, which was used for close quarters and for finishing a foe. Beowulf rips asunder the dragon with it, and Grendel's mother uses it on Beowulf in the struggle when he lies on the sand of the cavern. Some carried great axes, very heavy and long-handled; and the javelin, and bow with broad-headed arrows, especially among the thralls, were frequent weapons.

In the *Crafts of Men* we see the Smith at work on this armour:—

> One, a clever smith may for use in war,
> For the weapons' onset,[1] many (arms) make ready
> When he forges fast for the fighting of the warriors
> Either helm or hip-seax, or the harness of the battle,
> Or the sword sheer-shining, or the circle of the shield
> For to fix it firmly, 'gainst the flying of the spear.
> *Crafts*, l. 61.

At times an iron-bound club was carried, but the sword was the special weapon of all the nobler sort. It was also the noblest of all the pieces of armour, and it was fame for a smith to have forged one that would last, because of its fine temper, from generation to generation. If its maker was not known, and it was of the finest quality, its origin was referred to the elves, the dwarfs, or the giants. Magic runes were engraved on the blade by the smith, it was damasked, spells were muttered over it; it seems sometimes to have been dipped, when red hot, in blood, or in a broth of poison-twigs. The hilt was wrought with wires of gold, silver, or iron, interwoven like writhing snakes. Sometimes a blood-painted serpent, as in the Icelandic lay of Helgi and Swava, lay above the edges or on the ridge of the sword, whirling its tail round the hilt. Such a sword received a name of its own, and had, as it were, a living spirit in it that sorrowed and rejoiced.

Swords of this kind are named in *Beowulf*; "hard-edged and wonderful, damascened, and adorned with jewels"—Hrunting, Naegling, and the sword of the cave,—but of all these enough has been said. We touch on the proper literature of the sword in one of the *Riddles* of Cynewulf, where it is finely personified. Cynewulf conceives it as itself a warrior, wrapped in its scabbard as in a coat of mail; going, like a hero,

---

[1] I have translated *wæpenþracu*, not *wæpenþrague*.

into the battle; hewing a path for its lord into the ranks of the foe; praised in the hall by kings for its great deeds; and strangest of all, and most poetical (unless Prehn be wrong, from whom I take this explanation),[1] mourning when the battle is over, for its childless desolation, for the times when it was innocent of wars, for the anger with which the women treat it as the slaughterer of men. The power with which Cynewulf enters into the life of the things he treats of can scarcely go further, but this is not apart from Teutonic thought, which conceived a living being in the sword.[2] Here is the riddle. The Sword speaks:—

>   I'm a wondrous wight   for the warstrife shapen;
>   By my lord beloved,   lovelily adorned:
>   Many coloured is my corslet,   and a clasping wire
>   Glitters round the gem of Death   which my Wielder gave to me;
>   He who whiles doth urge me,   wide-wanderer that I am,
>   With himself to conquest.
>   Then I carry treasure,
>   Gold above the garths,   through the glittering day;
>   I of smiths the handiwork!   Often do I quell
>   Breathing men with battle edges!   Me bedecks a king
>   With his hoard and silver;   honours me in hall,
>   Doth withhold no word of praise!   Of my ways he boasts
>   'Fore the many heroes,   where the mead they drink.
>   In restraint he lulls me,   then he lets me loose again,
>   Far and wide to rush along;   me the weary with wayfarings,
>   Me the stout in battle. . . .
>   . . . Ranging largely, I'm a foe,
>   Cursed of all weapons.   Riddle xxi.

He is cursed of them, for he breaks through armour and beats down the spear and axe, but he pays the penalty. "No son have I," so mourns the Sword, "who shall avenge me;" his fate is, if he shape the

---

[1] *Composition und Quellen der Rätsel des Exeterbuches*, to which, both in the translation and explanation of the *Riddles*, I am throughout indebted.

[2] Eusebius, Ealdhelm, and Tatwine have all written riddles on the sword. Cynewulf has most followed the first; but Cynewulf adds all the imaginative work. It is he alone who represents the sword as a warrior, wearing armour of his own, showing his lord the way through the battle, and when the war is over, mourning like a shattered veteran over his lonely future.

work of war, never to have a bride, and the woman, whose joy he has lessened (by slaying her lover?), speaks to him words of reviling, strikes him with her hands, and sings to him an evil song. "I take no heed," she cries, "of the battle."

Another portion of the sword is also described, when Cynewulf, making a riddle on the scabbard, tells of its fourfold wood; and then, in his fancy, likens the sword-hilt to the Cross of Christ that overthrew the gates of Hell, and to the gallows tree on which the Outlaw is hung.

> In the hall I saw, where the heroes drink,
> Borne above the floor, four, in kind, of things :—
> Wondrous wood-tree, woven gold,
> Treasure skilful-wrought, and of silver part ;—
> Image of his Cross who of it for us to Heaven
> Lifted up a ladder, ere he of Hell's dwellers
> Broke the burg asunder. Of this beam can I
> Easily, before the earls, tell the ancestry—
> There was yellow holly, and the yew, the hard tree,
> And the oak and maple. To the Æthelings
> All of them were useful. One the name they had—
> "Wolf-head's tree." Riddle lvi.

The English Shield was circular, with a polished or gilded boss of metal, under which lay the aperture for the hand. *Rand sceal on scylde—faest fingra gebeorh* ("a boss shall be on the shield, firm refuge for fingers"). The woodwork was of yellow linden, covered with the skins of wild animals, fixed to the linden-board with studs, and strengthened with circular or intersected bands of iron, gilt or painted; and there may have been sometimes nailed on it the figure of a boar or the sacred animal of the family. Our nearest likeness to it is the Highland targe—

> There's brass on the target of barkened bull-hide,
> There's steel in the scabbard that dangles beside ;
> The brass shall be burnished, the steel shall flash free,
> At a toss of the bonnet of Bonny Dundee.

The shield is also personified by Cynewulf; but as its work in the battle is to bear strokes rather than to give them, it complains more than the sword. It is "sick of battles, no physician can heal its wounds, always it must endure the deadly strokes of swords." As we read, we feel the spirit speaking in the shield, and are even touched with pity,[1] so well does Cynewulf do this work—

> I am all alone,   with the iron wounded,
> With the sword slashed into,   sick of work of battle,
> Of the edges weary.   Oft I see the slaughter,
> Oft the fierceful fighting.   Of no comfort ween I,—
> So that, in the battle-brattling,   help may bring itself to me;
> Ere I, with the warriors,   have been utterly fordone.
> But the heritage of hammers [2]   hews adown at me,
> Stark of edges, sworded-sharp,   of the smiths the handiwork,
> On me biting in the burgs!   Worse the battle is
> I must bear for ever!   Not one of the Leechkin,
> In the folk-stead,   could I find out,
> Who with herbs he has   then should heal me of my wound!
> But the notching on my edges   more and more becomes
> Through the deadly strokes of swords,   in the daylight, in the night.
>   Riddle vi.

The same self-pity for its hard fate, which we find here in the shield, is also found in the riddle on the headpiece of the Helmet. Like the Antlers of the stag, in the 88th riddle, it complains of the bitter weather.

>   Wretchedness I bear;
> Wheresoe'er he carries me,   he who clasps the spear!
> On me, still upstanding,   smite the streams (of rain);
> Hail, the hard grain (helms me),   and the hoar-frost covers me;
> And the (flying) snow (in flakes)   falls all over me.
>   Riddle lxxix. 6-10.

In the same way the Spear (R. lxxii.) mourns

---

[1] The contrary view is given in the parallel riddle by Ealdhelm. There, the shield is a soldier proud of his wounds—
> Quis tantos casus, aut quis tam plurima leti
> Suscipit in bello crudelis vulnera miles?

[2] That which is left after the hammer work is done,—*homera life*, i.e. "the sword."

that it was taken away from the field (as a sapling of the forest land) where earth and heaven nourished it; that its nature has been changed, and forced to bow to the will of a murderer. Yet, as it learns to know its master better, it sees that he is no murderer, but one who will fulfil a noble fame. Then the spear changes its thought, and is proud of its small neck and fallow sides, when the glow of sunlight glitters on its point, and the warrior bedecks it with joy, and bears it on the war-path with a hand of strength upon its shaft, and knows its ways in battle.[1]

In the same way the Battering Ram wails for its happy life as a tree in the forest, and for all it suffered when it was wrought by the hands of man; yet at the end, like the spear, it boasts itself of its deeds of war, of the breach it has made for the battle-guest to follow, of the plunder which they take together.

I beheld a tree in woodland, towering on high,
Branchèd brilliantly; and its bole abode in joy.
Wood that waxed each day! Water and the Earth
Fed it faithfully, till far gone in days,
To another state it came, a most unhappy state.
Deeply was it down-stabbed, dumb was it in bonds,
O'er its wounds enwreathed, and with woful trappings
In the front 'twas fretted. For another false one,

---

[1] *Gar* is the usual word for "spear"—(gar-Dene = spear Danes). *Gar* was the javelin armed with two of which the warrior went into battle, and which he threw over the "shield-wall." It was barbed, but the other, shaped like a leaf, without a barb, was called the "*spere*," the lance, concerning which is Cynewulf's Riddle. This was shod on the top of the handle with a heavy metal ball to give it weight, just as the sword was. There are other names for the weapon. "*Franca*" is the javelin which, in the battle of Maldon, is whirled through the neck of a warrior. "*Waelsteng*" is the deadly shaft or stake of the spear, and poetry uses it for the spear itself. "*Darod*" is a dart, and "*darodaese*" an ashen spear; *ord* is the spear point. The shafts of all these weapons were of ash, and the poets came to call the spears "ashes," and the warriors who bore them the "ash-bearers" (*Genesis* 2041). Hrothgar says that he has guarded his folk for fifty years with ashes and edges, with spear and sword.—*Beowulf* 1773.

For another battle guest, through the beating of its head,
Does it ope the way. Oft do these together
Ravage ragingly the treasure. Fast and restless[1] then
Was its follower to follow, when the first had cleft its path!
None into the narrow strait now would dare to venture.
             Riddle liv.

There is a very different tone in the riddle that represents the Bow. The personification is just as vivid, but where the shield mourns, the bow exults. His force as a warrior, his slaughter of the foe, the deadly poison of his shafts are sung with a savage joy.

A. G. O. F. is my name, turned the other way;
And a wight well wrought am I, for the war enshapen—
If it hap I bend myself, and from out my bosom fareth
Venomous an (adder) sting— then I'm all on fire
Far from me to drive away a very death to life.
Whensoe'er my master, who has made me for that woe,
Lets aloose my limbs, I am longer than before,
Till I spit out from me, with death-sorrow blended,
That all-baleful poison that I erst uptook.
Nor shall any of the men easily escape,
Not a warrior of them all, from what I then outcry!
.   .   .   .   .
. . . Then a drink of death he buys
(Brimming) sure the beaker that he buys with life!—
If I am unbounden, I obey no man;
Only when with skill I'm strung— Say what is my name!
             Riddle xxiv.

Two other riddles belong to war—one on the Coat of mail, the other on the Horn. The first brings the iron from which the rings are wrought out of the bosom of the earth, out of the dewy meadow-land, just as Ealdhelm, from whom the subject of the riddle is taken, says of his mail-shirt—

> Roscida me genuit gelido de viscere tellus,
> Non sum setigero lanarum vellere facta,
> Licia nulla trahunt, nec garrula fila resultant:

phrases which Cynewulf expands into poetry. But

---

[1] Ragingly = most rapidly; restless = unwearied. Ealdhelm has a riddle on the Battering Ram which Cynewulf had before him.

the most remarkable line is that in which, with a sudden return to pagan thought, he makes the mail-shirt say: "Me the snakes wove not through the crafts of Wyrds"—a line which takes us into the heart of ancient heathendom, but which returns in the next to the real worms of which he, with Ealdhelm, speaks, "Nec crocea Seres texunt lanugine vermes."

> Me the well-wet meadow,   wonderfully frosty,
> Out of its inside,   in old time brought forth—
> Of myself I wot not   as enwrought of woolly fleeces,
> Nor of hairs through high-craft   of my heart a-thinking.
> I have no enwoven woof,   nor a warp have I,
> Nor resounds a thread of mine,   through the smiting of the loom,
> Nor the shuttle shoots through me,   singing (as it goes).
> Nor shall ere the weaver's beam [1]   smite from anywhere (on me)!
> Me the Worms did not weave   through the crafts of Wyrds,
> Those who gloriously [2] the golden,   godlike web bedeck.
> Yet before the Fighters,   far along the Earth,
> Many a man doth name me—   "marvellous delightful Weed." [3]
>   Riddle xxxvi.

The riddle on the *Horn* which begins the life of the thing from the bull, the "weaponed warrior" of the text, is even more vigorous than that on the war-shirt, and describes the doings and uses of the horn in war and peace.

> I a weaponed warrior was!   Now in pride bedecks me
> A young serving man   all with silver and fine gold,
> With the work of waving gyres!   Warriors sometimes kiss me:

---

[1] The word is *am*, which Grein translates as a "weaver's beam," but Bosworth and Toller, "the reed or slay of the weaver's loom."

[2] "With adornments."

[3] At Benty Grange, in Derbyshire, an Anglo-Saxon barrow, opened in 1848, contained a coat of mail. "The iron chain work consists of a large number of links of two kinds, attached to each other by small rings half an inch in diameter; one kind flat and lozenge-shaped about an inch and a half long, the others all of one kind, but of different lengths, varying from four to ten inches. They are simply lengths of square rod iron with perforated ends through which pass the rings connecting them with the diamond-shaped links; they all show the impression of cloth over a considerable part of the surface."—*Grave Mounds*, Jewitt, p. 254.

This seems to have been an ordinary mail-shirt, roughly made; but there were others, worn by the great leaders, and forged of as delicate links as that which Harry Wynd sold to Conachar's foster-brother.

Sometimes I to strife of battle,   summon with my calling
Willing war-companions!   Whiles, the horse doth carry
Me the march-paths over,   or the ocean-stallion
Fares the floods with me,   flashing in my jewels—.
Often times a bower-maiden,   all bedecked with armlets,
Filleth up my bosom;   whiles, bereft of covers,[1]
I must, hard and headless,   (in the houses) lie!
Then, again, hang I,   with adornments fretted,
Winsome on the wall   where the warriors drink.
Sometimes the folk fighters,   as a fair thing on warfaring,[2]
On the back of horses bear me;   then bedecked with jewels
Shall I puff[3] with wind   from a warrior's breast.
Then, again, to glee feasts   I the guests invite
Haughty heroes to the wine—   other whiles shall I
With my shouting save from foes   what is stolen away,
Make the plundering scather flee.   Ask what is my name!
                                        Riddle xv.

There is no riddle on the helmet, only on the Vizor of the helm, but we have many a slight description of it throughout ancient English poetry. "Grima," which is the mask, the vizor, was used as a name for the whole helmet and included the crest, when there was a crest. The grinning face-covering, the ear-pieces, the projecting jut on the crown of the helm are frequently alluded to, and were adorned with incised or raised images of the boar. A helmet, found at Benty Grange, "has on its crown an elliptical bronze plate, supporting the figure of a boar—much corroded, carved in iron, with bronze eyes,—standing rampant like the crest of a knight." Such seems to have been the ornament of the helmets which the thegns of Beowulf wore when they approached Heorot. The

---

[1] *Bordum* I do not take to be "on the tables," but *bordum behlyðed*—robbed of my covers, of the round tops, like shields, which shut down on the drinking horn, and were, because they were adorned with jewels and gold figures, wrenched away by the plunderers.

[2] Literally, "a fair war-ornament." I have translated it as above, because I want to give, in this place, the force of "fyrd," which is the militia; and here, I think, the levy *en masse* of the population for a war-expedition—the horn is part of the war-material, part of the ornamented things used in the Fyrd.

[3] *Swelgan* is literally "to swallow, drink in."

translation I give of this obscure passage follows Professor Skeat's reading of the text.

> High above the helmet's vizor,   O'er his glittering body,
> Many-coloured, did the Boar   fire-hardened, gold-adorned,
>   hold the guard of life.
>   *Beowulf*, l. 303.

On Hnaef's funeral pyre is laid his helm—"a swine all golden, a boar iron hard!" When Beowulf plunges into the sea he sets his bright helmet on, adorned with jewels, circled round with a chieftain's chains,[1] which a weapon-smith in days of old had wrought and wondrously forged, beset with swine likenesses (here the boars seem to be small, and fastened on like nails on the cheek-plates), "so that never after brand nor swords of battle should bite into it." Lastly, when Beowulf is telling his story to Hygelac, he bids be brought into the hall the "Boar head sign, the battle-steep helm."[2] Nor is it only in *Beowulf* we find the boar-helm. Later on it appears in Cynewulf's *Elene*. When Constantine lies dreaming in his tent, he wakes up "overcovered with the boar-sign," with his helmet. When the warriors of Helena land on the shores of Greece, "on every earl was seen a masked-helm, a costly boar-crest."

So were the warriors armed. They marched into the fight led by the king and chiefs, sometimes on foot, sometimes riding on horses, under their banners, their chain armour ringing, their long ashen spears in their hands, their swords by their sides, and around them their henchmen, armed also with sword and

---

[1] "Chains—" Gold links twisted like a coronet.
[2] See Kemble, *Saxons in England*, chapter on Heathendom, and Grimm's *Teutonic Mythology*, chapter on Freyr, for the connection these and other writers establish between the Boar-sign and the golden boar which Freyr rode, and his worship.

spears and shield, in close array. Before they joined battle, the leader spoke to his soldiers, throwing up his shield arm to call their attention.

>   'Fore the vanward of the warriors   sprang the war-host leader ;
>   Bold that promise-bringer was,   his shield-board upheaved.
>   *Exodus*, ll. 252, etc.

Then the trumpets blew, and singing their war-songs and clashing their spears on their shields,[1] while the horses stamped the earth, the main body of freemen, wolves of the battle covered with their "vaulted shields," making a "shield-burg" as they went, a "breast-net" of men, marched forward and let fly their javelins and arrows above the yellow linden shields—

>   Then with boldness they
>   Letten forth be flying   shower-flights of darts,
>   Adders of the battle,   arrows hard of temper,
>   From the horn-curved bows.   High aloud they shouted,
>   Warriors fierce in fighting, sending forth their spears
>   Through the host of hard ones.   *Judith*, l. 220.

A passage in the *Christ* describes the same beginning of the battle—

>   To another, luck in war
>   Gives he on the battle-ground,   when the javelin shower
>   Send the shooters forth   o'er the shelter of the shield—
>   Flickering flight of arrows.   *Christ*, l. 673.

All these expressions, and many more, of the glitter and rushing noise of battle are common phrases of the poets and reveal the joy and glory our forefathers had in war. Cynewulf paints the advance of the Franks and Huns—

>   Then (in battle byrnies)   were the men of bravery
>   For the fight well fitted ;   flickered then the spears,
>   And the wreathen shirts of war.   With war-words and shields,
>   Heaved they up their hosting banner.   *Elene*, l. 22.

---

[1] *Elene*, l. 50.

When Pharaoh's host draws nigh in the *Exodus*, this is what the Hebrews see coming up from the southways—

> Then they saw,
> Forth and forward faring,   Pharaoh's war array,
> Gliding on, a grove of spears;[1]   glittering the hosts!
> Fluttered there the banners,   there the folk the march trod.
> Onwards surged the war,   strode the spears along,[2]
> Blickered the broad-shields;   blew aloud the trumpets.
> *Exodus*, l. 155.

Around the march, on the battle-field, after the battle, the beasts and birds of war collected—the gray wolf, the swart raven, the dewy-feathered, horn-nebbed eagle,—choosers, like Valkyrie, of the slain. The first, and perhaps the finest, association of these war-creatures is in *Beowulf*. It is already translated, but I translate it again—

> But the raven wan,
> Eager o'er the fated,   oftentimes shall speak.
> Tell unto the earn   how at eating he had sped,
> When he with the wolf   tore away the flesh of corpses.
> *Beowulf*, l. 3024.

There is nothing better in the Anglo-Saxon poetry of war than this grim conversation. The wolf, the raven, and the eagle never become Christian in English song. They are just as savage in the later poems as they are in *Beowulf*, or in the fragment of the *Fight at Finnsburg*. When Pharaoh's host is on the march they accompany it all night, longing for the slaughter—

> Wheeling round in gyres,   yelled the fowls of war,
> Of the battle greedy;   hoarsely barked the raven,
> Dew upon his feathers,   o'er the fallen corpses;
> Swart that chooser of the slain!   Sang aloud the wolves

---

[1] *Oferholt wegan; oferholt* = "overwood." A parallel passage in *Beowulf* makes me translate it a "grove of spears"; otherwise it would be, "a cover, a shield."

[2] *Garas trymedon*—"the spears strengthened themselves;" "moved along like a wall" is perhaps the poet's thought; or, *spears* may mean the spearmen.

<pre>
    At the eve their horrid song,   hoping for the carrion.
    Kindless¹ were the beasts,   cruelly they threaten;
    Death did these march-warders,   all the midnight through,
    Howl along the hostile trail—   hideous slaughter² of the host.
                                              Exodus, ll. 161-168.
</pre>

Then we see them while the battle is raging. This is the description in *Genesis* of the fight between Abraham and the Elamites—

<pre>
    So they rushed together—   Loud were then the lances,
    Savage then the slaughter-hosts. Sadly sang the wan fowl,
    With her feathers dank with dew,   midst the darting of the shafts,
    Hoping for the corpses.   Hastened then the heroes,
    In their mighty masses,   and their mood was full of thought.
        .   .   .   .   Then was hard play there,
    Interchanging of death-darts,   mickle cry of war!
    Loud the crash of battle!   With their hands the heroes
    Drew from sheaths   their swords ring-hilted,
    Doughty of the edges!   Genesis, l. 1982.
</pre>

Again we meet these beasts when the Hebrews go forth from Bethulia at the call of Judith. "The warriors hurried, heroes under helm, and bore the banner of victory forth at the breaking of the day. Sounded then the shields, starkly clanging—"

<pre>
                         Then rejoiced the gaunt beast,
    In the wood the wolf;   and the raven wan,
    Slaughter-greedy fowl!   Surely well they knew
    That the war thegns of the folk thought to win for them
    Fill of feasting on the fated!   On their track flew fast the earn,
    Hungry for his fodder,   all his feathers dropping dew;
    Sallow was his garment, and he sang a battle lay;
    Horny-nebbed he was.   Judith, l. 205.
</pre>

We meet them also on the march and in the battle in Cynewulf's *Elene*, when Constantine fights with the Huns—

---

¹ *Carleasan* is "without care or sorrow, reckless." I have ventured to make *cear* stand for "pity."

² I have repeated *fyll* in the translation.

Forth then fared the folk troop,   and a fighting lay
Sang the Wolf in woodland,   wailed a slaughter-rune ! [1]
Dewy-feathered,   on the foes' track,
Raised the Earn his song.   *Elene*, ll. 27-30.

Loud upsang the Raven
Swart, and slaughter-fell.   Strode along the war host ;
Blew on high the horn-bearers ;   heralds of the battle shouted ,
Stamped the earth the stallion ;   and the host assembled
Quickly to the quarrel !   *Elene*, ll. 52-56.

At last the battle is joined, and Cynewulf is all pagan in his description—

                    Sang the trumpets
Loud before the war hosts ;   loved the work the raven :
Dewy-plumed, the earn   looked upon the march ;
    .   .   .   .
Ranger [2] of the holt !   Rose the Terror of the battle ! [3]
There was rush of shields together,   crush of men together,
Hard hand-swinging there,   and of hosts down-dinging,
After that they first encountered   flying of the arrows !
On that fated folk,   full of hate the hosters grim
Sent the showers of arrows,   spears above the yellow shields ;
Forth they shot then [4]   snakes of battle
Through the surge of furious foes,   by the strength of fingers !
Strode the stark in spirit,   stroke on stroke [5] they pressed along ;
Broke into the wall of boards,   plunged the bill therein :
Thronged the bold in battle !   There the banner was uplifted ;
(Shone) the ensign 'fore the host ;   victory's song was sung.
Glittered there his [6] javelins,   and his golden helm
On the field of fight !   Till in death the heathen,
Joyless fell ! [7]   *Elene*, l. 109.

---

[1] *Waelrune ne mað* ; literally, "hid not the slaughter-rune." The slaughter-rune was the howling of the wolves.

[2] *Holtes gehleða*—" comrade, indweller, of the holt."

[3] This phrase is like the picture of Terror and Strife and Rout in the 4th book of the *Iliad*.

[4] I repeat *forð onsendan* in the translation.

[5] *Stundum* is "at times," hence "eagerly." I have combined both meanings in *stroke after stroke*.

[6] I have put *his* in, because I think Cynewulf meant the Emperor's spears and helm.

[7] Nor does Cynewulf leave them there. The Huns are driven in flight to their camp, but are beaten from it. "Some, half alive, guarded their lives in the rocky cliffs, some Drowning" (like an evil witch), "seized on in the river stream." I have wondered as I read the description whether the poet may not have remembered, as he wrote, the fight where Penda fell, and the flooded waters of the river that swept away the Mercians and their king. "Then," he continues, "was the host of the brave-hearted rejoiced ; they chased the stranger

One more example shows the birds of war gorged with carcases after the battle. Abraham in the *Genesis* vowing to the King of Sodom that he will not take seat or shilling from him, save that part which Aner and Mamre and Eshcol have fairly won in the brunt of ashen spears, tells him that he need no longer disquiet himself concerning the Northmen—

> For the birds of carrion,
> All along the mountain ledges,   sitting blood bedropt,
> Crammed and glutted are   with the corpse-flesh of the host.[1]

The picture of the vultures, thus sitting, dripping blood, on the ledges of the cliffs travels beyond the conventional description, of which we find another example in a war-song written when poetry had decayed, but which has attained a high reputation because it happens to be one of the few pieces of Anglo-Saxon poetry known to Englishmen—

> Behind them they left   to have lust of the dead
> Him of the sallow coat,   him the swart raven,
> Horny-nebbed fowl;   and the ash-feathered one,
> White-tailed, the earn,   to rejoice in the carrion,—
> And the greedy war-hawk,   and that grizzled beast,
> Wolf of the weald.   *Brunnanburh*, ll. 60-65.

from break of day till evening fell. The snakes of battle, the ashen darts, flew after them. Few of the host of the Huns came back to their home. There it was seen that the King Almighty gave victory to Constantine, magnificence and dominion through His rood-tree." These are lines that may well resemble those sung after the fight of Winwaed by the bard of Oswiu. Did Cynewulf, more than a century afterwards, enshrine, under the victory of Constantine the victory of Oswiu ; under the tale of the swollen Danube, the drowning of the host of Penda?

[1] Under beorhhleoðum   blódig sittað
    þeodherga wael   þicce gefylled.   *Genesis*, l. 2159.
"Under the precipices of the mountain" is, of course, on the ledges at the bases of the cliffs ; *wael* is often the battle-field strewn with corpses, the whole slaughter of the fight ; and "crammed and glutted" is to express the repetition of *þicce gefylled*.

CHAPTER IX

THE SETTLEMENT IN POETRY

WHEN, after the year 613, the Conquest was practically complete, the English had settled down over all the open country into an agricultural life, family by family, kinsfolk by kinsfolk, collected into hamlets round the heads of their houses. They hedged and ditched their villages, built their farm-steads, each with its garth and outhouses, laid out the arable land and the meadow outside the hedge, organised their village government, and established the places where the folk met for religious worship and for council. As to the Roman-British cities which they had sacked and burned, these remained in ruins, to be haunted by the owl and the fox. A long time passed by before this agricultural people cared to live in towns. They were like the Douglas; they liked better to hear the lark sing than the mouse squeak.

There was no further war with the Welsh, except upon the marches of the north, west and south, or when a Welsh king like Cadwallon united his forces with a king like Penda against another English king. The wars which were now waged by the English were those of English king with English king for overlordship. Even amidst these wars agriculture went steadily on, and the arts of peace were developed in home and village life. The English forged the ploughshare rather than the sword. They built weirs, and fished, and set up water-mills by the rivers.[1] Boat-building, brewing, leather-tanning, pottery, dyeing, weaving, the working of gold and silver, and embroidery, grew and soon began to flourish. The days of merchandise succeeded the days of piracy and plunder; life became gentler, nearer in spirit to the homes of England as we now conceive them. The main struggle was closed.

There are many records in Anglo-Saxon poetry which have to do with this daily life of the people—life inland, life on the seaboard, life on the sea, customs and manners, implements, hunting, tilling, and war. Of war and arms I have already written. This chapter and that which follows it are intended to bring forward such of these records as have a literary interest of their own, and will at the same time illustrate the English settlement as well as the English life on the sea. Most of them belong to a time when Christianity had been thoroughly established, but the manner of life and the matters mentioned in them were much the same in the sixth and seventh as in the eighth and ninth century. The fresh gentleness which Christianity added scarcely touches the things which are here discussed. Being thus independent of date, it is more convenient to bring these records together under such a title as—The settlement of the English, in poetry.

These records are found in short poems, such as the *Riddles* of Cynewulf, and in scattered lines

---

[1] *Mills.*—Corn was usually ground by the women in stone querns, but we find water-mills in a problematical charter of 838 (Ecgberht). "Et unam molinam in torrente qui dicitur holan beorges burna."—Earle's *Charters*, p. 288.

in the midst of longer poems. To turn aside and notice them in the midst of the general history of literature would confuse the main narration. To omit them, on the other hand, would be to leave out some striking pieces of early English poetry. But I hope my readers will understand that these chapters are not intended to be a treatise on the Settlement, or an attempt to discuss all that pertains to the manners and customs of the English. Such a treatise belongs to the historian and the antiquarian, and has been admirably done by others. My object is to set in this framework the descriptions of the early English life, of its habits and way of thinking which are to be found in the poetry of Northumbria, and I shall not travel beyond this aim. I say the poetry of Northumbria, because I believe it was in that part of England that poets chiefly wrote; and the scenery, the manners, the spirit of the people described in such records as the *Riddles*, belong rather to the Angles than to the Jutes or Saxons.

Inland, then, in the seventh century, the Angles were settled along the rivers, on the plains overlooked by moor and down, by the sea, and among the fens. Their hamlets rose on the site of the Roman villas, on either side of the Roman roads, wherever the Romans had drained the marshes, in every fertile vale or plain where the provincials had cultivated the land. The masses of forest country, the moors and mountains were left unoccupied by this agricultural people and were haunted by giant and elf and monster. But when the better sites were filled, the land, as the English pushed their advance by the water-paths, was cultivated up to the edge of the forest-waste, and day by day the axe and the plough wore their way into it and reclaimed it. The poorer and the more outcast set up their solitary huts on the banks and islands of the fens, and made a precarious living by fishing and trapping. They were, in fact, squatters; and it was only afterwards when pieces of the folk-land were allotted to the king's comrades and others that these men might come into employment on an estate.[1]

Of the kind of scenery among which these settlers in the fens lived we have a slight sketch in the sixty-first riddle of Cynewulf. It tells of a desert place near the shore, traversed by a channel up which the tide flowed, and where the reeds grew which were made into the *Reed-Flute*, which is the answer to the riddle. I translate the whole. The picture, at the end, of the lover talking in music to his sweetheart, music that none understood but she, is full of human feeling, but the point on which I dwell is the scenery. It is that of a settlement where only a few scattered huts stood amid the desolate marsh. Such, at first, were the homes of the Gyrwas among the fens. It is the Reed that speaks—

> On the sand I stayed,   by the sea-wall near,
> All beside the surge-inflowing!   Firm I sojourned there,
> Where I first was fastened.   Only few of men
> Watched among the waste   where I wonnèd on the earth.
> But the brown-backed billow,   at each break of day,
> With its water-arms enwrapt me!   Little weened I then,
> That I ere should speak,   in the after days,
> Mouthless o'er the mead-bench. . . .
> Only for us two,   utter boldly there,
> Message in my speech,   so that other men
> Would not be aware [2]   of my words to thee.

---

[1] Kemble quotes a passage from a translation of St. Augustine's *Soliloquia*, which illustrates the text: "But it pleaseth every man, when he hath built himself some cottage on his lord's laen, with his assistance, for a while to take up his rest thereon, and hunt and fowl and fish, and in divers ways provide for himself upon the laen, both by sea and land, until the time when, by his lord's compassion, he can earn a bocland and eternal inheritance."—Kemble, vol. i. p. 312.

[2] Literally, "Should not repeat our words."

There is another passing sketch of the same kind of scenery in the twenty-third riddle, when men come riding to the sea-channels on war-horses. The flood is too deep, and the press of the tide between the steep banks too strong for their passage. They mount a strange wain, proudly carrying their spears on their gray war-stallions. The answer to the riddle is obscure (Prehn thinks it to be *the Month*), but the scenery is clear. It is of a broad, deep-ditched channel, the stream of which in the fen-lands meets the rough incoming of the tide.[1] Near such a place on the shore where it fell to the sea Cynewulf would see the sight he describes in another riddle, "wood enrotten, heaps of weed, lying, flung together, vilely on the earth;" and more inland, in the hollows of the earth, "the black-faced fen that smelt so evilly of filth, where the fen-frogs swiftly leaped into the dark water," where the Elk-sedge, as the *Rune Song* sings, "waxed in the water, wounding and burning" every man who touched it. We are brought into another part of the country, probably the borders of Cumbria, where in riddle lxxi. the Ox speaks, and tells how weary he was among the rough paths of the border moorland. "I was silent," the Ox says (and it is in Cynewulf's manner to sympathise in this fashion with the suffering and joy of animals); "I never told any man when the point of the goad was bitter to me, but I was

> With the swart herdsman.   Farther I journeyed,
> Wended Welsh marches,   wandered the moors
> Bound 'neath a yoke-beam."

The swart herdsman is a Welsh slave. Swart is the usual epithet of the Welsh as against the fairer

---

[1] The stream shall in the waves, in the sea-floods mingle.—Gnomic Verses.

Englishman. In another riddle (xiii.) a "black-haired Welshwoman presses and shakes the ox-hide." Also in riddle liii. the "Welshwoman of dark tresses" carries to and fro the buckets from the well, and in another we hear of the "swart thegn with the dusky face" who works with the student in the monastery. Evidently in Northumbria there was a crowd of Welsh used as servants in the farmhouses and the convents of the eighth century.

A great part of the country was forest, that is, wood and wild land, heath and moor, and a supernatural terror brooded over it. In the moor-pools dwelt the water-elves, and in the wreathing mists and driving snow on the fells men saw mighty moor-gangers stalking, fiends of the lonely places, such as their fathers saw in the land from which they came. Grendelsmere was not a name given without reason. "The Thyrs"—that is the giant—"dwells alone in the fen," that is, in the morasses of the mountains. Dark elves haunted also the hills and moors. We hear of *beorg-aelfen, dun-aelfen, muntaelfen*. The howling of the wolves filled these waste hills at night, and many a wanderer, lost on them, was devoured. "Him shall the wolf eat," says the poem on the Fates of men, "the grizzly heath-tramper; his mother shall wail his death." In the caves of the moor-cliffs the outlaw lurked, as Grettir did in Iceland, and the British who fled from the sacking of the towns took refuge in them, and miserably starved and died. Sometimes in Christian times the hermit seeking a religious solitude exiled himself among these solitudes. The demons, who have taken the place of the giant and the elf, contend with him for the possession of these green hills which they grieve to leave, and reproach him bitterly for depriving them of their homes, as Caliban reproaches Prospero. In the same wild solitudes lived the Dragon of our forefathers' imagination, couched over his hoard of gold, terrible in the dreadful recesses of the cave—

<blockquote>Horridus horriferas speluncae cumbo latebras—</blockquote>

a phrase of Eusebius which is not apart from the lines in the Gnomic Verses: "The Dragon will dwell in the barrow on the hill, old, and proud of his treasures." Even down to Shakspere ran the tradition—

<blockquote>Like to a lonely dragon, that his fen
Makes fear'd, and talk'd of more than seen.
Coriolanus, Act iv. Sc. i.</blockquote>

The pathless woodland was, however, nearer to the life of the English than the moor. A great number of the settlements were on the outskirts of the wood forest. It was covered with beech[1] and oak, ash and maple, linden and birch. Alders clung to the banks of its streams and pools. A thick undergrowth of thorn and holly blocked it up and climbed the ledges of the cliffs within it, where the great birds of prey had their home. The English likened this vast covering of forests to curly locks upon the head and shoulders of Earth. In the Riddle on *Creation* Earth has no need of wimple or cape—

<blockquote>For upon me wonderfully   waxeth on my head,
So that on my shoulders   they may shimmer bright,
Curly locks full curiously.</blockquote>

This is paralleled by the Icelandic imagery, and we

---

[1] Earle shows very good reason for his belief, not only that the beech existed in these times, but also the fir, though Caesar had denied both these trees to Britain. Geologists would not agree with Caesar, who must have been misinformed.—*Land Charters*, p. 474.

ourselves may compare Keats' lovely phrase of the pines—

> Those dark clustered trees
> Fledge the wild-ridgèd mountains steep by steep.

The Yew, "an unsmooth tree, holding fast to the earth, a herd of the fire," grew in the wood and on the ridges of the hills. The oak woods fed men as well as swine, and the English saw in them the future ship—"the strength that would resist the sea." Wherever the birch grew, the English admired it. Even though it was fruitless it was beautiful. "High is its helm—'tis decked out with beauty—laden with leaves—in touch with the air."[1] But the chief feeling with regard to the woods was dread. These were desperate solitudes where the "bitter worm-wood stood pale gray" (Cynewulf, R. xli.), and the "hoar stones lay thick." The horror of their sunless and murky depths was a superstitious horror. Giants also dwelt in them, and black elves. These claimed the forestland as their own and hated the spread of agriculture, as Grendel hated the sound of the harp and the joy of men in Heorot. There too at times were seen the light elves, in contrast with the black, and of exceeding beauty. Caedmon, describing the loveliness of Sarah, says she was "sheen as an elf" —but, light or dark, they were the natural foes of men. There were water-elves, who were, I presume, impersonations of the disease-striking powers of the forest-fen and marsh.[2] Most diseases were thought

---

[1] These phrases are from the *Rune Song*.
[2] I daresay the "water-elf disease," a leechdom for which I quote, for it contains an old verse-charm, was a boil and blain plague such as the elves of stagnant waters smite on men. Grimm thinks it a burning fever, and Fever is thought to be an elf who rides the man with whip and spur. "If a man" (here is the charm) "is in the water-elf disease, then are the nails of his hand livid and his eyes tearful, and he will look downwards. Give him for this a leechdom"

to be demoniac possessions, and this meant to the Christianised Englishman dwarf or elf-begotten. Other elves rode in the air and shot deadly arrows; and the Scotch phrases, "elf-arrows," "elf-bolt," "elf-flint," are survivals of the English dread. We might perhaps imagine that elves lived in the trees, for an English gloss translates Dryads by *wudu-aelfenne*; and in order to divert their capricious anger whole groves were sometimes dedicated to the elves. We hear, moreover, of the *wudu-maer*, the "wood nymph," "a record of the time," thinks Tylor, "when Englishmen believed, as barbarians do still, that the Echo

---

(and many herbs are mentioned), "to be soaked in ale and holy water," and sing this charm over them thrice—

I have wreathed round the wounds,	Nor be wicked wounds,
The best of healing wreaths;	Nor dig deeply down!
That the bane-sores may	But he himself may hold
Neither burn nor burst,	In a way unto health!
Nor find their way further,	Let it ache thee no more
Nor turn foul and fallow,	Than ear in earth acheth!
Nor thump and throb on.	

Say also this many times—"May Earth bear on thee with all her might and main." These charms a man may sing over a wound. Cockayne, whose translation is here given, conjectures that the phrase "May Earth," etc., "is meant to quell the Elf." Diseases, and no doubt the Elf that caused them, were frequently—in folk-tales—buried in the ground. One of the leechdoms, translated from Sextus Placidus, holds in it a remnant of the Teutonic belief in dwarfs as the cause of sickness. "*To do away a Dwarf*" (*i.e.* convulsions or ague caused by a Dwarf's possession). "Give the man the dung of a white hound pounded to dust, and baked into a cake, *ere the hour of the dwarf's arrival*, whether by day or night it be. His access is terribly strong, and after that it departeth." I may add to this note on elves and dwarfs that Ariel may be compared with the sheen, the glittering elf of our forefathers. Ariel is the free wind of Heaven, whether in storm, or in play with the flowers or the sand of the seashore; and his music is the wind-music. A shoal of elves are his companions; and he has some power over the elements, over fire and air. Indeed his life is the life of the air. Such a life, rudely conceived, belonged to the Old English bright Elf. Ariel is not, as an Anglo-Saxon would have made him, a natural mischief-doer to man, but he does take pleasure in mischief and in plaguing men at Prospero's command; and though he is subdued by Prospero's magic to serve him, he is "not human," and has no sympathy with men. He is of the pure element alone. Even his desire for freedom is not human, but elemental—the desire to be wholly the unchartered air. The whole conception is more in harmony with Old English than with Celtic or French ideas of the elves. Indeed I may hazard the opinion that the fairies and elves of later England, of Shakspere and Milton and Shelley and many others, are not merely romantic but genuine English descendants of the sheen-bright elves of the Angles.

is the voice of an answering spirit"; and the word *mare* for Spirit appears in an Anglo-Saxon charm as the Mare which harms a man. I conjecture also that the wild, hairy wood-sprites which we find in German and Norse legends were also part of our forefathers' forest-superstition, and that it was strengthened by the apparition now and again of a Welshman who had fled into the woods to dwell. The lines in the *Andreas* may refer to the poet's memory of a time when the woodland was as yet haunted by unsubdued bands of Welshmen,—"All the markland (*i.e.* the forestland) was with death surrounded, the snares of the foe." We certainly find in *Solomon and Saturn*, in a passage which Kemble thinks is redolent of heathenism, that the fiends "haunt unclean trees," and, "changing themselves into a worm's likeness, sting the neat and destroy the cattle going about the fields, and hew down the horses with horns"—verses which are a remnant of the way in which a farmer, living on the outskirts of the wood, would think, when any misfortune befell his cattle.

A far fiercer inmate of the wild wood was the Wolf[1]-man, the outlaw—the companion of the wolf of the wood. In these terrible solitudes he met his fate by starvation, by the wolves, by losing himself, and by the "dark weather" in which English verse places the thief. There is a description of him in the Gnomic Verses—(Exeter MS.)

```
147. Friendless, doth a woeful man      take him wolves for comrades;
     Often does that comrade tear him,   very crafty is the beast!
     Of that gray one, dead-man's-grave, grisly fear shall be.
     . . . . Never truly doth the gray wolf  for his slaughtering weep,
     For the murdering of men ;          but the more of it he wishes.
```

---

[1] The gallows is called in a Riddle of Cynewulf's the wolf-head's tree ; and in the Middle Ages the outlaw was said to bear a wolf's head— *Caput lupinum.*

Sometimes the outlaw climbed a high tree to see his way or to escape the wolves, like the adventurous youth in the folk-tales; and feeble, fell headlong. Caught in the boughs, he hung between heaven and earth till he died. Here is such a one sketched in the *Fates of Men*—

> 21. In the holt shall many a one   from the high-topped tree
>   Featherless fall down;   yet in flight shall he
>   In the lift still hover,   till no longer he is held
>   Like a fruit upon the tree.   Then to the root-stock
>   Sinks he, slowly dying,   of his soul bereft;
>   Falleth on the field of earth!   On a faring is his spirit.

At times he was seized, as he roamed the wood, by the outlying shepherds of some township, judged, and hung on the gallows, which seems, by some at least of the English families, to have been kept up at a little distance from the village in the forest. There he became the proper prey of the raven. "One shall on the wide-stretched gallows ride," sings the *Fates of Men*, "till his bloody corse shall be all broken up. Then shall the dark-coated raven take his eyes, nor shall his hands guard him from that thievery. Wan on the tree, he waits his weird, o'ershrouded with a death-mist. Outlaw is his name." Now and then, even a woman, driven from her home by her enemies, was forced to take refuge in the forest; and we have a picture of a wild place where such a one takes refuge, in the *Wife's Complaint*—

> Men have garred me dwell   in a grove of woodland,
> Under an oak tree,   hidden in an earth-cave.
> Old is this earth-hall: I am all outwearied!
> Dark are all the dens,   high the duns above,
> Bitter my burg-hedges,   with the briars overwaxen,
> A delightless dwelling . . . .
> When in early dawn,   all alone I go
> Underneath the oak,   round my earthy lair,
> There I sit and weep   all the summer-lengthened day.   l. 27.

In the woods also were hosts of wild animals. Herds of wolves roamed through them, and so long did they last, and so formidable was their increase, that they were not killed out in England till the end of the fourteenth century. The bear, the Teutonic king of beasts, was perhaps an unfrequent inmate of the caves, and was met upon the moor. "The bear will be on the heath old and terrible," says an early English verse.[1] The wild cat was numerous and formidable in the woods. The wild boar "strong with the strength of his tusk," wandered through the undergrowth and grew fat upon the acorn and the mast. In Cynewulf's Riddle on *Creation* he paints the beast in a few lines (Rid. xli.)

<pre>
And I am everywhere   than a boar more daring,
When he stands at bay,   furiously enraging ;

 .   .   .   .   .   .

Than a well-stuffed Swine am I stronger, am I fatter ;
Than a boar that grunts him   in the beechen woods,
Black, and rooting up—   one that lived in joys.
</pre>

Great herds of wild cattle also roamed the forest, and their huge horns were used for drinking cups, for blowing notes in battle, and for warning of approaching war. The loud roar of these horns, warning of the approach of a foe, was heard from village to village of the kinsfolk on the skirts of the forest. Some of the dark Celtic shorthorns probably lingered in the woods after the expulsion of their masters. They were the only domestic cattle known to Roman Britain. The large cattle with red ears, white bodies,

---

[1] "The Bear," says Boyd Dawkins (*Early Man in Britain*, p. 493), "has left no traces of his existence of a later date than the Roman occupation." Unless the passage quoted above and the other one in the Gnomic Verses be remnants of verses made on the continent—the bear was still in England during the early English occupation. The Gnomic Verses, 175, after describing how ill it is to live alone, illustrates this by saying how much better it is to have a brother if "they should meet a boar, or when together a bear." "That," he adds, as if he had known of it, "that is a savage wild beast."

and great horns, now represented by the Chillingham breed, were brought over in their ships by the English, and soon got into the woods. It is also possible that in the wilder woods there lingered scattered descendants of the Urus of the prehistoric period. Then, across the streams which traversed the woodland, the beaver built its dam and was trapped for its fur—we find them trapped even as late as the twelfth century. Concerning the stag, another wild dweller of the woods, we have two elaborate Riddles from Cynewulf (lxxxv., lxxxviii.). They are really concerning the stag-horns which were used to adorn the gables of the halls, and for the insertion into them of stone and iron weapons. Cynewulf makes one of the horns speak, and bestows upon it, in his vivid manner, human pleasure and regret. "Full oft the holt covered us; the helm of forest trees shielded us against storms in the gloomy nights. Now I stand on wood at the end of a beam" (that is, at the end of the roof-ridge of a hall). "Brotherless, I keep my place at the end of the roof-board; my brother is not here. Where he is, who once beside me dwelt, I know not, in what region of the earth, in possession of what men?" The other Riddle (lxxxviii.) incidentally describes the forest life of the stag. "At whiles I climbed the steep hillsides, mounting to my dwelling. Then again I went into the deep dales to seek my food — my strengthening, strong in step. I dug through the stony pastures when they were hard with frost, then, as I shook myself and tossed my head, the rime, the gray frost, flew from my hair." Scott himself could scarcely say it better—

> But ere his fleet career he took
> The dewdrops from his flanks he shook.

It may be that when the English first came over, the reindeer was still to be found in the north of England; but this is mere conjecture, founded solely on the story, in the Orkneyinga Saga, which relates that the jarls of Orkney hunted the reindeer in the north of Caithness in the middle of the twelfth century. Once more, on this beast life in the literature of the woods, we are placed on the edges of the hills where the badger has his hole, and Cynewulf throws himself as fully into the life and passions of the animal for his home and children as he does into the eagerness of the hunter. The Badger speaks

> White of throat I am,   fallow gray my head;
> Fallow are my flanks,   and my feet are swift:
> Battle-weapons bear I!   Bristles on my back,
> Like a sow's, stand up: from my cheeks two ears
> O'er mine eyes prick up.   With my pointed toes
> Through the green grass step I!   Great is then the grief
> Fated to me if a fighter,[1]   fierce as death in battle,
> Findeth me concealed   where I keep the house,—
> With my bairns the building   . . .
> . . . .   When he comes, that deadly guest,
> (Digging) to my doors,   death is doomed to them.
> . . . .
> So full stoutly must I,   with my foreclaws working,
> Through the mountain steep   make myself a street.
> By a hidden way,   through the hole of the hillside
> Lead my precious ones, my children.   Then I shall no more
> Fear in anywise   war with the Death-whelp.
>
> If the greedy battle-seather   in the straitened way
> Seeks me on my gang-slot; then he shall not miss
> War-mote on the (mark)-path   where the fighters meet.
> When I rise at last,   through the roofing of the hills,
> And I furiously deal strokes   with my darts of war
> On the loathly foes   whom I long had fled!   Rid. xvi.

The darts of war are the badger's teeth, and Cynewulf paints him as a hero. It is in these short poems—

---

[1] The hunter whom he afterwards calls the Death-whelp. In this riddle I have left out several lines.

in this sympathetic treatment of the beasts of the wood, as afterwards of the birds; in this transference to them of human passions and of the interest awakened by their suffering and pleasure—that the English poetry of animals begins. Of course, the temper of mind shown towards them here is connected with the beast-epics and beast-stories, and with the humanising of the beasts in the folk-tales, and in such short poems as the *Cock and Fox* of Chaucer and the fables of Henryson. But the difference between the beast-poems of this class and those of Cynewulf will be felt at once. In the one the beasts talk and act like men and women, in the other the poet feels from above with their life itself,—pitying or loving them. His sympathy is even more than that of Shakspere in his outside description of the horse or the hare. The note is rather the note of Burns and Coleridge, Cowper and Wordsworth, and is strangely modern in feeling.

Such is the forest and its indwellers in English literature. Along its outskirts lay the hamlets of those settlers who had pushed their way into it from either side of the river, or who had from the plains arrived at its edge. By slow degrees the circling scoop they cut into it grew larger, till at last enough land was cleared for all the kinsfolk and their slaves. If we wish to picture to ourselves the aspect of such a settlement, let us imagine a wandering singer coming through the untilled woodland to one of the villages, to sing his songs, and to pass on to another. He would blow his horn and shout as he walked to show that his aims were honest and peaceful, otherwise he might be slain as an outlaw and lie unavenged. And he would have to do this at the distance it may be of some miles from the village.

for he might meet the slaves and the poor freemen of the village lords in the distant glades or on the uplands in the forest, tending the sheep, cows, oxen, and mares near the folds, lying out during the gloomy winter nights from Martinmas to Easter. Close by he might pass in some dark recess the tree which served the village for the gallows—the wolf's-head tree—and startle the ravens at their feast. Nearer still he would meet in the more open glades, under the shade of the great beeches and oaks, the watchers of the swine, the huge herds that devoured the acorn and the mast, and the lean dogs that were with the watchmen; woodmen also, gathering wood for the fires, or cutting down the young trees to repair with them house and plough and hedge. Yet closer still, on the very skirts of the wood, where he began to see the light of the open space beyond, he might chance upon the remains of the sacred grove once dedicated to the dwelling and the worship of a god; or if the settlement were still heathen, as it might have been in Mercia under Penda, catch through the trees a glimpse of the rude temple—a hall within a wooden fence—and of a householder going up to do the worship of his house; or if the settlement were in some still earlier time, hear the song of the woman who kept the temple. But if it were a large hamlet, after Christianity had come, our wandering poet might hear the chanting of the priest in the church; or if a small forest village, such as we have chosen here to describe, he would see no church, but the cross set up beside one of the trees of the forest, chosen of old for its great size and splendour, and still retaining, it might be, the carved figures of birds or beasts, or even runes such as would tell him that in his father's days the gods of heathendom were worshipped beneath its shade. After the Danish occupation, such a wandering singer would most frequently find these dedicated trees. We have traces of such names in the charters. Kemble translates the *Wonac* and the *Wonstoc*, as Woden's oak and Woden's post; *Tcowesþorn*, *Frige daeges treow*, as Tiw's thorn, Frea's tree. Such a tree would also be the limiting tree, the mark-tree, and would tell him that all beyond it was village land.

Or he might, near at hand, set up also to define the edge of the clearing, see a cluster of rude, hoary stones, remnants of the old indwellers, past which at night the thrall or the poor freeman passed in fear of the spirits that haunted them. There too, and certainly if there were no river near, he might drink and rest, where, under the eaves of the mark (*gemearcodan acfsan*—"the branches that dripped their rain on the skirts of the clearing"),[1] the native spring or well which served the township bubbled up, and which, lived in by a deity, was even yet worshipped. As he drank of its waters, he would see the whole clearing before him, the wide pasture lands, common to all, the undivided possession of fine grass, fed over by the horses, cows, goats, sheep, geese of the village; short, sweet sward, such as Cynewulf called the noble green floor of the earth; and beyond that, the arable land of the town, fenced into fields, and the fields divided into long furlong strips, subdivided into acres and half-acres—the allotments of the cultivators. The wide balks between were covered with grass or

---

[1] The *mark* was properly a sign, a line of division; hence a boundary line and also the belt of wild land round the cultivated area of a village: afterwards the march, or the width of neutral land between two communities.—Earle, *Land Charters*, p. 454.

brake, and scattered over the whole were the men at work, dyking and delving, ploughing and clodding. Beyond that, and nearer to the town, was the home pasture where the folds of the lambs and calves and foals were set, and this ran up to the mound and the wattled fence on its top—which enclosed the "town" itself, and from which the "tun" derived its name,—the place which was tyned or girded with a fence of rods. At the other side from where he stood, the river, instead of the forest (in the village we conceive), formed the boundary of the occupied land. In it the "salmon roved and darted in the pools," and higher up, in the thick of the wood, the beaver built his dam across this stream. Then, our wandering singer (whom I will now call Cynewulf, because all the illustrations of village life which I shall quote are from his riddles), listening, heard the rushing of the water past the wattled weirs built out from its sides for the fishing, and saw the bridge of wood that crossed it, and perhaps mills by its side that ground the corn of the settlement, and thinking of the millstone made it the subject of his fifth riddle.

It might be, when he arrived, that the leading men had determined to take into the plough-land a portion of the common-pasture, and to extend the pasture in proportion by clearing more of the bounding wood; and then Cynewulf would see exactly what he described in his riddle of the Plough, where he calls the plougher (whom we see as if he stood before us) "the grayhaired enemy of the wood" (Rid. xxii.)

Netherward my neb is set,   deep inclined I fare;
And along the ground I grub,   going as he guideth me
Who the hoary foe of holt is,   and the Head of me.
Forward bent he walks,   he, the warden at my tail;
Through the meadows pushes me,   moves me on and presses me,

> Sows upon my spoor.   I myself in haste am then.
>
> Green upon one side   is my ganging on;
> Swart upon the other   surely is my path.

It is a vivid picture of an old English farmer labouring on the skirts of the woodland, leaving behind him the furrow, black where the earth is upturned, green where the share has not yet cut the meadow. Then on the tilled land Cynewulf saw the gardeners wielding the rake, tending the vegetables which the little colony enjoyed, beans and onions and the rest, or dragging out the hurtful weeds from the pasture. "It is a thing"—riddles Cynewulf of the Rake—"that feedeth the cattle. Well does it plunder and bring home its plunder"—as if it were a forager. The riddle is dull, but it ends with the poet's pleasure in the meadows—"The Rake leaves firm the good plants" (Rid. xxxv.)

> Still to stand fast   in their stead in the field,
> Brightly to blicker,   to blow and to grow.

While he lingered, watching, he saw, perhaps on this very day, a common incident which he made into a riddle. Among the cattle on the pasture, the young bull was tethered. With his close sympathy with animals the poet paints him as rejoicing in his turbulent youth, and fed with the four fountains of his mother. Suddenly he saw the beast dash loose and rush from the pasture into the tilled land. Then Cynewulf let his imagination loose also, and pictured the bull breaking up the clods of earth left by the plough, as a monster might break up the hills.

> Of the kind that is weaponed   a creature I saw,
> Of the gladness of youth was he greedy;   for a gift unto him
> The Defender of Beings   let four welling fountains
> Glittering, spring.

> Then spoke a man, who said unto me—
> "If the beast should escape, it will break up the hills,
> If itself be up-broken, 'twill bind up the living."[1]   Rid. xxxix.

Then all the clearing was full of birds. He had heard as he came along the pleasant noise of the vast multitudes of the wood-birds which were then in England, and the cries of the water-fowl in the forest pools and streams; but now in the open he would see them. He saw the eagle, the raven, and the hawk, floating in the open air above the clearing. They had come from their homes in the "Nesses of the woods" —the steep cliffs in the forest, or the rocky banks of the stream—and Cynewulf would think of the last battle in which he had fought, and of these fierce followers of the slaughter. Among them, but not of them, he watched the falcon, the most noble of all birds to an Englishman, soaring to overtop the crane or the heron that built on the islands in the river.[2] And then, on the meadows near the stream where the fishers plied their craft from pool to pool, he saw the chief of the family of the township riding with the gray bird on his fist. And he remembered the riddle (lxxviii.) he had made, in which he had marked the aristocracy of the bird—

> I an Ætheling's arm-companion am;
> Am a wanderer with the warrior; well-belovèd of my lord,
> Of a king the comrade. Oft a queenly woman—
> One of golden locks- lays her hand on me,
> Daughter of an Ætheling, if she be right noble.
> On my breast I bear that which blossomed in the grove.
> On a stately battle-steed sometimes I may ride

---

[1] That is, its hide will form leather strips for binding captives.
[2] The falcon is never represented, like the eagle, as haunting the battlefield, as a devourer of the dead. In contrast to the eagle, who is the dark, the demoniac bird, it is brilliant and divine, the bird of heroes, nobles, and the happy gods.

With the host, at head of it!	Hardened is my tongue.
Often to a singing seer,	when he hath sung well,
Do I give a word-reward.[1]	Good is then my guise!
I myself am sallow-hued.	Say what I am called!

The English lord, like the Norman knight, had in his household those who tamed the falcon; and in the poem on the *Fates of Men* there is a description of this which has some poetical feeling. To call the falcon a Welsh, a stranger bird (*falco peregrinus*), makes one imagine that the best kinds were brought from the northern cliffs, where the *Menologium* says that the "hawk in the sea-cliff lived wild,"

One shall the wild bird	make tame on his wrist,
The proud-hearted hawk,	till this prey-thirsty swallow
Gentle become;	then girds he on varvels,[2]
And in fetters so feeds	the feather-proud fowl,
With little morsels	this Lift-speeder weakens,
That at last the Welsh bird,	in weeds and in deeds
To its food-giver	is friendly become.

But if the noble used the falcon, all the freemen, even of the poorer sort, made use of the ordinary hawk for hunting birds. The hawks were so numerous, long after the time of which we are speaking, that in a late Anglo-Saxon dialogue we hear that they were let loose in the spring, and young ones freshly caught and tamed in the autumn. During the winter these winged servants pulled down the numberless water-fowl that nested in the river banks. One of the noblest of these, no prey indeed for the hawk, but the food of the eagle, was the swan; and once on a time Cynewulf, who may now have seen it flying over the forest to some inland pool or fen, described it in one of the finest of his riddles—marking especially that old tradition of its song, not before its death, but when it

---

[1] Reward, *i.e.* for song. I suppose the falcon is made a present to the singer.
[2] Silver rings round the foot.

left the village to fly over the great world. Nor did it sing with its throat. Its *feathers* sounded melodiously as the wind went through them, a form of the myth which might easily arise among a people who knew of swan-maidens whose robe of feathers had a magical existence of its own and could be done off or on at pleasure. Cynewulf may have had, when he wrote this riddle (viii.), some form of the heathen myth in his head—

> Voiceless is my robe   when in villages I dwell,
> When I fare the fields,   or drive the flood along.
> Whiles, my glorious garments   and this lofty Lift
> Heave me high above   the housing place of heroes!
> When the Craft of clouds   carries me away
> Far the folk above,   then my fretted[1] feathers
> Loudly-rustling sound,   lulling hum along,
> Sing a sunbright song,   when stayed to earth no more,
> Over flood and field   I'm a spirit faring far.

That has the modern quality. Phrases, like "the strength of the clouds," "the spirit that fares over flood and field" (*flóde and foldan férende gaest*), the melodious rustling of the fretted feather-robe, the sense of a conscious life and personality in the bird and its pleasure in its own beauty, are all more like nineteenth century poetry in England than anything which follows Cynewulf for a thousand years. But it is not only the greater birds that are drawn with a vigorous pencil by the early English poets. Cynewulf, as he stood at the edge of the clearing, heard the Cuckoo shouting, and he sketched the bird in one of his riddles. But the sketch has no poetry in it; it is only when speaking of the Starling and the Nightingale that he feels the gentle influences of the singing

---

[1] *Fractwe* is originally carved, fretted things; hence an ornament—anything costly; here, then, "my rich garment of feathers." *Craft* is, of course, power.

fowl. He saw the Starlings,[1] as we suppose, upon this day, rising and falling in flocks over the hills and cliffs, above the stream where the trees stood thick, and over the roofs of the village, and the verse tells how happy he was in their joyousness, their glossy colour, and their song (Riddle lviii.)

>Here the Lift beareth wights that are little,
>O'er the hill-summits; and deep black are they,
>Swart, sallow-coated! Sweet is their song!
>Flocking they fare on, shrilly they sing,
>Roam the wood-nesses, and whiles, the burg-halls
>Of the children of men. Let them call their own name!

And now the evening falls, and as the traveller enters the town a flood of song bursts from the woods, and the English "earls" stop to listen, or sit silent in the doorways, while the "ancient evening singer," as Cynewulf calls the nightingale, pours forth his song. The bird himself speaks, proud of his power over men, and the whole thought of the riddle is the same as Wordsworth's—

>Over his own sweet voice the Stock-dove broods.

>Many varied voices voice I through my mouth.
>Cunning are the notes I sing, and incessantly I change them.
>Clear I cry and loud; with the chant within my head;
>Holding to my tones, hiding not their sweetness.
>I, the Evening-singer old, unto earls I bring
>Bliss within the burgs, when I burst along
>With a cadenced song. Silent in their dwellings
>They are sitting, bending forwards.[2] Say what is my name.
>   Riddle ix.

---

[1] Starling; at least so Prehn dissolves the Riddle. I am not sure he is right. The stare is not particularly a *little* bird, nor is its note sweet. Does it call its own name? The bird seems to answer best to the Martin; others say that *Gnats* is the solution, but this seems out of the question.

[2] I quote here the whole of Ealdhelm's riddle *De Luscinia* in order to confound those who say that Cynewulf in his *Riddles* is a mere imitator of the Latin. In the Latin there is not a trace of imagination, of creation. In the English both are clear. In the one a scholar is at play, in the other a poet is making.

>Vox mea diversis variatur pulcra figuris,
>Raucisonis nunquam modulabor carmina rostris,

Making this song our supposed Cynewulf passed through the gate in the hedge and entered the village. The main road was probably paved, and led straight to the hall of the kinsfolk set in the midst and surrounded by a piece of meadow-land. Many narrow paths, on either side of the main-way, went to the separate houses of the freemen, each with its farm buildings, each surrounded by its own hedge, and within the hedge, its orchard, or vineyard; perhaps fig-trees, or mulberry from which the morat was made; and many beehives. These stood under the apple-trees, or leaning against the out-houses of the farmer's home; and in the garth Cynewulf watched with pleasure, and afterwards described, the draw-well and the water-bucket rising into the air, then the black-haired Welshwoman carrying on her shoulders the yoke from which the water-buckets hung, "two hardy bondsmen," as he calls them in his fanciful fashion, "fast fettered together," which she bears under the roof of the hall (liii.). He saw the women spinning at the doors (xxvi.), or feeding the dogs and hens (li.). He saw the cobbler lay by his tools (xiii.), and the smith cease to labour at the sword (xxi. 6) and the war-shirt, and the jeweller at the ornamenting of the horn and the cup, the collar and the bracelet; he saw the carpenter leave the half-finished house, and the hedger lay aside his bill, and he made verses on them all. The paths were full of the men returning from work, the swine-

---

Spreta colere tamen, sed non sum spreta canendo.
Sic non cesso canens, fato terrente futuro :
Nam me bruma fugat, sed mox aestate redibo.

Almost every riddle, the subject of which Cynewulf took from Ealdhelm, Symphosius, or Eusebius, is as little really imitated as that. Even the Riddle *De Creatura*, the most closely followed of them all, is continually altered towards imaginative work.

herd and the woodward, and the hewers of wood from the forest, and the hunter with his spoil; the watchers of the cattle from the common pasture next to the wood, the plougher and sower and gardeners from the arable land, the tenders of the lambs and colts and calves from the meadows nearest to the town, the miller and the eel-fishers, the weir-wards and the fowlers from the river-side. The town was full. He moved with the crowd, and soon saw shining in the red light of evening the high, horned gables of the hall of the kin, standing in the midst of the central meadow, and near it the moot-mound, or the two or three huge trees left to mark the place of assembly when the town was planned. All the freemen we picture now, were there, perhaps in their armour, their long hair floating on their shoulders, hearing and judging causes, making their own laws, taking counsel for war or peace, commanding and forbidding. The chosen head of the kinsfolk, with his comrades and the chief freemen, stood on the top of the mound as the wandering singer came through the crowd. When the moot was over and the evening star shone (the star the English called the "star of the swains"), and the loud horn "called with its voice the warriors to the wine-feast," the hall was opened, the torches were lit, the smoke rose from the great fires in the midst. The men sat down to eat and drink, and as Cynewulf took his place, one of the women had finished a great web at the loom and brought it to the head of the kin into the hall, and Cynewulf, seeing this, made a riddle about the loom, which, to please his hearers, he likened to a noble warrior making and enduring a hard fight. Now his fancy paints the bed of the loom smitten by the restless and wrathful beam, "the fighting warrior"; now he sympathises with that part on which the web is stretched, and which is pierced by spears—perhaps, too, he thinks of the dartings of the shuttle,—then we see at last the "leavings of the battle," the finished web, borne into the hall. This is the riddle, but it is very difficult to translate, and many are its renderings—

> I was then within, where a thing I saw;
> 'Twas a wight that warred, wounded by a beam,
> By a wood that worked about: and of battle-wounds it took
> Gashes great and deep! Very grievous were
> To this wight the darts; and the wood with war-gear
> Fast was bound about. Of its feet
> One was fastened down, but the other active toiled,
> Leaping through the lift, then the land anear!
> And a tree was touching it, where it towered in light,
> All behung with leaves. Then I saw the leavings
> Of the Doing of the darts to the dwelling borne
> Where men met a-drinking; where my master is.
>   Riddle lvii.

When Cynewulf had sung this riddle (if I may continue my presentation of him as a wandering singer), he would be offered mead and ale, borne to him from the small table at the end of the hall where the drink was placed. Inspired with the draught, we may well fancy him making two other riddles to make gay the feast. The first, on the *mead*, begins with the bees bringing honey from the hills and dells, and then draws a vivid picture of the drunkard—

> Far and wide I'm found, and of worth to men;
> Carried from the copses, from the city's heights,
> From the dells and from the downs. Feathers daily bore me
> All along the air. Artfully they bore me on,
> Under Heaven's high roof. Then the heroes (took me)
> In a butt they bathed me! Now I am a binder,[1]
> And a scourger then: soon I'm an o'erthrower!

---

[1] In a riddle concerning the Ox hide, it is said, speaking of its use as a leathern jug—a "black jack." "I give the heroes drink from my bosom, I bind the swart Welshman and many a worthier man," *i.e.* the liquor binds them into slavery.

Oft an ancient churl   on the earth I fling,
And he finds at once   if he fight with me,
That with back (and shoulders)   he must seek the ground !
If from that unrede   he escape him not,
He's bestolen of his strength,   in his speech is strong,
Of his mood not master,   of his might bereft,
Powerless in feet and hands.   Find out what I'm called.
I who thus to earth   bind the hireling down,
Dullard by my dinting,   even in the day !

Riddle xxviii.

The solution of the next riddle (xxix.) is, according to Prehn, a wine vat. The better answer has occurred to many. It celebrates "Old John Barleycorn." The things said, even to the very order of their saying, are so curiously like those said in the old ballad, that I am induced to conjecture that this impersonation is extremely old, and that Cynewulf's riddle and the ballad are both forms of a much older original. I translate the riddle, and a vigorous thing it is ; and I give below [1] the version which Burns made of the ballad—

---

[1] JOHN BARLEYCORN

There were three kings into the east,
  Three kings both great and high,
And they hae swore a solemn oath
  John Barleycorn should die.

They took a plough and plough'd him down,
  Put clods upon his head,
And they hae swore a solemn oath
  John Barleycorn was dead.

But the cheerfu' Spring came kindly on
  And show'rs began to fall ;
John Barleycorn got up again,
  And sore surpris'd them all.

The sultry suns of Summer came,
  And he grew thick and strong,
His head weel arm'd wi' pointed spears,
  That no one should him wrong.

The sober Autumn enter'd mild,
  When he grew wan and pale ;
His bending joints and drooping head
  Show'd he began to fail.

His colour sicken'd more and more,
  He faded into age ;

And then his enemies began
  To show their deadly rage.

They've ta'en a weapon, long and sharp,
  And cut him by the knee ;
Then tied him fast upon a cart,
  Like a rogue for forgerie.

They laid him down upon his back,
  And cudgell'd him full sore ;
They hung him up before the storm,
  And turn'd him o'er and o'er.

They filled up a darksome pit
  With water to the brim,
They heaved in John Barleycorn,
  There let him sink or swim.

They laid him out upon the floor,
  To werk him farther woe,
And still, as signs of life appear'd,
  They toss'd him to and fro.

They wasted, o'er a scorching flame,
  The marrow of his bones ;
But a miller us'd him worst of all,
  For he crush'd him between two stones.

> There's a portion of the earth,   prankt most gloriously
> With the very hardest   and the very sharpest
> And the very grimmest   of the goods of men!
> Cut and rubbed about,   rolled around and dried,
> Bound and twisted,   bleached and softened,
> High-adorned, bedecked,   dragged along from far
> To the doors of men!   Dear delight is in it
> For each living creature.   It increases jollity [1]
> In the aged who, living long,   have of old enjoyed
> Each the bliss he wished for—   and abuse it not.
> Then it, after dying,   to declaim begins,
> Things to tell in many ways!   Mickle food for thinking
> To a wise man is,   what this wight may be! [2]
>
>   Riddle xxix.

Many things took place as the feast wore on. We know its general customs from *Beowulf*. But we hear other matters from the *Riddles*. Sometimes a

---

> And they hae ta'en his very heart's blood,   "Twill make a man forget his woe;
>   "Twill heighten all his joy;
> And drank it round and round;   'Twill make the widow's heart to sing,
> And still the more and more they drank,   Tho' the tear were in her eye.
>   Their joy did more abound.
>
>   Then let us toast John Barleycorn,
> John Barleycorn was a hero bold,   Each man a glass in hand;
>   Of noble enterprise,   And may his great posterity
> For if you do but taste his blood,   Ne'er fail in old Scotland!
>   'Twill make your courage rise.

[1] *Clenged* is here taken as a substantive.

[2] I have already mentioned the drinking habits of our early ancestors, and mocked at the accusation of a special barbarism levelled against them on this account—as if they were not in the eighth century the most cultivated people in Europe. In all Anglo-Saxon poetry, in these *Riddles* written by a wandering Bohemian, there is a tone of contempt for the drunkard. He is a captive, a degraded freeman; and the delight and inspiration which Cynewulf places in "jolly good ale and old" only make his reproof of excess seem the stronger. It is the same in other Anglo-Saxon poetry. The most vigorous description of drunkenness is in the *Judith*. But it is the Pagan Holofernes and his thegns who drink themselves into the brutality which the poet scorns. There is another passage in the *Fates of Men* which sketches the view the ordinary Englishman (for I do not believe a monk wrote it), took of heavy drinking—

> From another on the mead-bench   shall the edge of sword
> Take his life away!   With the ale made wrathful,
> With the wine besotten,   far too hasty was his word!
> Another at the beer,   through the beer-out-pourer's hand,
> Is a man mead-mad.   Then he may not mete
> Any measure to his mouth,   by his mind's (discreetness).
> But his life shall lose   in a loathly fashion;
> From delight disparted,   suffer dreadful ill!
> And the men in talking   of the mead-enmaddened's drinking
> With their mouth shall say—   "Murderer of himself."
>
>   *Fates of Men*, ll. 48-57.

messenger came in, bringing tidings. Sometimes the lord called for his ancient sword and displayed its hilt and sheath and told of its great deeds. Sometimes he drew an old-time cup out of his treasures. "Often shall I," cries such a cup, "serve with joy in the joyous hall, when, glittering with gold, I am borne into the house where heroes are drinking." Sometimes bitter quarrels rose, men mocked and stabbed as in the Icelandic tales. Sometimes the boaster broke out into tales of his own, while the women poured out the ale. When the eating was over, the warriors, sitting blithely in the beer-hall, played at games or at throwing the dice, and so excited did they become that they forgot all the pain and sorrow of life. "They twain," say the *Gnomic Verses*, "shall sit o'er the dice while their misery glideth away from them. They forget their sad fate. They have their pleasure on the board." Often enough, when the drinking was hard, as it was likely to be after a battle, but not in the peaceful assembly of everyday life, the evening ended tumultuously. There is a vigorous description of such a feast in a poem (*Bî manna môde*, ll. 13-20), where a contest arises among the warriors as to who stood firmest in the battle. "Many a one," it says, "is full of talking and praises; prideful war-smiths who in their wine-burgs sit at the feast and tell sooth stories, to and fro barter their words, and set their mind to know who of the warriors, on the spear-stead, holds out the best. Then the wine whets the breast-thoughts of fighters, and midst of the throng wild shouting arises, a varied tumultuous outcry." But chiefly it was playing and song which lightened the evening. Cynewulf, who we suppose was in our imagined hall this night, may have heard other instruments than the harp, for he has riddles on the reedflute which the lover plays for his mistress, and on the bagpipe and the psaltery. The bagpipe sits at the banquet, waiting till it can make known its skill. "Pleasant speech is in its foot and a sweet voice. Ornaments enrich its neck, and it is proud of its rings"; but the psaltery "sings through its side, and is haughty, and of a bright countenance, rejoicing in the use of men."

At last the feast is over, the men go to their homes, the "helm of night" covers the village, but the house is not yet still. Cynewulf hears the men and maid-servants chattering, and household work being done, before the fires, and sketches the master of the home seeking his treasure-press at midnight, either to lay by some new booty, or to look at the goods which he had of old won in battle. Then there was silence; but as the poet lay down to rest a new riddle came into his head. He had seen, before he had gone into the hall, the new moon with the old moon in her arms in the "broad Burg" of Heaven, above the clearing. And his imagination likened the moon to a young warrior returning with his spoil between his horns, who would build his hall in the very citadel of Heaven. But another and a greater warrior—the sun—was at hand, who, rising over the horizon's wall, would take the booty of the moon and drive him homewards with great wrath. Then the sun also would hasten westwards, and the night would come again with mist like dust and falling dew. So he made the 30th riddle.

It is characteristic of Cynewulf, who probably derived his first idea of this riddle from that of Eusebius on the same subject, that he departs altogether from the way Eusebius treats the subject. In Eusebius, sun and moon are friendly. Here they are enemies,—their strife is renewed each night and day. Defeat and victory and pursuit are incessantly interchanged. The little poem is a true piece of imaginative and mythical Nature-poetry, and the end is as terse and rapid as it would be in the hands of Tennyson—

> I have seen a wight   wonderfully shapen,
> Bearing up a booty,   in between his horns,
> A Lift-Vessel flashing light,   and with loveliness [1] bedecked;
> Bearing home this booty,   (brought) from his war-marching!
> He would in the burg   build himself a bower,
> Set it skilfully,   if it so might be.—
> Then there came a wondrous wight   o'er the world-wall's roof—
> Known to all he is   of the earth's indwellers—
> Snatched away his war-spoil,   and his will against,
> Homeward drove the wandering wretch!   Thence he westward went,
> With a vengeance faring,   hastened further on!
>   Dust arose to Heaven,   dew fell on the earth,
>   Onward went the night.   And not one of men
>   Of the wandering of that wight   ever wotted more.

Early in the morning he rose and went on his way. Now as he passed through the town it chanced that in one of the garths the household were gathered together and were troubled, for the hive was empty; the bees had swarmed, and they knew not where they were. Then Cynewulf, who knew the old songs and charms, leant over the hedge and said to them, "I will do this thing for you, take some earth and, throwing it with your right hand under your right foot, say—

> "So I take it under foot—   I would find (the swarm)!—
>   (*he sees the swarm*)
> Lo! this earth be strong   'gainst all wights whatever,
> And against all grudging,   and against forgetfulness,
> And against the mickle tongue   of the (mighty) man." [2]

---

[1] Skilfully, *listum*; therefore "beautifully."

[2] All these *Charms* which I treat of now, and in the *Note* at the end of this volume, will be found in Cockayne's *Leechdoms*, and in Wülker's edition of the Anglo-Saxon poetry, under the title of *Zaubersprüche*. They are full of Folk-lore

And then the folk saw the place where the bees hung, and Cynewulf cried to them, "And now throw gravel over the bees as they swarm, and say this verse of the old time which our kin sang of old"—

> Sit ye, Victory-women,   sink ye to the earth!
> Never to the wood   fly ye wildly more!
> May ye be as mindful   of my good to me
> As is every man   of his meat and home.[1]

And the women smiled, and when they had sung the old lay, the bees swarmed. Then Cynewulf laughed with pleasure, and, as the folk thanked him, said, "Take veneria[2] and hang it to the hive, then the bees will not fly away, and if you wish to keep them safely, lay a plant of madder on the hive, so will no man be able to lure away the bees, nor can they be stolen the while the plant is on the hive."

So he walked on, thinking of the old days and the many strange charms which still prevailed in the land, though the Christian priests were hard on them; and now he had passed through the gate and saw a farmer who was giving a herd of cattle into the charge of one of his servants; and he was reciting a kind of spell to prevent them from being stolen from the forest pastures.

---

interest, but they are also well worthy of a place in English literature. They have a childlike ancientry which is delightful. They smell of the earth and the woodland and the village life. Now and then the natural imagination works finely in them, without consciousness of itself, as in the charm against the shooting elves. No history of poetry can afford to neglect them any more than it can neglect the Ballad of which things of this kind were one of the origins.

[1] This is plainly a heathen charm. When it says, "Let this Earth be strong against all wights," it goes back to that most ancient time when Mother Earth was perhaps the sole goddess of Angle-worship—the strong and faithful protector of men, and of all their agricultural work. The "Sigewif," the Victory-women, Grimm mixed up in some way or other with the Valkyrie; but the phrase belongs, I think, to a world which did not know the Valkyrie, but did put a living spirit into beasts, birds, and into those insects which were bound up, like bees, with the daily life of men. "Sigewif" here seems to me to be a term of flattering endearment, such as we find in our nursery song, "Lady Bird, Lady Bird, fly away home."

[2] These are fragments of old Charms.

Cynewulf stayed to listen, and this is what he heard. Part of it, chiefly the part in verse, was very old, but it had been Christianised.

"Neither stolen nor hidden be aught of what I own, any more than Herod might (steal or hide) our Lord. I thought on Saint Helena, and I thought on Christ hung on the rood; so I think to find these beeves again, not to have them wandering far, and to know (their fold), not to have them mischieved, or led astray, but tenderly cared for."[1] Then the farmer began to sing a spell, putting in the name of God into the old verse—

<pre>
Garmund,   of God the thegn,
Find the cattle   and fare out the cattle,
And have the cattle   and hold the cattle,
And bring back   the beeves to their home.
</pre>

The rest has no value. It is a spell against a reaver of cattle, and ends—"Let him be all wary as wood is wary of the fire, as the thigh of bramble, or of thistle, who may think him to mislead or to drive away this cattle."

When he had heard this, Cynewulf went onwards, and now he had gotten among the acres, where, near at hand, he saw a little knot of men upon a piece of plough-land of a hungry look; and drawing near he heard them reciting the *spell for bewitched land*, to which he had listened when he was a boy, and which he was told had come with the Angle out of their fatherland beyond the sea. But now it was mingled up with Christian words and rites, and with Christian names, and it sounded very old and curious; and so old it was that the meaning of *Erce*, one of the heathen names, was even then unknown. They had

---

[1] This is not literal; but it is, I think, the meaning.

just begun as he came up. The night before, ere the day-dawning, they had taken four turfs in four parts of the acre,[1] and dropped thrice into their place oil and honey and barm, and milk from each kind of cattle that fed on the land, and a piece of each kind of tree, except the hard trees (oak and beech), and a piece of every well-known wort except buck-bean; and scattered holy water on them, and had said these words, "Wax and grow, and fill this earth"; and they had taken the turfs then to church and let a mass priest sing four masses over them and turned the green side to the altar; and afterwards, before the down-going of the sun, had taken the turfs to where they were before. And they wrote on each end of four crosses, "Matthew and Mark, Luke and John," and laid the cross of Christ on the lower part of the pit and said, "Cross! Matthew," etc. etc. Then they took the turfs and set them down therein and said nine times as before "Wax and increase, and fill this earth," and the Paternoster as often, and then turned eastward, and louted down nine times humbly and said—

> To the East I stand,   for the gifts-of-use I bid me;
> So I pray the mighty One,   so I pray the mickle Lord,
> So I pray the Holy One,   Ward of Heaven's Kingdom.
> Earth I also pray   and the Heaven above
> And the sacred   sooth Maria,
> And the might of Heaven   and its high-built Hall,
> That I may this magic spell,   by the favour of the Lord,
> Open from my teeth   through a thought firm-grasped;
> Waken up the swelling crops,   for our worldly need;
> Fill the fielded earth   by my fast belief.

---

[1] It is plain that we have here a heathen ceremony with Christian rites and names added to it. The turfs were taken to the shrine of the god, and the green side turned to his symbol, and runes written on bast, and a song, of which we have a portion in the verse, sung to Earth and Heaven. These are the old sacrificial rites of the ploughing, and there are many similar observances, some of which will be found in the chapter on Charms in Grimm's *Teutonic Mythology*.

> *Prank the turfed plain with fairness,* as the Prophet quoth—
> That he had on earth his honour whoso had praiseworthily,
> By the grace of God, given out his alms.[1]

And now they were met to fulfil the charm. And the owner of the land stood and turned himself round three sun-courses, and stretched himself out longways and said many litanies and Christian hymns and prayers; but the last song he sang was to Mother Earth, for himself and for all who were under him. Then he brought unknown seed which he had got from beggar-men, and for which he had given them twice as much as he had taken, and gathered all his plough-tackle together. And he bored a hole in the plough-beam and put into it (stor-) styrax, and fennel, and soap, and salt which had been hallowed, but the seed he set upon the body of the plough. Then Cynewulf listened to the ancient lay—

> Erce, Erce, Erce—Mother of Earth! [or, O Earth, our Mother]
> May the All-Wielder, Ever-Lord grant thee
> Acres a-waxing, upwards a-growing,
> Pregnant (with corn) and plenteous in strength;
> Hosts of (grain) shafts[2] and of glittering plants!
> Of broad barley the blossoms,
> And of white wheat ears waxing,
> Of the whole earth the harvest!
> Let be guarded the grain against all the ills
> That are sown o'er the land by the sorcery-men,
> Nor let cunning woman change it nor a crafty man.[3]

---

[1] This is the least heathen of all the poetic fragments in this charm; but I have italicised, in the translation, the verses which seem to have formed part of the ancient Earth and Heaven worship.

[2] A very long note on this will be found in Wülker.

[3] These last three lines have been shortened. *Cunning woman* might be better translated "talkative woman," and *crafty* is of course "powerful." This is nearly altogether a very old heathen invocation, used, I daresay, from century to century, and from far prehistoric times, by all the Teutonic farmers. Who *Erce* is remains obscure. But the *Mother of Earth* seems to be here meant, and she is a person who greatly kindles our curiosity. To touch her is like touching empty space, so far away is she. At any rate some godhead or other seems here set forth under her proper name. In the Northern Cosmogony, Night is the mother of Earth. But Erce cannot be Night. She is

And when he had thus sung he pushed on the plough and cut the first furrow; and then he stayed himself and, looking on the upturned earth, he sang again a very ancient verse—

> Hale be thou, Earth,   Mother of men!
> In the lap of the god   be thou a-growing!
> Be filled with fodder   for fare-need of men!

Then the farmer took of each kind of meal and let knead a broad loaf with milk, and laid it under the first furrow and sang again—

> Acre, full fed,   bring forth fodder for men!
> Blossoming brightly,   blessed become!
> And the God who wrought the ground   grant us gift of growing,
> That the corn, all the corn,   may come into our need.

And when he had so sung, the work was done, and he drove the plough on through his acre. But Cynewulf (if Erce be a proper name) bound up in this song with agriculture. Grimm suggests *Eorce*, connected with the Old High German *erchan* = "simplex." He also makes a bold guess that she may be the same as a divine dame in Low Saxon districts called Herke or Harke, who dispenses earthly goods in abundance, and acts in the same way as Berhta and Holda—an earth-goddess then, the Lady of the plougher and sower and reaper. In the Mark she is called frau Harke. Montanus draws attention to the appearance of this Charm in a convent at Corvei, in which this line begins " Eostar, Eostar, eordhan modor." Nothing seems to follow from this clerical error. The name remains mysterious, and I am glad of it. As to the rest of the song, it breathes the pleasure and worship of ancient tillers of the soil in the labours of the earth and in the goods the Mother gave. It has grown, it seems, out of the breast of Earth herself. Nor are the next four lines less remarkable and less heathen. Earth is here the mother of men. The surface of Earth is the lap of the goddess; in her womb let all growth be plentiful. Food is in her for the needs of men. "Hale be thou, Earth!" I daresay this hymn was sung, ten thousand years ago, by the early Aryans on the Baltic coasts. The next four lines—Acre full-fed—are partly heathen, partly Christian.

On the whole, we are placed in these songs in that early time, after settled agriculture had begun, when the "Cornfield," as Professor Rhys says, "is the chosen battlefield where the powers favourable to man make war on those other powers that would blast the fruits of his labour." And if we wish to bind up this ancient English Earth Religion with Northern names of gods, we may think of Frigg, Woden's wife, who is the Earth goddess, and of Thor her son, the god of husbandry, "the farmer's friend," whose bolt cleaves the storm-clouds that threaten the grain and disperses the blighting mists, who marries Sif, the yellow-haired goddess of the cornfield. Beyond this there is a literary quality in this old song, and in the Stitch-Charm that follows it, which, from its delightful naturalness, from its close clinging to the subject, and from its contrast to the conventional Christian poetry, pleases the ear and the imagination.

walked on, nor was he fated to leave the place till he had heard something more heathen still. For now a little way in the wood he came to a hill whence the trees had been cleared, and he saw a man crouching doubled up upon the ground in sudden pain of a stitch caused by witchcraft; and another, who stood by, held a shining linden shield over him as if to guard him from weapons shot at him, and was anointing him with a salve made of fever-few and the red-nettle, which had grown through a fence,[1] and waybroad (*plantago*), which it was his habit, for he was a witch-doctor, to keep by him, having first boiled it in butter, that he might heal those whom the fierce elves shot with their spears. So Cynewulf drew near to listen, hiding in the fringe of the wood, and he heard the man singing this pagan song, which told of fierce witch-wives riding over the hill and flinging spears—[2]

Loud were they, lo, loud,   as over the land they rode;
Fierce of heart were they,   as over the hill they rode.
Shield thee now thyself;   from this spite thou mayst escape thee!
   Out little spear   if herein thou be![3]
Underneath the linden stood he,   underneath the shining shield,
While the mighty women   mustered up their strength;
And the spears they sent   screaming through the air!
Back again to them   will I send another

---

[1] Through a sieve. The Romans had this custom. They laid a sieve in the road, and used the stalks of grass that grew through it for medical purposes.— Grimm, Chapter on Herbs.

[2] Elf-shooting, etc., is a common superstition in England. Indeed, it ranges from Shetland to Cornwall. Here is a Scandinavian instance: "That same autumn Hermund gathered a party and went on his way to Borg, intending to burn down the house with Egil in it. Now as they came out under Valfell, they heard the chime of a bowstring up in the fell, and at the moment Hermund felt ill, and a sharp pain under his arms, and the sickness gained on him."

[3] "In dock—out nettle.—Nettle in, dock out."—*Troilus and Cressida*.
In Sussex a poor woman is cured of a scald on a Sunday evening by an old wife who bows her head over the wound, crosses two of her fingers over it and breathes upon it, repeating these words—

    There came two angels from the north,
    One was Fire and one was Frost,
    Out Fire, in Frost,
    In the name of Father, Son, and Holy Ghost.
      Folk-Lore: Northern Counties (Henderson), p. 171.

Arrow forth a-flying	from the front against them ;
Out little spear	if herein thou be !
Sat the smith thereat,	smote a little seax out ;

. . . . .

Out little spear	if herein thou be !
Six the smiths that sat there—	making slaughter-spears :
Out little spear,	in be not, spear !
If herein there hide	flake of iron hard,
Of a witch the work,	it shall melt away.
Wert thou shot into the skin,	or shot into the flesh,
Wert thou shot into the blood,	(or shot into the bone),
Wert thou shot into the limb—	never more thy life be teased !
If it were the shot of Esa,	or it were of elves the shot,
Or it were of hags the shot ;	help I bring to thee.
This to boot for Esa-shot,	this to boot for elfin shot,
This to boot for shot of hags !	Help I bring to thee.
Flee, witch, to the wild hilltop	. . . . -
But thou—be thou hale,	and help thee the Lord ! [1]

Then the strange chant ended, the witch-doctor bid the man take the seax and dip it into water; but Cynewulf had heard enough, and we bid him farewell as he entered the forest paths.

---

[1] I have taken Sweet's reading.

CHAPTER X

THE SEA

THE English, at least in the north of England, were close observers not only of the natural aspect of the Earth, but also of the Sky and the Sea; and the proof of this lies in the number of words they invented to express the different appearances of these two great creatures. The changes of the Dawn from the first gray tinge of the heaven to the upward leap of the Sun; the changes of the Evening from the light left by the setting sun to the last glimmer of it before dead night, have each their own specialised words. The fiercer phases of natural phenomena were also watched and described with minuteness by the poets. Cynewulf dedicates eighty lines to the story, hour by hour, of the birth, the growth, and dying of the Tempest. But no natural object engaged them so much as the Sea, and for no object have they so many names. Their treatment of it in verse deserves a chapter in a history of English poetry. Such a chapter will bring together a number of descriptive passages, so varied in form and in imaginative sentiment that we shall be able to estimate the range of the natural description of the Angles, its limits and its excellence. No critical analysis of mine could make this estimate or give this insight into the way in which the English saw nature, half as well as the series of examples which I shall translate, and which describe the doings of the great Being who of all the living things of the world awakened in them the most profound emotion.

A shoal of simple terms express in *Beowulf* the earliest sea-thoughts of the English. But, still uncontent, the singers compounded these simple terms with other words, in order more fully to image forth the manifold impressions they had received of the doing of the great waters. Double, sometimes treble words were used to picture, if possible, the waves in storm and the ships that rushed through them. Many more than those in *Beowulf* were invented by Cynewulf, whose imagination wrought like the surges he described; but at present our task is confined to the sea and the seamen as they appear in *Beowulf*.

The simplest term is *Sae*, our sea, and it has the general meaning which we attach to the word. To this they added *Waeter*, the great wet world beyond the land, which, when the adjectives *deep* and *wide* were prefixed to it, meant, it seems, the ocean. Then came *Flod*, our flood. This was the outpoured sea which flowed into and filled the hollows of the earth. The same word expressed anything that flowed—the tide, a river, the rush of an inundation. Correlative with this was *Stream*, which, when used of the Sea, probably meant the ocean river that went round the world, then the general flowing of the deep, and especially the apparent movement of the whole body of the sea in waves to the coast. Again, the term *Lagu* belonged to the Sea, as to all waters. The Sea was the great Pool, and considered as lying in a hollow, this word for it seems to express in poetry the sea at peace. There are certainly no words compounded with it in Anglo-Saxon poetry which suggest water in great disturbance.[1] *Mere*, another ancient term for the Sea, is of frequent occurrence, and means the desert waste of waters. Another word is *Holm*. As men stood on the beach or on the ship's prow they saw the wide waters raised up, as it were, around them, or lifted into a mound on the horizon, and this common aspect of the Sea they called *Holm*. It was the up-mounding of the Ocean; and Hunferth exactly expresses this when he says that the *Holm* bore Breca up on the strand. Hence it came to mean the high waves, each wave like a rounded height, and then the whole high going of the waves, and further the deep ocean itself, which was conceived as heaved upwards, like the coil of a great serpent, from the abyss below. This abysmal bottom of the deep was *Grund*, a word which, in connection with certain other words, is mixed up with a sense of dread, with that which was unfathomably unknown —the great cavernous bed of ocean, the hiding-place of primæval and deadly creatures, born of the slime, the grounded-dust that covered the foundation rock of the world. One giant line in *Lycidas* gives me this ancient impression—

> Visitest the bottom of the monstrous world.

Another name for the Sea, *heaðu*, may also embody the conception of the high mass of water, the deep

---

[1] *Lagu-flod* and *lagu-stream* are, however, two components, and these may be instances of that use of *lagu* for flowing water on which Earle dwells in his notes to the Anglo-Saxon charters, though I do not understand how *lagu* can ever come to mean a flowing thing. Compounded with *flod* and *stream*, it means, I think, the flowing sea in its peace.

ocean, and then pass on to express the high tossing of the waves.

Sund used for the Sea is representative of another thought. We say a Sound of the Sea, but the earlier English who lived on the inlets and among the islands knew only the short stretches of sea which a man could swim across. Afterwards, when they knew the greater water, they transferred the name of the part to the whole. Perhaps they thought of it as the great swimming-place for their ships. *Brim* is another word, and if I may judge from *Brimi*, the surf-hall of the giants in Volospa, it is the Sea when it breaks in raging surf upon the margin of the shore, or the Sea breaking in foam on the deep. The Sanskrit word *bhram* ("to agitate") is compared with it; and in Dorsetshire I have found that the surf-borne sea sand is called Brim-sand. Generally then it means, I think, the rough sea furiously tumbling into foam, either far out on ocean or on the beach.

Garsecg, a frequent term in *Beowulf* and afterwards, is a very ancient name of the Ocean; the great encompassing sea that embraces the world. "Our forefathers," said Ælfred, translating and adding to Orosius, "divided into three parts all the globe of this mid-earth which the Ocean that we call Garsecg surrounds." Sweet says that it means the Rager[1] and this—the stormy-tempered giant of the Ocean—is close to the Northern thought. There are two words used for the sea in *Beowulf* which seem to belong to traditional conceptions of the Ocean as the dwelling-place of a living Being. These are *Eagor*,

---

[1] *Garsecg*, by transposition of *r* and *s* is the same as *gasric*, and *gas=gais*. Old Norse, *geisa*, to chafe, to rage (*Eng. Stud.* vol. ii. 315). This is indeed far better than deriving it from *gar*, a spear, and *secg*, a man, and connecting it with Poseidon and his trident!

compounded with *Stream*, and *Geofon*. Ægir, who in Norse mythology has by Ran, the net-wielding goddess who weaves destruction for sailors, nine daughters who are the waves, and whose song is the roaring of the surf, is, according to Grimm, an older god of the giant-kin, not one of the Æsir; and his name signifies the Terrible One. The word means, in Scandinavian poetry, the Sea itself; and the Anglo-Saxon term *Eagor* may be related to *ege* (awe), and *egesa* (horror). *Eagor-stream* might then possibly be translated the stream of Eagor, the awful terror-striking stormy sea in which the terrible giant dwelt, and through which he acted.[1]

Fifel is perhaps, Grimm thinks, another and obsolete name of Eagor. But *Fifel* seems to mean nothing more than a giant or monster, and it would be to push personification too far to make *Fifel* a personage because an Anglo-Saxon called the sea *fifel-stream* or *fifel-waeg*. There is more to be said of *Geofon*. The word does seem to gather personality round it in Anglo-Saxon poetry. It is used independently for the sea in *Beowulf*: " Geofon boiled with waves " (l. 515); as afterwards in the *Exodus* (l. 447): " Geofon threatened death." It may have some relation to the fierce sea of winter, and Geofon be the same as Gefion, the ocean-goddess whom we meet in the *Loka-Senna*, who, like Odinn, knows the fates of all men. At any rate we have in these names the conception of the Sea as an awe-producing, wrathful living thing. " Then Terror rose from the deep " is a frequent phrase used in describing storms at sea, as if a great giant

---

[1] The English term *Eagre* still survives in provincial dialect for the tide-wave or bore on rivers. Dryden uses it in his *Threnod. August*. " But like an Eagre rode in triumph o'er the tide ; " and Camden uses it when he speaks of the *bore* on the Severn. Yet we must be cautious in dwelling on any relation of these words to the Anglo-Saxon *Eagor*.

pushed his head out of the billows. There is a half-line in *Beowulf* which seems to speak of a fierce being who makes an onset on those who tempt the depth of the sea. When the hero is borne into the cave by Grendel's mother, it is said that the "sudden treacherous grip of the Flood can no longer reach him." When Caedmon describes the deluge he says: "The sea gripped fiercely on the fated folk," as if it were a giant that choked them.

These are the main names of the sea in *Beowulf*, and each of them describes some thought concerning it, or some one of its aspects.[1] They are more than words, they are pictures. A number of them are indifferently used together in one passage in *Beowulf*, with no distinction of meaning. They have become, it seems, mere poetic interchanges. It is too much the fate of words originally individual and noble. But the passage is sufficiently interesting to translate—

>   Art thou that Beowulf   who battled with Breca
>   Swimming a match   on the far spreading *sea*
>   When in pride of your hearts   ye proved the vast *fords*
>   And on the *deep water*   in a vaunting, like fools,
>   Risked each your lives?   .   .   .   .
>   .   .   .   .   There ye swam on the *Sund*,
>   Arm after arm   over *Eagor-stream* laid;
>   Measured the *mere-streets*,   moved your hands to and fro,
>   Glode o'er the *Garseeg*!   Tossed *Geofon* in waves,
>   A Welter of winter.   In *Water's* vast power
>   Seven nights ye strove.   In swimming he beat thee,
>   More was his might!   Him then at morn-tide,
>   Heaved up the *Holm*   on the Heathoremes' land.
>   *Beowulf*, l. 506.

Compounded with these single terms are other words such as *faroð*, which itself sometimes means the

---

[1] I need scarcely mention the metaphorical names for the sea used in *Beowulf*. It is the *Hron-rad*, the *swan-rad*, the *segl-rad*, the *ganotes-bað*—the "whale-road," the "swan-road," the "sail-road," the "gannet's-bath."

sea, but is in composition the moving of the sea
and is used now and then for the racing of the waves
towards the coast. The chief of these secondary words
is *wylm*, the upwelling, the tossing of the billows.
Its most remarkable use in *Beowulf* is in conjunction
with ice to express the tumbling of broken ice and sea
together in a roaring welter; and in symbolism (so
much had the tormented sea entered into Anglo-Saxon
thought) it is compounded with care and sorrow.
Lastly, the word *yð* (wave) is combined with others to
image the various passions and actions of the sea
in storm. We have *yð-geblond*, the confused blending
of the waves; *yð-geweale*, their tossing to and fro;
atol yða geswing, their dreadful swinging; and *yð-gewin*, their tumultuous battling and onset like armies.
Nor are more detailed descriptions of sea-scenery
wanting in *Beowulf*. There is the hithe at the
beginning of the poem and the ship waiting for the
body of Scyld; the two voyages of Beowulf to Heorot
and back again; the sea seen from the great cape
where he is buried—the misty sea and the ships sailing in it. These I have already given. A few more
remain which are worth quoting. The first describes
in Beowulf's own words an adventure on the Northern
Sea, night and fierce weather, and the peace of the
morning on the waves—

> When we swam on the Sound   our sword was laid bare,
> Hard-edged in our hands;   and against the Hron-fishes[1]
> We meant to defend us;   nor might Breca from me
> Far o'er the flood-waves   at all float away,
> Smarter on ocean;   nor would I from him—.
> There we two together,   were (tossed) on the sea,
> Five nights in all,   till the flood apart drove us:
> Swoln were the surges,   of storms 'twas the coldest,

---

[1] Whales?

> Dark grew the night, and northern the wind,
> Rattling and roaring,[1] rough were the billows.
> Then was the mood of the mere-fishes roused.
> *Beowulf*, l. 539.

There is also a light sketch of another kind of coast, not of cliffs, but of a wide flat of sandy shore, when Beowulf arrives at home. He " went with his following "—

> All along the sand, treading the sea-plain,
> Seabanks stretching far! Shone the candle of the world,
> Sloped the sun was from the south.[2]
> *Beowulf*, l. 1964.

One more description tells of the longing of an exiled seaman for his home, while he waited for summer, held from his sailing by the fierce winds of winter and the ice-fettered sea. Hengest was mindful of his land, though he could not drive o'er the sea his ring-equipped bark—

> Surged the sea in storms,
> Wrestled 'gainst the wind. Winter locked the waves
> In an icy bondage, till another year
> Came unto the garths . . .
> Weather glorious-bright. Then was winter gone,
> Lovely was the lap of Earth. *Beowulf*, l. 1131.

Such is the strong and stormy sea (*mere-strengo*, "strength of the sea," or "strength of the warriors on the sea," *Beowulf*, l. 533) which is heard breaking in the background all through the action of the poem of *Beowulf*; and those who first sung its verse were masters of the Ocean and its lovers. The sea was their patrimony, as it was the whale's. The young men went out on adventure from every settlement on the coast to fight and to plunder, and when they amused themselves with trading it was in reality the exchange of plunder for

---

[1] *Heaðogrim and hwearf.* If we put *and* on to *hwearf* we must translate "fierce blew in our faces," and so I have translated in a previous page.
[2] That is, it was near mid-day.

plunder. When they were not fighting they were
hunting the sword-fish, the walrus, the seal, and the
whale in the icy seas, or struggling for wagers to excel
one another in the battle with the elements. The Ocean
was itself a mighty monster with whom they fought for
life; and in it, as we see, were orcs and tusked terrors and
witches of the waves, and wolves of the deep, hideous
half-human brutes like Grendel and his dam, shapeless
fish-like things which attacked man, wrathful at
their home being invaded; and memories of these
superstitious creatures lasted on into the Christian
poetry. But the sea-rovers of Beowulf's time cared
for none of these things. They were true sea-dogs,
the forerunners of the men who sailed in wasp-like ships
from the southern harbours of England to the Spanish
main. They were probably a separate class, not to be
mingled up with the farmers, the thegns and the lord,
who dwelt in burgs like Heorot or in the cultivated
lands; but most of the young men of spirit seemed to
have joined for a time at least the ships of the sea-
harriers. Beowulf talks of his class as distinct from
those to whom he spoke in Heorot : "We sailers of the
sea," he says. Ongentheow retires to his fort "that
he might be able there to withstand the seamen, and
shield his hoard from the seafarers." It is a phrase
which a Spanish Don might have used when he heard
that the ships of that devil, Drake, were seen in the
offing. They are called "travellers of the wave" and
"dwellers of the deep." There is no trace in *Beowulf*
of any dread of the sea, even in its worst moods, nor
do the men complain of the labours of the ocean,
or its icy weathers. They are rather comrades of its
storms, and it is their glory to sing their daring
while they overcome its anger. What Sidonius said

of the pirate Saxons would have been true of Beowulf and his sea-crafty men: "They know the dangers of the ocean as men who are every day in touch with them. In the midst of tempests, and skirting the sea-beaten rocks, they risk their attack with joy, hoping to make profit out of the very storm." And this is all the plainer from the number of names given to the ship—names which speak their pride and their affection. It is the Ætheling's vessel, the Floater, the Wave-swimmer, the Ring-stemmed, the Keel, the Well-bound wood, the Sea-wood, the Sea-ganger, the Sea-broad ship, the Wide-bosomed, the Prow-curved, the Wood of the curved neck, the Foam-throated floater that flew like a bird.

This fearlessness, this friendship with the waves, this love of their vessel as of a mistress, passed away with their settlement in our England. Such, at least, seems the evidence of Anglo-Saxon poetry. The first arrivals on the coasts of Southern and Northern Britain were the roving pirates, the young sea-heroes and their bands. These went inland and became great land-warriors. Those who came after them and those who settled on the coasts, were probably the agricultural freemen and warriors of Engle, or Saxons from the inland who were unaccustomed to the sea. The South Saxons did not even know how to fish when Wilfrid came among them; and we know the difficulty that Ælfred had in working up a fleet (he was probably his own shipbuilder), and how ignorant of naval war Englishmen had become in his days. The temper in which the ordinary Northumbrian seaman looked upon the sea was not at all the sea-dog temper, but that of the common merchant sailor who, while he sailed the waves, dreaded their dangers and complained of their hardships. There is not a trace of that audacious sense of lordship over the sea which the sea-rover possessed. The passage in the *Gnomic Verses*, though it seems to speak of a Friesland home, may well have arisen concerning one of the Frisian band which seems to have settled to the north of the Tweed, and at least the collector of these scattered verselets adapted it to the case of those for whom he edited the lines. It is plain that the true home of this man and his type is on shore and not on sea—

<pre>
                    Dear the welcomed one
To the Frisian wife,   when the Floater's drawn on shore,
When his keel comes back,   and her churl returns to home,
Her's, her own food-giver,   And she prays him in,
Washes then his weedy coat, and new weeds puts on him,
O lythe¹ it is on land to him, whom his love constrains.
</pre>

Fearlessness and peace are found on the land, but on the ocean terror and disquiet. The beginning of the *Seafarer* is full of this temper. The old man must tell,—he says, of his voyages, how often he outlived hours of pain, bitter care in his breast, sailing in his ship through seas of sorrow, amid the frightful whirling of the waves, keeping the anxious night-watch on the prow, his feet pinched with the frost, his beard hung with icicles, hunger in the heart of him, sea-wearied, far from his beloved, hearing only the scream of the sea-mew and the high flood thunder on the cliffs. No man on land can think what woes he suffers who fares far forth upon the wanderings of the sea. Yet even in that poem, which I keep for separate treatment, the attraction also of the sea appears, the longing of the young sailor to go on voyage, the pull of the ocean life upon the heart. But for all that, nothing of the Viking spirit is found in it; mourning

---

¹ Pleasant, soft.

and fear, not joy and daring, fill its lines. Again in the *Andreas* the shipmaster tells Andrew that he who tries a sea-journey has a hard life, and the comrades of St. Andrew are terrified when the storm begins. It is only the overmastering duty of the thegn to his lord which prevents them from asking to be set on shore. The "Water Terror" which rises from the waves is made much more of in these later poems than it is in *Beowulf*. In the great riddle on the Hurricane there is a picture of a ship with its crew aghast for fear, almost unable to work in the horror of the tempest. The sailor in the *Gnomic Verses*, "who rows against the wind is weary." When the timid sailor is threatened of the captain, "he loses his courage, and his oar drieth on board." Everywhere it is the merchant sailor and not the sea-warrior who speaks. Nevertheless, in Cynewulf's poem of *Elene*, one of the last he wrote, another note is struck, a reversion to the old heroic strain concerning the sea ; and the voyage of Helena is described as if it were a Viking expedition. I cannot do better than illustrate these remarks by passages from the *Andreas* and the *Elene*, and all the more because, in these passages, I think that the scenery of the Northumbrian coast is represented.

God appears in a vision to Andrew, and bids him set sail for Mermedonia to deliver Matthew from prison, and Andrew answers that God's angel would do the business better ; for he knows the going of the seas and ocean's salt streams, and the swan-road, and the war of the waves on the shore, and the water-terror

        But to me the war-ship's streets [1]
 O'er the water cold are not known at all. *And.* l. 200.

[1] *Herestræta* would mean, on land, the military roads ; hence the "main streets." Andrew means that he did not know what every seaman knew, the well-known routes across the sea.

"Alas, Andrew," answers God, "that ever thou shouldest be slow to this journey!"

> Yet thou shalt assuredly,   at the early dawn,
> Even at to-morrow,   at the ocean's ending,
> Climb upon thy keel,   and o'er water cold
> Break along the bathway.   *And*. l. 220.

Andrew, now steadfast, sets forth with the rising of the day, and the description of his path to the sea has often recalled to me the approach to the seashore, over the dunes of sand near Bamborough—

> Then he went him at the dawning,   at the earliest day,
> O'er the sandy hillocks,   to the sea's inflowing,
> Daring in his thinking;   and his thegns, beside him,
> Trampled o'er the shingle.   Thundered loud the ocean,
> Beat the surges of the sea.   *And*. l. 235.

When they come to the shore they see a boat drawn up, amid the breaking of the surf, and the ship-master seated on the bulwark, and two sailors with him. They are Christ and two angels, and the dialogue, which I shall speak of afterwards, ends in the embarkation of Andrew and his comrades. The waves are high and whirling and the storm begins to rise. In short, vigorous lines the poet describes it, and the terror of Andrew's companions—

>   Then was sorely troubled,
> Sorely wrought the whale-mere.   Wallowed there the Horn-fish,
> Glode the great deep through;   and the gray-backed gull
> Slaughter-greedy wheeled.   Dark the storm-sun grew,
> Waxed the winds up,   grinded waves;
> Stirred the surges,   groaned the cordage,
> Wet with breaking sea.   Water-horror rose
> With the might of troops.[1]   Then the thegns
> Cold with terror grew,   nor thought any one
> That alive he should   win at last the land.
>   *And*. l. 369.

---

[1] *Þreata þrydum* ("with the strength of armies"). This seems an impersonation almost too fine for so early a time. It is quite in the manner of the modern imagination. It is Kemble's translation, and Grein's is more probable, though I do not like to surrender the other—*Mächtig durch die Massen*.

A fine passage follows in which the thegns of Andrew refuse to leave him, and the steersman bids him break the length of the journey by telling how Christ acted in the gale that so the young men may be comforted. "Long is our journey still over the fallow flood, very far the land we seek," and now "the sand is upblended, the ocean bed with the shingle," a phrase which puts us in mind of the lines in the first book of the *Æneid*.[1] Whereat Andrew strengthens them with words. "The Water Terror shall become gentle, as of old it was with us upon the Lake of Galilee"; and he tells the story of Christ's calming of the sea. Cynewulf paints it from nature, and the sea he describes is not that of Gennesaret, but of the German Ocean—

> So of yore it fell   that on sea-boat we,
> O'er the war of waves,   ventured (ocean's) fords,
> Riding on the flood.   Perilous and dread
> Seemed the sea paths then.   Eagor's streamings now
> Beat upon the bulwarks;[2]   billow answered billow,
> Wave replied to wave!   And at whiles uprose,
> From the bosom of the foam   to the bosom of the boat,
> Terror o'er the Wave-ship.
>
>   *Andreas*, l. 438.

Meanwhile the Almighty slept in his brightness on "the Rusher through the sea," but when the fearful called, arose and stilled the weltering waters—

>   He rebuked the winds:
> Sank the sea to rest.   Strength of ocean-streams
> Soon did smooth become!   Then our spirit laughed
> Whenso we had seen,   underneath the skiey path,
> All the winds and waves   and the Water-Fear
> Full of fear become   for the fear of God the Lord.
>
>   *Andreas*, l. 451.

---

[1] "His unda dehiscens
  Terram inter fluctus aperit; furit aestus arenis."—*Æn.* i. 106, 107.

[2] *Bordstaeđu* means, I think, the bulwarks of the ship. Compare here "Deep calleth unto deep, because of the noise of the water floods," etc.

Therefore, he says (almost quoting a passage from *Beowulf*, save that God is substituted for Wyrd), "the living God will never forlet a man if his courage avail." And when they heard this tale, Andrew's comrades fell asleep, and "the sea grew calm, the rush of the waves, the rough rage of the deep returned," like a giant who had been roused from the depths, "whence it had come."

Now Andrew and the steersman, whom he does not know to be Christ, are alone left awake. " I would," says Andrew, who is amazed at the skill of this divine sailor, " thou wouldest teach me how thou guidest the swimming of this wave-floater, foamed over by the ocean, of this stallion of the sea." Then, either because the poet wishes to give local colour and invents voyages for Andrew, or, as I would fain believe, introduces his own personal experience of the deep and imputes it to Andrew, he tells how he has been sixteen times at sea, and contrasts these old journeys with his present one—

> 'Twas of old and now   fate of mine to be
> In a ship at sea,   for sixteen of times;
> Frozen were my hands   which the floods were moving,
> Ocean's streaming tides!
>
> Never have I seen   any hero like to thee
> Steer so o'er the stern!   Roars the swirling sea;
> Foaming Ocean beats our stead;   full of speed this boat is;
> Fares along foam-throated,   flieth on the wave,
> Likest to a bird.
>
> Almost like it is,   as if in a landlocked bay [1]
> Still it stood at rest;   where the storm may move it not,
> Nor yet wind at all,   nor the water-floods
> Break its beamy prow—   yet o'er breaking seas it rushes,
> Snell beneath its sail.   *Andreas*, l. 489.

"Answer me, thou hast the answer of a sea-playing

---

[1] *Landsceap* cannot mean our *landscape*; but some place where ships were drawn to shore; some land-edge, or as I have put it above.

earl." And the steersman replies with a touch of the old Viking spirit, but also with the more modern fear of the sea—

>   Oft it doth befall,   that on ocean's pathways we,
>   In our ships with seamen,   when the squall comes up,
>   Scour the bathway o'er   with our stallions of the foam.
>   But at whiles on waves   wretched is our fate
>   On the (weary) sea ;   though we win the voyage through,
>   Comrades courageful.   *And.* l. 511.

But the flood tossing cannot let us against the will of the Lord who bindeth the brown waves, and now because thou art a messenger of God, terror has been stilled for thee; the wide-bosomed wave and all the fords have sunk to rest.

In all this passage concerning the sea, we do not catch, as I said, the note of *Beowulf*. The spirit of the merchant sailor and not of the warrior is shown in its verse. We hear a different note in a later poem, in the description of the expedition of the Empress Helena to find the True Cross—

>   Quickly then began   all the crowd of earls
>   For the sea to ready.   Then the stallions of the flood
>   Stood alert for going   on the ocean-strand,
>   Hawsered steeds of sea   in the Sund at anchor.
>   .   .   .   .   .   .
>   Many a warrior proud,   there at Wendelsea,
>   Stood upon the shore.   Over the sea marges
>   Hourly urged they on,   one troop after other.
>   And they stored up there— with the sarks of battle,
>   With the shields and spears, with mail-shirted fighters,
>   With the warriors and the women— the wave-riding horses.
>   Then they let o'er Fifel's wave   foaming stride along
>   Steep-stemmed[1] rushers of the sea.   Oft withstood the bulwark,

---

[1] I take this to mean the steep sides, or the up-curved and lofty prow of the ships. It curved back from the sea-level, steep as a hillside. The Anglo-Saxon *brant* or *bront*, and the Swedish *brant* is to be found in Northern England (*brant* and *brent*) to signify the steep (side of a hill). The Icelandic is *brattr* (steep). *Brandr*, a fire-brand, or the blade of a sword, also means the raised prow, the beak of a ship, and may be connected with the adjective *brattr.*—*Icelandic Dict.*, G. Vigfusson. *Wendelsea* is the Mediterranean.

<pre>
O'er the surging of the waters,   swinging strokes of waves ;
Humming¹ hurried on the sea !   Never heard I ere or since,
Or of old, that any lady   led a fairer power
O'er the street of sea,   on the stream of ocean !
There a man might see   (who should mark the fleet²
Break along the bathway)—   rush the Billows'-wood along,
Play the Horse of flood,   plunge the Floater of the wave,
'Neath the swelling sails.   Blithe the sea-dogs were,
Courage in their heart.   Glad the Queen was of her journey,
When at last to hithe,   o'er the lake fast-rooted,
They had sailed their ships,   set with rings on prow,
To the land of Greece.   Then they let the keels
Stand the sea-marge by,   driven on the sandy shore,
Ancient houses of the wave.   *Elene*, l. 225.
</pre>

In these two sets of passages from the *Andreas* and the *Elene*, we hear the double note of which I have spoken. The last is, I suppose, the work of the imagination only ; it is not likely that the poet ever joined a war-fleet ; the first is imagination backed up by personal experience. But a man who loved the sea wrote them both. And this love, in which Caedmon, to a certain slight extent, seems to have shared, is confirmed by the new terms which Cynewulf invented or used for the sea, and by the new compounds he and his school added to those we find in *Beowulf*. Some of these are full of that poetry which grows up into expression when generation after generation live in constant vision of a vast natural power like the Sea. *Sund-helm* is used for the Ocean, the great covering helmet of the earth. *Arwela* is another name for the Sea, and its meaning—" the realm of the oar "—has come down to modern English poetry. *Hop* is the ocean seen, perhaps, as the vast Ring or

---

[1] *Sae swinsade*—

<pre>
    The humming water shall o'erwhelm thy corse
    Lying 'mid simple shells.
</pre>

[2] Literally, the voyage, the path ; hence, as I think, the voyaging fleet, the whole expedition.

hoop which embraces the world.[1] Then the adjective sea-still (*mere-smylte*) is used in comparison. A thing is said to be as quiet as the broad calm of the sea. Sea-bright (*mere-torht*), the burning sheen of the sunlit sea, is also used. A very cold thing is sea-cold (*brim-ceald*). A vast expanse or a broad-beamed thing like a ship is called *sae-geap* (sea-broad). *Holmeg* means, perhaps, stormy as the sea. Then as we had in *Beowulf*, *mere-strengo* (the strength of the sea), so now we hear of the might of the sea (*holm-maegen*) or, as it may be translated, the vast fulness of the deep; and with a similar meaning, *Lagu-faesten* the fastness of the deep, the fortressed sea, or the firm-set sea.

With the exception of *sea-calm* and *sea-bright* used as adjectives, there is no record of any fair and beautiful impression. The sea is always the dark and troubled waters of the German Ocean. It is never warm; a common phrase for it is the ice-cold sea. Its colour is never blue or green. It is always wan, black, or murky. The waves are brown or flood-gray. It is a flint-gray flood which in the gale hurls itself upon the cliffs (Riddle iv.) This gray colour of waters when they foam in flood dwelt in the eyes of the English. They settle on it as the hue of mountain streams in spate. "Water," the *Gnomic Verses* say, "shall rush gray in flood from the hills." In the same *Verses*, and in the *Wanderer*, the waves are fallow, dun-yellow, like withered ghosts of leaves, the frequent colour of the sea after storm as seen from the Northumbrian coasts. Indeed, as in *Beowulf*, what most the

---

[1] I fear, however, that this is quite unauthorised. See Grein's Dict. "Hop." New metaphorical words are now used for the sea. It is called *hwales-edel* (the patrimony of the whale), *fisces baeJ* (the fish's bath), *seolh-wadu* (the seals'-path).

English felt was the impression of the wild turmoil of the billows, and they added words for this to those already used. *Hop-gehnaest* expresses the crashing of the spreading waves on the cliffs; *waroð-faruð* the surge as it breaks on the shelving beach; *waroða gewcorp* is the dashing of the waves themselves upon the shore; *holm-þracu* the tossing and beating together of the tormented sea far from shore. *Sund-gebland* and *carh-gebland* are other forms of the same thought —the blending of wave with wave in the gale,—and *stream-gewin*, the warring of the waves with each other, is another word for this terrible surging.

Then there are a few more words compounded with *yð* a wave; *yða gepring* is the crushing together of the billows; *yða gepraec* the thronging of the waves; *yða-ongin* the onset of the waves on the shore, or on a ship. It may be also that *sac-beorg* signifies the whole mountainous advance of the billows of the sea, or any one mountain of water. The same image, with a different word (*dûn ofer ðýpe*), is used in the *Riddle* of the hurricane.

The whole mass of the onward rushing waves—as in the deluge—is called the host of Eagor. "I shall never lead again," answers God to Noah, "Ocean's army (*Egor-here*) over the wide land" (*Gen.* l. 1537). For the whole expanse of the sea, the word *Lagu-faeðm* is used, the embrace of ocean, the bosom of the deep; and out of it rises *wacter-stefn*, the voice of waters. Then there are new words in which the old mythological conceptions are contained — *waeg-þrea*, terror on or of the sea; *wacter-broga*, *wacter-egesa*, the water-horror, which rises from the depths when storm is on the surface. Through this went the ships, and a new name for them is *wacter-þisa* the rusher through the water. So also they are called *sae-hengest, sae-mearh* sea-stallion, sea-horse; *sae-flota, sae-genga, sae-wudu* sea-floater, sea-goer, sea-wood. *Brante ceole, hea hornscipe,* "with the steep-sided keel, the high-horned ship," describes the ships as they plunge through the deep, dipping their lofty figure-head in the waves. *Geofon-hus* and *mere-hus*, ocean and sea house, are other words for them, and are used of the ark in Caedmon. A passage in the *Guthlac* brings a number of these ship names together. It is the description of the voyage of Guthlac's disciple to tell his sister of her brother's death. He climbs on board the boat, and then—

> Urged the *Stallion of the wave*, and the *Water-rusher* ran
> Snell beneath the sorrow-laden. Shone the blazing sky,
> Blickering o'er the Burg-halls. Fled the *Billow-wood* along
> Gay and gleaming on the path! Laden, to the hithe,
> Flew at speed the *Flood-horse*, till the *Floater of the tide*,
> After the Sea-playing, surged upon the sea-land,
> Ground against the shingle-grit. *Guth.* l. 1303.

"Whence come ye," says one in the *Andreas*, "solitary floaters on the wave, on your Sea-rusher?" And another passage uses this imaginative phrase: "The high-stemmed boat, the snell sea-horse, *woven round with speed*, bore us hither with the flood over the road of the whale."

There are other new words for all these matters, but let these suffice, while we turn to the direct things said concerning the sea in the later English poetry. Caedmon—I use the word for the poems under his name—has nothing like the range of treatment of the sea which is so characteristic of Cynewulf. His allusions to the great Element, in those parts of the poem which may have been really composed by him, are very much those which a quiet monk who saw the gray northern sea from the heights of Whitby in calm and in storm, would be likely to make out of an impression weighty from its continuance. It is only when he describes the Flood that we find the sea in presence, for the description of the vast water of Chaos may be drawn from ancient sources. That vast water is called *Garsecg*. "Garsecg o'er covered, swart in the endless night, far and wide the gloomy waves." In the tale of the deluge he speaks of the smiting and pushing of the black sea streams, of their warring or mounting on the shores, of the dusky waves, of the thunder noise of the whole deluging deep, of the Water-Terror that dared not lay his hand upon the Ark, of the hosted waves of Ocean, of the ebbing, of the foaming Wave-stream, until we seem to be standing with him in a north-east gale upon the cliff of Whitby. One other touch in the poem, perhaps from Caedmon's hand, is where God speaks to Abraham and tells him that his seed shall be like the stars for multitude. Caedmon makes these stars shine on the wide calm bosom of the deep, as, when peace was on that stormy northern sea, he may have watched them on a summer night from the edge of the lofty headland where his monastery stood—

On the Heaven gaze,   count its glorious gems,
Count the stars of Æther,   that, in space, so pure,[1]
Ever-glorious fairness,   now so far are dealing!
O'er the billows broad,   see, they brightly glimmer.
Genesis, l. 2189.

These are from the *Genesis*. In the *Exodus*, a poem which seems to have none of Caedmon's work in it, there is of course a great deal about the sea, but it is the sea treated miraculously. The phenomena

---

[1] "Spaciously gentle," perhaps.

described have no relation to reality, and, indeed, I seem to detect in it that the writer had not much personal acquaintance with the ocean. It is quite another matter when we look into the *Andreas*, the *Guthlac*, and the *Elene*, and into such poems as the *Seafarer* and *Wanderer*. These were written by poets in Northumbria who were well acquainted with the Deep. We have already told, in the lines from the *Andreas*, what the writer saw upon the mid sea as the ship ran over the surges, and the personal touch in it is as unmistakable as its vigour; but it has often occurred to me, though I only give it as a vague conjecture, that the passage which describes the awaking of Andrew on the land near the coast and the first sight of the town, may be also a record of a personal experience. It is just the sight a sailor, coming towards land in the morning, near Bamborough for instance, would have seen from the sea,—the plain, the city gates, the steep rock, the glittering tiles, the wind-swept walls. Andrew lies sleeping on the highway—

> Until, now, the Lord   let the lamp of day
> Sheerly bright to shine,   and the shadows sank away,
> Wan below the welkin.   Then there came the Weather-torch,
> And the light of Heaven serene   o'er the houses blickered!
> Then awoke the war-hard man,   looked upon the wide-spread plain,
> Lying 'fore the Town gates.   Towered there the steep hills
> With high-hanging cliffs,[1]   O'er the hoary rock
> Stood the gay-tiled houses,   stood the towers up,
> And the wind-swept walls.   *And.* l. 835.

It may have been also in one of these conjectured voyages that it occurred to Cynewulf to imitate, but with many a change, the riddle of Symphosius on the Ship. This is "a work of skill that grinds into the gravel and yelling fares along; which has neither

---

[1] I have punctuated these two lines in a new fashion.

face nor hands, shoulders nor arms, but moves on a single foot (its keel) over the fields of ocean and has many ribs and a mouth in its midst." Nor is this a war-ship as a Norseman would have described, but a merchantman. It brings "food and gifts that rich and poor desire, every year, to men." When it enters the bay, the anchor is let go; and the vigour and fire with which Cynewulf makes another riddle on the Anchor has all the spirit of a sailor in it. The Anchor is a strong and warring hero, following in this Symphosius from whom the idea of the riddle is taken. But Cynewulf's Anchor-hero is more feelingly impersonated than that of Symphosius. A touch of sorrow, as Prehn thinks, of a sad weird laid upon him, belongs to a phrase like this which tells how the Anchor felt in the solitude of the ocean-bed—"Strange is that home to me." Here are the first lines (Rid. xvii.)—

> Oft shall I with waves be warring, and with winds be fighting.
> And against sea-tangle [1]— whensoe'er I plunge to seek
> Earth with surges over-shrouded. Strange such homeland is to me!

These are the doings on the Sea, but there are also a number of passages which might have been written by a settler on the coast who looked on the Sea from the shore. One, the description of Andrew passing over the sand-dunes to the beach, has already been quoted. There is another in the *Wanderer* (l. 46), where the lonely man wakens from his dream of joy and beholds the image of his own sorrow in the wintry waters—

> And he sees before him [heave] the fallow waves,
> And the sea-birds bathing, broadening out their feathers,
> And the hoar sleet hurtle down, snow with hail commingled.
> . . . . . Care is then renewed

---

[1] Or "I contend against both of them."

> For the man who many times   must with passion send
> All his spirit sorrow-laden   o'er the sea-floods interchaining.[1]

The birds of the sea, as in this passage, are not neglected. The tern, the "sea-swallow icy feathered," the "sea-eagle, dewy feathered and barking among the cliffs," the "swan as it sang its song" in flight over the waves, and the gannet and the sea-mew shrieking in the storm, are all brought together in the *Seafarer*. In the *Andreas* there is a vision of sea-eagles—

> Us sea-weary   sleep o'erwent;
> Then on came earns,   o'er tossing waves,
> Fast in flight,   in wings exulting.   *And.* l. 862.

The 11th riddle of Cynewulf describes, as I believe, the Barnacle goose, and only a man who was well acquainted with the sea and its dwellers could have done the thing as well. It is so interesting, even from an historical point of view—since it puts back old Gerarde's tradition so far—that I give it entire [2]—

---

[1] "O'er the binding of waters."
   When the midnight moon is weaving
   Her bright chain o'er the deep.

Byron means that the moonlight on the faintly-rippled sea makes, as it were, a silver coat of mail—chain-mail—over the deep. But the poet of the *Wanderer* means, I think, the interlocking of the waves, their knitting together into a net which weaves together all the waves of all the oceans. That it should mean, as some think, the bond of the ice sheet over the sea, does not accord with the context.

[2] The answer Prehn gives to this riddle is *See-furche*, and he connects it with the 13th Riddle of Symphosius, and with Ealdhelm's, iv. 11. The reasons he gives for this answer are not sufficient to induce me to give up my own answer, which seems to fit at every point. One would scarcely talk of the neb of a *sea-furrow*. The clinging with the body to a drifting wood is not one of the habits of the hollow between two waves. When the foam flies from the wave it is not a living creature, nor is it clothed in fine ornaments (*hyrste*, a word used for the feathered robe of the swan). The furrow of the wave may be black and white, but in that condition it is not borne into the air, nor far and wide over the sea. But the Barnacle is almost altogether in black and white. "The bill is black, the head as far as the crown, together with cheeks and throat is white the rest of the head and neck to the breast and shoulders black. The upper plumage is marbled with blue-gray, black and white. The feathers of back and wings are black edged with white, the underparts are white, the tail

> In a narrow was my neb, and beneath the wave I lived;
> Underflowen by the flood; in the mountain-billows
> Low was I besunken; in the sea I waxed
> Over-covered with the waves, clinging with my body
> To a wandering wood———.
> Quick the life I had, when I from the clasping came
> Of the billows, of the beam-wood, in my black array;
> White in part were then my prankéd garments fair,
> When the Lift upheaved me, me a living creature,
> Wind from wave upblowing; and as wide as far
> Bore me o'er the bath of seals— Say, what is my name!

But the chief thing which engaged the dwellers in the stormy north was the fierce weather on the sea. The whole of the descriptions which follow make me almost certain that Cynewulf lived for a great part of his life on the sea coast. It seems quite impossible that an inland person—and there are those who hint at his being a Mercian—could have described the doings of the deep so accurately. Descriptions of this close quality—all the right things said and the unnecessary details left out—are only made after long experience.

In the *Andreas* the weather of Northumbria is described, and it is as wild and hard as that of which we hear in *Beowulf,* and are told of in the *Seafarer.*

---

black." Then the rest of the Riddle agrees with the old account given in Gerarde's *Herball,* which I quote here: "There is a small Ilande in Lancashire called the Pile of Foulders, wherein are found the broken peeces of old and brused ships, some whereof have been cast thither by shipwracke, and also the trunks or bodies with the branches of old and rotten trees, cast up there likewise: whereon is found a certaine spume or froth, that in time breedeth certaine shels, in shape like those of the muskle but sharper pointed, and of a whitish colour, wherein is conteined a thing in form like a lace of silke finely woven, as it were, together of a whitish colour; one end whereof is fastened unto the inside of the shell, even as the fish of Oisters and Muskles are; the other end is made faste unto the belly of a rude masse or lump, which in time commeth to the shape and forme of a Bird. When it is perfectly formed, the shel gapeth open, and the first thing that appeareth is the foresaid lace or string; next come the legs of the Birde hanging out, and as it groweth greater, it openeth the shell by degrees, till at length it is all come foorth, and hangeth only by the bill, in short space after it commeth to full maturitie, and falleth into the sea, where it gathereth feathers, and groweth to a foule, bigger than a Mallard, and lesser than a Goose; having blacke legs and bill or beake, and feathers blacke and white, and spotted in such a manner as in our Magge-Pie."—Gerarde's *Herball,* p. 1391 [pub. 1597].

It is the description, as will be seen, of one who dwelt near the sea—

Snow did bind the earth
With the whirling winter-flakes ;   and the weathers grew
Cold with savage scours of hail ;   while the sleet and frost—
Gangers gray of war were they—   locked the granges up
Of the heroes, and folk-hamlets !   Frozen hard were lands
With the chilly icicles ;   Shrunk the courage of the water ;
O'er the running rivers   ice upraised a bridge ;
And the Sea-road shone.   *Andreas*, l. 1255.

The same kind of weather is spoken of in the *Wanderer* and the *Seafarer*. "The storms lash the overhanging cliffs, the falling sleet binds up the fields, the wan terror of the winter comes, the shadow of night comes darkling on, and out of the north sends the fierce hailstorm for the troubling of men."—So says the Wanderer, and the Seafarer mourns the like upon his ship. His feet are bound with the bands of frost, he is hung with icicles, the hail flies round him in showers, the sea is icy cold. All the poetry is full of the fury of the hail. Even in the *Rune Song* the poet, when he has called it, conventionally, the "whitest of corns," passes on, thrilled by what he has seen, to describe how when the tempest is at its height, the hail is whirled through the lift, as if it were snow—mingled and tossed by the squalls of wind,—for so I must translate *windes scura*, showers of wind. A similar passage in the *Gnomic Verses* speaks of the shower coming up the sky blended into one with the wind. Midst of this weather, were the desperate tempests of the Northern coast, and a short passage in the same *Verses* brings together with some force the universal disturbance of sea and sky and waters of the earth in the fierce gale. "The salt sea shall toss in waves, and the helm of the air, and the water-floods; and o'er every land rush down the mountain

streams." But it is Cynewulf who chiefly loves the
tempests. He paints, with all the vigour of the North,
the ice-floe plunging and roaring through the foaming
sea, and shouting out, like a Viking, his coming to the
land, singing and laughing terribly. Sharp are the
swords he uses in the battle (the knife-edges of the ice),
grim is his hate, he is greedy for the battle.[1] He breaks
into the shield walls (the sides of the ships ranged along
with shields), binds, like a wizard, runes of slaughter.
"Such a hero," says Prehn, to whom I refer,[2] "may
well boast of his ancestors." "My mother," he cries,
"is of the maiden-kin; my daughter is waxen strong."
His mother was the water, and his daughter was also
the water—mother and daughter the same. Symphosius and Tatwine dwell on this fancy with regard to
snow and ice. In the *Ænigmata veterum poetarum*
we meet it —" Mater me genuit, eadem mox gignitur ex
me." And again " Quam mater genuit, generavit filia
matrem." But Cynewulf only brings in this fancy at
the end of his riddle. The rest—the audacious Ice
Viking, victoriously dashing through the sea, with all
his ship ringing as it goes, and he himself shouting
on the prow,—that is Cynewulf's alone, and it is
another illustration of the absurdity of those who pass
over these riddles of his as a mere imitation of the
Latin. Here is the Riddle (xxxiv.)—

> Came a wondrous wight   o'er the waves a-faring;
> Comely from his keel   called he to the land.
> Loudly did he shout,   and his laughter dreadful was,
> Full of terror to the Earth!   Sharp the edges of his swords,

---

[1] Grein translates, *Zum Kampfe geneigt*. "Sluggish to the battle" seems the literal meaning, but Grein evidently felt that this was not in harmony with the text, though I do not understand what reading he conjectures. It might, however, mean slow in beginning the war, but when engaged, bitter in battle-work, and the phrase might well apply to an iceberg.

[2] *Komposition und Quellen der Rätsel des Exeterbuches*, p. 205.

> Grim was then his hate. He was greedy for the slaughter,
> Bitter in the battle work; broke into the shield walls;
> Rough and ravaging his way; and a rune of hate he bound.
> Then, all-skilled in craft, he said, about himself, his nature—
> "Of the maiden kin is my mother known;
> Of them all the dearest, so that now my daughter is
> Waxen up to mightiness."   .   .   .   .

That is a particular aspect of storm, but Cynewulf draws the storms themselves, with all their characteristics on land and sea, and with such extraordinary force and fire that it seems as if these three short poems concentrated into their space all the storms he had seen in his life. The first describes the storm on land, the second at sea, and the third the universal tempest—the living Being who rises from his caverns under earth, and does his great business, first on the sea, then on the cliffs and ships, then on the land, and then among the clouds, till he sinks to rest again. They are all worth translating, chiefly for their poetry, but also because they are full of remnants of heathenism, of mythical images of natural phenomena, of phrases which those who care for natural folk-lore would have pleasure in illustrating. Here is the first—A Storm on land (Rid. ii.)—

> Who so wary and so wise of the warriors lives,
> That he dare declare who doth drive me on my way,
> When I start up in my strength! Oft in stormy wrath,
> Hugely then I thunder, tear along in gusts,
> Fare[1] above the floor of earth, burn the folk-halls down,
> Ravage all the rooms! Then the reek ariseth
> Gray above the gables? Great on earth the din,
> And the slaughter-qualm of men. Then I shake the woodland,
> Forests rich in fruits; then I fell the trees;—
> I with water over-vaulted— by the wondrous Powers
> Sent upon my way, far and wide to drive along!
> On my back I carry that which covered once
> All the tribes of Earth's indwellers, spirits and all flesh,
> In the sand together![2] Say who shuts me in,
> Or what is my name— I who bear this burden!

---

[1] *Fere* may be "terribly."   [2] The water of the Flood.

The next (Riddle iii.) is the Sea-storm—

Whiles, my way I take, how men ween it not,
Under seething[1] of the surges, seeking out the earth,
Ocean's deep abyss: all a-stirred the sea is.
Urged the flood is then, whirled the foam on high;
Fiercely wails the whale-mere, wrathful roars aloud;
Beat the sea-streams on the shore shooting momently on high,
On the soaring cliffs with the sand and stones,
With the weed and wave.[2] But I, warring on,
Shrouded with the ocean's mass, stir into the earth
Into vasty sea-grounds! From the water's helm
I may not on journey loose me, ere he let me go
Who my master is.—[3] Say, O Man of thought,
Who may draw me (like a sword) from the bosomed depths of ocean,
When the streams again on the sea are still,
And the surges silent that shrouded me before?

The next Riddle (iv.) is yet finer than these. Cynewulf was not one of those small poets whom a single effort on one subject exhausts. Moreover, he has not yet treated the work of the wind among the clouds and sky, and this he will now do, combining it with entirely new descriptions of the storm as it traverses the land and upraises the ocean. We scarcely expect that unconscious art, which is often the highest, in an early Anglo-Saxon poem, but the order and unity of this poem is admirable. The imaginative logic of its arrangement is like that which prevails in the "Ode to the West Wind," to which, indeed, it presents many points of resemblance, even to isolated phrases.

---

[1] *Geþraec* is "thronging," the fierce crowding together of the waves. I have put, "seething," for the sake of alliteration.

[2] A similar passage occurs in the *Christ* describing the cliffs withstanding the waves. The fire of judgment has passed over the earth, and while the cliffs melt in the heat Cynewulf recalls how he had seen them of old—

Tumble down in ruin
All the broken burg-walls, and the mountains melt,
And the high cliffs that of old, 'gainst the heaving sea,
'Gainst the floods fast rooted, guarded all the field of earth;
Strong and steadfast stood, bulwarks 'gainst the surges,
'Gainst the war of waters. *Christ*, l. 977.

[3] Or, "Who my master is on every journey."

Shelley tells of his wind—which, as in Cynewulf's poem, is a living being—first, as flying through the forests and the land, then of its work among the clouds, then on and in the sea, then on his own soul. Cynewulf tells of his storm-giant rising from his lair, rushing over the sea, then over the land, and then in the sky, but not of the storm in his own breast. That is the one modern quality we do not find in this poem of Cynewulf. It was natural for him—being closer to Nature-worship than Shelley—to impersonate his Hurricane, to make the clouds into stalking phantoms, to make them pour water from their womb and to sweat forth fire; and his work in this is noble. Shelley, who was himself an ancient Nature-worshipper born out of due time, a maker of Nature-myths, and as innocent as a young Aryan in doing so, is on that account very like Cynewulf when both are writing about natural phenomena. Both of them write as the people talked in old time about the Wind, and the Clouds, and the Sea; and in Cynewulf's case this is all the plainer when we compare his work with the riddles on the same subject which Ealdhelm and Eusebius put forth, which use the classical conventions, and which gave to Cynewulf nothing but the theme of his poem—

1. Oftenwhiles my Wielder   weighs me firmly down,
   Then again he urges   my immeasurable breast
   Underneath the fruitful fields,   forces me to rest.
   Drives me down to darkness,   me, the doughty warrior,
   Pins[1] me down in prison,   where upon my back

---

[1] "Pins me down" is, literally, "dashes, and presses me down." Compare with these lines, and with 13-16—

   In a cavern under is fettered the thunder,
   It struggles and howls at fits.   *The Cloud.*

Also—

   Hic vasto rex Æolus antro
   Luctantes ventos tempestatesque sonoras
   Imperio premit ac vinclis et carcere frenat.
   Illi indignantes magno cum murmure montis

> Sits the Earth, my jailor.   No escape have I
> From that savage sorrow—   but I mightily shake then
> Heirships old of heroes!   Totter then the hornèd halls,
> Village-steads of men;   all the walls are rocking
> High above the house-wards.

This is the introduction; the great giant power, clamped, like Enceladus, below the earth in the prison of dark caverns, the Earth seated on his back. Like Enceladus too, whom Cynewulf seems to have in mind, the giant turns and heaves in his sorrow, and then the earthquake is among the homes of men. Now his master lets him loose, but before he comes, air and sea are still—

> 10.   Calm abideth
> O'er the land, the lift;   lullèd is the sea;
> Till that I from thraldom   outwards thrust my way,
> Howsoe'er He leads me on,   who of old had laid
> At creation's dawning   wreathen chains on me,
> With their braces, with their bands,   that I might not bend me
> Out of his great Power   who points me out my paths.

The Storm now begins to work upon the sea, and Cynewulf introduces human interest in the ship—

> 17. Sometimes shall I, from above,   make the surges seethe,
> Stir up the sea-streamings,   and to shore crush on
> Gray as flint, the flood;   foaming fighteth then
> 'Gainst the wall of rock, the wave!   Wan ariseth now
> O'er the deep a mountain-down;[1]   darkening on its track
> Follows on another   with all ocean blended.
> Till they (now commingled),   near the mark of land and sea
> Meet the lofty linches.[2]   Loud is then the Sea-wood,
> Loud the seamen's shout.[3]   But the stony cliffs,
> Rising steep, in stillness wait   of the sea the onset;
> Battle-whirl of billows,   when the high upbreak of water
> Crashes on the cliffs.   In the keel is dread expecting[4]

> Circum claustra fremunt. . . .
> Sed Pater omnipotens speluncis abdidit atris
> Hoc metuens, molemque et montes insuper altos
> Imposuit. . . .   *Æneid* i. 56.

There are many phrases in Cynewulf's poetry which lead me to think that he was not unacquainted with Virgil. See the next note.

[1] *Insequitur cumulo præruptus aquae mons.* *Wan* is of course "black."
[2] *Hlincas* ("linches, *i.e.* the cliffs"). See Halliwell and Skeat. Dictionaries.
[3] *Insequitur clamorque virûm stridorque rudentum.*
[4] This is an extremely difficult passage, and I have varied considerably from

With despairing striving, lest the sea should bear it
Full of living ghosts on to that grim hour (of death) ;[1]
So that of its steering power[2] it should be bereft ;
And of living crew forfoughten,[3] foaming drift away
On the shoulders of the surges. Then is shown to men
Many of the terrors there of Those I must obey—
I upon the storm-path strong ! Who makes that be still ?

Now follows the way of the tempest in the air, the war of the clouds, and then the terror upon earth—

36. Whiles I rush along thorough that which rides my back,
Vats of water black : wide asunder do I thrust them
Full of lakes of rain ; then again I let them
Glide together. Greatest that is of all sounds,
Of all tumults over towns, and of thunderings the loudest,
When one stormy shower rattles sharp against another,
Sword against a sword. See, the swarthy shapes,
Forward pressing o'er the peoples, sweat their fire forth ;
Flaring is the flashing ! Onward fare the thunders,
Gloomed, above the multitudes, with a mickle din ;
Fighting fling along ; and let fall adown
Swarthy sap of showers sounding[4] from their breast,
Waters from their womb. Waging war they go,
Grisly troop on troop ; Terror rises up !
Mickle is the misery 'mid the kin of men ;
In the burgs is panic when the phantom pale
Shoots with his sharp weapons, stalking (through the sky).
Then the dullard does not dread him of the deadly spears ;
Nathless shall he surely die, if the soothfast Lord
Right against him, through the rain-cloud,
From the upper thunder, let the arrow fly—
Dart that fareth fast ! Few are they that 'scape
Whom the spear doth strike of the Spirit of the rain.
I beginning make of this gruesome war

---

other translators. *Slidre sæcce*—" with slippery (Grein makes it 'dangerous'), with feeble striving "—may, I think, mean what I make it, with a hapless, ill-fortuned, and therefore a despairing strife against the elements. Some are paralysed in expectation, some struggle ; *that* is, I think, the meaning.

[1] *On þá grimman tíd* may, of course, mean " in that grim hour ; " but I think it alludes to the moment in which the ship would be driven on the cliffs.

[2] Is *Ríce* from *rien* (" direction ") ? Did Cynewulf see the steering oar whirled from the hands of the steersman, or does he mean that the ship was driven out of its true course ?

[3] *Bifohten*. The verb *bi-feohtan* means to deprive one of anything by fighting. The ship was deprived of its living souls by the war of the wind and sea with it.

[4] I should like to have in English the German word *summen*, which answers here to *sumsend*, and translate this *sümming*. " Sounding " does not give the humming hiss of the rain.

> When 1 rush on high   'mid the roaring shock of clouds,
> Through their thundering throng to press   with a triumph great,
> O'er the breast of torrents![1]   Bursts out with a roar
> The high congregated cloud-band.[2]
>   Then my crest again I bow,
> Low the Lift-helm under,   to the land anearer;
> And I heap upon my back   that I have to bear,
> By the might commanded   of my mastering Lord.

And now he ends with a passage which, with a fine art, collects together all the action of the Tempest, and brings it back to its cavern, having had a great joy, in obedient quiet—

> 67. So do I, a strongful servant,   often strive in war!
> Sometimes under earth am I;   then again I must
> Stoop beneath the surges deep;   then above the surface-sea
> Stir to storm its streams.   Then I soar on high,
> Whirl the wind-drift of the clouds.   Far and wide I go,
> Swift and strong (for joy).   Say what I am called,
> Or who lifts me up to life,   when I may no longer rest;
> Or who it is that stays me,   when I'm still again.

Such was the way a great Northern gale impressed a Northern poet who had dwelt by the sea, and who himself, as I believe, had gone down into the sea in ships and battled with the storm.

---

[1] The word I here translate torrents is *byrnan* ("of burns or brooks"). Torrents is quite fair, for the word is connected with *byrnan* ("to burn"). The upsurging and boiling of fire is attributed to the fountain and stream. Cynewulf is not thinking of the quiet brooks of the land, but of the furious leaping rivers which he conceives as hidden in the storm clouds over which the storm giant passes on his way.

[2] *Hlod-geerod. Hlod* is the name given to a "band of robbers from seven to thirty-five," hence any troop or band of men. *Geerod* is "a crowd," "a multitude." Thus compounded the word means, I think, a crowd made up of troops; of troops of clouds! Then the word "high" put with *hlod-geerod* and the context prove sufficiently that Cynewulf was thinking of the piled-up clouds of the storm; and no doubt the notion of ravaging and slaughter connected with *Hlod* pleased his imagination, for his Tempest is a Destroyer.

I quote the line from Shelley which suggested my use of the word "congregated." The two lines which follow may also be compared with the previous passage (ll. 42-48)—

> Vaulted with all thy congregated might
> Of vapours, from whose solid atmosphere
> Black rain, and fire and hail will burst. O, hear!

Compare also—

> The triumphal arch through which I march
> With hurricane, fire, and snow.

The passages, out of the *Elene* and the *Christ*, with which I close this chapter, and which we are certain Cynewulf wrote, not only go far to prove that their writer was the writer of this fourth riddle, so closely do they parallel it, but are also examples of the symbolic use of the sea and the storm in Christian illustration; of the use by the poet in his old age of the wonderful things he had observed when young.[1] The first, like the passage in the Riddle, thinks of the giant wind pressed down in his cavern, and perhaps of the mythic wild-hunt in the clouds—

> Wealth below the sky shall fail; all the splendour of the land
> 'Neath the welkin vanisheth; to the Wind most like
> When he, over heroes, high and loudly mounts the sky;
> Through the clouds he hunts, hurries, raging on;
> Then, upon a sudden, silent is again,
> In his prison cave narrowly pressed down,
> Overwhelmed with woes. *Elene*, l. 1269.

The last I give is full of personal interest, of an old man's remembrance of his sea-voyages; of his troubles like the troubles of the world's stormy sea, of gratitude to God who piloted his bark to the haven where he would be, of longing such as age may have for the fulness of his rest—

> Mickle is our need
> That in this unfruitful time, ere that fearful Dread,
> On our spirits' fairness we should studiously bethink us!
> Now most like it is as if we on lake of ocean,
> O'er the water cold, in our keels are sailing,

---

[1] It has been said that elaborate similes are not to be found in Anglo-Saxon poetry. It should be understood that the remark only applies to the earlier poetry. Cynewulf uses a number, of which the two above are examples. There are many more in his work. There is one also in the *Genesis*, but its age is doubtful. I give here another which belongs to the subject of this chapter, and which is to be found in the *Gnomic Verses*. I daresay it is of the ninth century—

> As the sea is smooth,
> When the wind waketh it not,
> So are the people at peace, when they have settled their strife!
> In happy state they sit, and then, with comrades, hold,
> Brave men, their native land. *Gn. V.* (Exon.) l. 55.

```
    And through spacious sea,      with our stallions of the Sound,
    Forward drive the flood-wood.     Fearful is the stream
    Of immeasurable surges       that we sail on here,
    Through this wavering world,      through these windy oceans,
    O'er the path profound.     Perilous our state of life
    Ere that we had sailed (our ship)     to the shore (at last),
    O'er the rough sea-ridges.      Then there reached us help,
    That to hithe of Healing       homeward led us on—
    He the Spirit-Son of God!      And he dealt us grace,
    So that we should be aware,      from the vessel's deck,
    Where our stallions of the sea     we might stay with ropes,
    Fast a-riding by their anchors—     ancient horses of the waves!
    Let us in that haven then     all our hope establish,
    Which the ruler of the Æther      there has roomed for us,
    When He climbed to Heaven—      Holy in the Highest!
                                                         Christ, l. 848.
```

To compare these lines, written when Cynewulf was advanced in years, with the poem of the *Hurricane*, written when he was young, has more than a transient interest. And no artist can read both at the same time without having a higher pleasure than the ordinary reader. He will feel the same personality in both, but working, with how different a life behind the poetry, with how different an impulse; in how different a fashion and from how changed a character! Youth, moved out of itself by Nature, and looking neither before nor after, is in the earlier poem. The passion in it is untouched by the weight of the sorrows or duties of manhood, or by the sense of sin and the cry for redemption. These pains and burdens, on the contrary, as well as the soul wrapt in self-consciousness, are present in the later verses. Such a contrast makes Cynewulf real to us; and the change—I will not call it artistic progress, though at certain points it is so—does at least enable us to say, This man was an artist.

CHAPTER XI

CHRISTIANITY AND LITERATURE

THE matters of which we have treated in the three previous chapters do not belong especially either to heathenism or Christianity. They may rather be called secular. All that had to do with the affairs of arms was as much heathen as Christian; and the same may be said with regard to the greater part of the poetry quoted to illustrate the daily life of our forefathers. We cannot altogether say this when we consider the poetry of natural description. I do not think that the remarkable descriptions of the sea and its storms and of various aspects of nature could have been written by the heathen English. The temper of these poems is not at all the old Teutonic temper. They are too contemplative for English heathendom. Nevertheless some of their spirit goes back to other heathendoms than the Teutonic, and goes back through the advent of Christianity. It was the Celtic missionaries who evangelised Northumbria, and through them the Celtic feeling for nature was imported into English poetry. Along with this, Latin Christianity brought with it Roman poetry, and Virgil and Ovid gave to the Northumbrian poets a fresh and kindling impulse to the observation and love of Nature.

Beyond these impulses, however, the coming of Christianity poured into the river of the English imagination a multitude of new tributary streams, enlarged its waters, enriched its constituents, purified, mellowed, and deepened it. It did more; these new streams were of various elements, and though, at first, they did not isolate themselves into distinct currents, yet, as time went on, and they assimilated what was necessary for their separate existence, they became self-conscious streams of poetry within the general stream. What Christianity thus did for literature, what it modified of the past, what it originated for the future, what powers it added to that emotional life from which poetry urges itself upwards into form, what it weakened and strengthened, restricted and enlarged, is the subject of this and the following chapter.

When we consider Christianity in contact with those heathen elements, so many of which, as pregnant motives of poetry, have continued in our literature, the first thing to be said is that, owing to the manner in which Christianity was propagated in England, it did not root out heathen ideas so much as change them. Its growth was left to the will of the people; to persuasion and not to force. The sword had no part, as on the Continent, as among the Northmen, in the evangelising of England. In no modern land that Jesus won was his conquest so gentle, so marked by tolerance and good sense. Hence Christianity was subject for a long time to interruptions and reactions. For nearly eighty years the heathen and Christian faiths were in close contact, and each preserved its freedom of development. The old battle songs were sung side by side with the Christian hymns, the sagas of the English heroes with the saga of Christ; the Christian Church, on the hill or by the river, saw during a varying term of years, and without any fierce religious fury, the heathen temple in the neighbouring grove. There was a long mingling then, in a peaceful fashion, of Christian and heathen thought; and through the mingling ran a special temper of tolerance and wisdom and good-breeding. These two things, both of which were vital influences on English literature, are best illustrated by a brief but necessary account of the various changes which marked the conversion of England.

It was in the year 597 that Augustine brought the gospel to Kent, and King Æthelberht (partly prepared by his wife) listened to it graciously. A speech of his, which Erasmus might have fathered, strikes the keynote of the manner in which Christianity was spread in England by the kings, and indeed by the bishops.[1] "Your words," said Æthelberht, "and promises sound very good to me, but they are new to us, and of uncertain meaning; I cannot so far yield to them as to abandon all that I and the whole English people have for so long observed. But since you are strangers and have come from a far land, and desire to tell us what you hold to be true and good, we will do you no harm, but will give you food and a place to dwell in, and you

---

[1] There were but few exceptions. Episcopal violence seems to have been retained between Christian and Christian, not between Christian and heathen. Augustine was gentle enough, though he was a vain man, with Æthelberht and the Kentish heathen, but his manners with the Welsh monks were not of the same type. But then the Welsh were Christians, not heathen, and they were not in harmony with Rome. It would not have been politic for Augustine to have anything to do with the Welsh. It was more easy for Rome to be tolerant to ignorant heathen than to Christians who differed from her formulae. And the keeping of Easter at a different date from Rome was a very serious thing; it touched the headship of Rome. Even Baeda seems to lose his temper over it.

may speak to my people and win over as many as you can to your belief"; which things he did, and was himself shortly afterwards, with many of his people, baptized. But he "compelled none to embrace the faith," so that many still remained heathen.

In 604 the East Saxons, under Saeberht, Æthelberht's nephew, were converted, and Æthelberht founded St. Paul's in London for his nephew. Eadbald, son of Æthelberht, became King of the Kentishmen in 616. He had refused to receive the faith of Christ. Even when he became Christian, he was unable to take any strong measures against idolatry (*E. H.*, ii. 6); and I think it possible that Kent in a large measure relapsed. It is plain that London went back into heathendom when Saeberht died. His three sons were all pagans, and the wild disturbance they made in the church—crying out to the bishop who was administering the Eucharist, "Why not give us the white bread you gave to our father?" —illustrates how close the English world was then to Paganism, how little the fear of Rome was in their hearts.

When we travel North we find much the same wavering state of things. Eadwine of Deira was baptized, 12th April 627, with all his people, by Paullinus. When he died in 633, a whole year passed by before Oswald came to the throne and Northumbria slipped back into heathenism, but after Oswald's accession the conversion of the country went on steadily. Paullinus, it is true, had fled, but Oswald sent messengers to the elders of the Scots who had baptized him when in exile, and Aidan descended from Iona to teach Northumbria. At Lindisfarne his bishop's seat was set, and from that desolate rock he and his successors evangelised Northumbria;[1] but in all the wilder and more inaccessible parts the people long continued heathen. Meanwhile the half-and-half condition of England can be further illustrated by the story of Raedwald. Raedwald, who was King of East Anglia till about 627, had become a Christian in Kent, but on his return home his wife seduced him back to heathenism. Nevertheless he made the best of both worlds; for he set up two altars in the same temple, one to Christ and another to his gods. One of Baeda's contemporaries had seen these altars when he was a boy. His son Eorpwald became a Christian, but was slain by a pagan, under whom the province was again heathen for three years. Then Sigeberht came to the throne, who, having embraced the Christian faith in Gaul and become a man of learning, made all East Anglia Christian in the years between 631-634.

In 635 the West Saxons, who were confirmed pagans, received the faith in the person of Cynegils their king, under the influence and in the presence of Oswald, who took the West Saxon "to son" at Dorchester, a town which for about forty years was the ecclesiastical centre of Wessex. His son Coenwalch was still a heathen on his accession in 643, but three years later was baptized. He is the traditionary founder of the great church at Winchester, a town which in after years was the cradle of English prose; and he secured Glastonbury for England with all its venerable traditions and its names so dear to after literature. In the meantime, Kent, under Earcomberht,

---

[1] They went also through other parts of England before the Synod of Whitby, but their chief work was in the North; and it must always be remembered, as one of the causes of certain elements in the Anglo-Saxon poetry of Northumbria, that the religion of the North—that is, the greatest source of popular emotion—came to the people through the Celtic character.

son of Eadbald, had become altogether Christian. This king, succeeding his father in 640, uprooted heathenism. It took then forty-three years to make Kent, where the faith was first preached, completely Christian.

In 653 the East Saxons, who had relapsed under those three stormy young men, were brought back to the faith by Sigeberht and by the preaching of Cedda ; but a pestilence breaking out among them in 665, a great number of them restored the old temples, but were reconverted—an unstable and fierce folk—within the year. Five years, then, before Caedmon wrote, heathenism had not been forgotten. This becomes still plainer when we think of the state of Mercia during this time. Penda, king of that province, came into lordship over it in 626. From that date till 655, when he was slain, he fought with stern consistency for the faith of his fathers—the terror and the admiration of Middle and Northern England. The wars he urged were, however, more political than religious. No persuasion could change his faith, but he ceased to persecute the Christians. He did not even prevent the preaching of their faith. He contented himself with sneering at those Christians who did not live up to the commandments of their God. His son Peada, whom he made viceroy of the Middle Angles, became Christian in 653 and introduced four Northumbrian priests into his province. Penda did not stand in the way, but I cannot help feeling that the old heathen suffered sorely when he felt his strife had been in vain. Two years after he was slain near Winwaed, and on his death all Mercia became Christian. Nine years later (664)—a date always to be remembered—the whole of Christian England came, after the Synod of

Whitby, into the Roman observance of Easter. The short career of Celtic Christianity closed. It had lasted from 635—a period of twenty-nine years—and its spirit continued a little longer in the persons of those bishops and priests of its race who, choosing to stay when the others went back to Scotland, retained their charges and conformed to the Roman custom. Five years later (in 669-671) Theodore of Tarsus and Hadrian of Africa came from Rome to England, the first to be Archbishop of Canterbury, the second as his sub-deacon. These two not only brought Greek learning to England; they also began Latin-English literature in the south, and we shall discuss their work in its proper place. All we have to say here is that with the arrival of Roman and Greek literature in England any future development of purely heathen poetry received its deathblow; and that this blow was given over the whole of England—for Theodore, before he died in 690, had welded all England into one spiritual kingdom, in one National Church, under one form of belief and practice. Now, when the Church was one, one spirit began to pervade all literature. Yet it was not till within four years of his death that we can say that all England was Christian. In 681 the South Saxons were still heathen to the number of seven thousand families, though their king and some of his comrades had been baptized. These were now delivered by the preaching of Wilfrid from the "wretchedness of eternal damnation." One small space of land yet existed in darkness—the Isle of Wight, a colony of Jutes. It was conquered in 686 by Caedwalla of Wessex, and he handed the place over to Wilfrid for evangelisation. That, then, is the date in which the long strife, which had begun in 597,

between Christianity and heathenism, finally closed in
England. It closed among all the upper classes, but
among the small farmers and labourers in the remote
parts of the country, in hamlets of the woods and
moors, heathenism for a long time retained its influence.[1] For a still longer time heathenism and
Christianity intermingled. Many men, like the bards,
lived, I think, in both worlds; the rites and beliefs of
either religion took one another's clothing; the people
reverted to heathen practices and then back again to
Christian in times of trouble; the laws right up to
the time of Cnut are still "forbidding heathendom,
the worship of heathen gods, of sun and moon, rivers
and wells, fire, stones, and trees."

This account fully confirms the long contemporary existence of Christian and heathen elements;
and during their mutual ebb and flow there was a
continual mingling and interpenetration of Christian
and heathen legend, of Christian and heathen poetry
which had its influence on literature. The two worlds
of song met and knew one another. Heathen ideas
and expressions entered into Christian poetry, and it
is possible that the heathen sagas and lays were penetrated by some of the Christian gentleness. We cannot say how much of this interpenetration was left
behind in the whole body of popular poetry of which
we have no record, nor how much has filtered down to
us. At least, as I shall proceed to show, the whole

---

[1] Baeda tells, in his *Life of Cuthbert*, chap. iii., how, when the boats bringing wood to the monastery near the mouth of the Tyne were swept out to sea,
and the monks tried in vain to rescue them, the multitude of country folk who
stood on the shore mocked the servants of God,— they deserved, they said, to suf-
fer this loss, since they had left off the old ways of life. Cuthbert reproved them,
and they answered angrily, "Nobody shall pray for them; may God spare none
of them; they have taken away from men the ancient rites and customs, and how
the new ones are to be attended to, nobody knows." If this could be said at
Tynemouth, what must have been said far inland in the wilder parts?

body of popular thought and feeling, out of which the unwritten poetry of the emotions arises before it is shaped into a written form, was filled with the interwoven ideas of Christianity and heathendom.

It would have been a pity, in the interests of Literature, if the romantic elements of the old heathendom, especially those which arose out of the personification of the savage or gentle forms of the life of Nature, had been blotted out by Christianity. To have wholly lost the image of the dark, relentless, and all-compelling Wyrd would have weakened the root of imaginative poetry. To be no longer able to see the sun hasting up the sky like an eager youth, or the moon building her treasure-house in the topmost Burg of Heaven, to hear no more the rustling sound—*daegred-woma*,—the "thrill of Nature which precedes the dawn," to fear or cajole no more the beings who moved in the storm cloud or drove the waves, the creatures who dwelt in streams or trees, in wells, among the gray stones of the moor, in the mist, and the secret places of the waters—would have drained dry the river of the love and awe of living Nature, which, long flowing only among the uneducated people, has, at last, in these later days, risen to the surface even of society, and still moves forward a fuller and a fuller stream in the Poetry of England. Our modern passion for a soul in Nature is a recurrence to the original heathen type. Myth incessantly revives in the poetry of Nature, and the greater its recurrence the better is that kind of poetry. In England these romantic, mythical elements were, I think, preserved in better form than elsewhere. The long intermingling, the soft interchange of heathenism and Christianity did not exile the captured deities, or utterly destroy the old habits of worship, but took them into service, gave them new names, and clothed them in Christian garments. The great Nature-festivals of the heathen, Yule and Eostra-tide, were now bound up with the birth and resurrection of Jesus Christ. The festival of Midsummer lasts in many Christian observances. New Christian feasts were made to fall on heathen holidays. A great part, then, of the emotions of the past, of the pleasant rustic joy, of the ancient poetic imaginations was retained in the new religion, and made more permanent by the Celtic spirit in that religion. Being retained, it became a continuous power in national sentiment, and therefore in all our literature. Nor did the new Christianity let slip away the associations which belonged to the time-honoured religious customs. The Church was built where the heathen temple had been, and the people walked to the shrine of Christ by the same well-worn path by which they had sought the sacred enclosure of the god. Where the consecrated tree had stood rose now the Holy Rood. The groves, devoted to the Nature-god, became the groves of the convent. The hills, the clear wells, the eyots in the river which had been dedicated to heathen deities of flood and field, were now called after the saints and martyrs; and the old emotions were retained unimpaired, though the names were changed. The minor gods and heroes which the various wants of men had created to preside over and to satisfy those wants were replaced by saints who did precisely the same work. The personages were different, but the Polytheism, with all its romance, remained. Even the nature myths were often continued in the legends of the saints. Moreover, "laws and usages," says Grimm, "ordeals and oath-takings, beating of bounds, consecrations, image processions, spells and formulas were clothed in Christian forms, but their heathen character endured. The old was interwoven with the new." Thus Christian stuff was heathenised, heathen stuff was Christianised.

Again, what was gracious and beneficent in the doings of the heathen gods was kept in the Christian thought, but it was now done, not by Frea (if the earliest English worshipped Frea), or by goddesses who were kind to men, but by Jesus Christ and the Virgin. On the other hand, the dark and dreadful elements of Nature, personified in giant and monster, were not lost as poetry, but added to the conceptions of the devil and his harmful host, among whom were now included the Elves, the wood creatures, and the dwarfs; even all the gentle beings who, in old days, wished well to man, and who afterwards emerged from this devilish connection into the kindly and tricksome fairies. The Church grew sharper against the gentlehood of heathendom as time went on. Up to about 800 A.D. piety was, however, not importunate. But after that time the ancient and nobler ancestor deities, in order to destroy their moral character, were all, by means of the transference of their attributes to the devil, made hideous or absurd. Yet, though their moral character was destroyed, what was poetic in their history lived on in legends, or, in a better way, in a number of fantastic words and images in common use among the people.

Another form of transference is seen in the case of the most widespread of the heathen myths. The war of Day and Night, the still greater war of Summer and Winter, of the radiant Sunny-Gods and the Frost-Giants, of the healing and harmful powers of

Nature—that war, which is one of the ever-during roots of poetry, became now, in varied forms, the war between Christ and Satan, between eternal Light and eternal Darkness, between the Church and Heathenism, between the Saint and his Tempter, between God in the Universe and the old Dragon who claimed the dominion over Earth and Air,—but whatever shape the changes took, the original spirit of the myth is preserved. Its poetry—the poetry of a fierce, adventurous, unending war, various as are the fates and characters of men, shared in by all the spiritual powers beyond our world, a battle in which Earth, Heaven and Hell were mingled—the mightiest Epic the wit and passion of men have ever conceived—was not made less but more imaginative by Christianity; and the range of the subject was extended. In this world-wide war which transcended the local wars of tribe with tribe and kingdom with kingdom, Jesus was the King, his Apostles were the King's thegns, and so were all the saints and martyrs, nay, every one who fought against the Dragon. Satan is the great foe whose seat is in the North before he falls into Hell. Hell is the dark-Burg which Christ attacks, Heaven the light-Burg to which he returns in victory. The supper of the Lamb is laid for his warriors in the great hall, amid the singing of the Angels who are the poets of the battle. When the Apostles are celebrated, as they are in a poem in the Vercelli book, they are heroes who go forth to war and their work is told as if it were a Viking expedition. "Great proof of valour gave these Æthelings; far spread the might and glory of the King's thegns over the earth. Bold in war was Andreas; not tardy was James, nor a laggard on the journey. Daring was the adventure of Thomas in India; he endured the rush of swords." Simon and Thaddeus, "warriors brave in battle, valiantly sought the Persian land; not slow were they in the fight, in the play of shields." Andrew in the *Andreas* is "the hero stout in battle, the steadfast champion," even the "beast of battle" (*hilde-deor*), "the hero hard in war." These are a few expressions out of many in which the heathen terms of war are transferred to the apostolic soldiers of Jesus. Round about them are collected their thegns, those who accompany them on missions; and all the devotion which tied the thegn to his lord in heathen war, all the disgrace which befell the thegn who was unfaithful, are transferred to the relation of the Apostles to Christ, and of their followers to the Apostle and the Saint. Nor was the war only in the present or the future, nor only since the time of Christ. All the past since the beginning of the world was filled with it. David, Moses, Noah, Adam replaced the English demigods, and were their national heroes. A trace of this is found in the genealogy of Æthelwulf as given in the *Chronicle*. He is brought back from Woden to Sceaf, and Sceaf is the son of Noah, born in the Ark, and Noah carries the line back to Adam; that is, the patriarchs become one with the ancestral heroes. Even before time, when man was not, this war that filled their imagination had prevailed, and the battle in Heaven of Christ with Satan is described in Caedmonic poems in much the same terms as the contest of Beowulf with Grendel. Thus little of the imaginative passion of war was lost to the Christian Englishman, and nothing of the worship of heroic and divine ancestors. The field open to their warlike imagination was doubly expanded; nor was it only the noble or the freeman who could join in this fight and find fame in it, but all men and all women, no matter how common their position or enslaved their work.

The central point of the war was the victory of Jesus, and round this, as well as the final finish of the war in the second coming of the King, the force of the poetry collected. Only one other point was as poetical. It was the beginning of the war in Heaven, at the time of the creation of man. That beginning is treated, as we shall see, in the *Genesis*. The victory of Christ and the Judgment are best done by Cynewulf. The Incarnation and the Crucifixion are fully treated but the Resurrection is scarcely touched in Anglo-Saxon poetry. That which more attracted English imagination was the Harrowing of Hell, the legendary event that followed the Resurrection,—and this, with the return in triumph to the heavenly home, is described in images such as belonged to heathen war and victory. In a similar saga fashion the end of the war is described—the Doomsday—the final overthrow of evil, the final victory of righteousness.

The change, then, retained a good deal of the old poetic elements. Nevertheless there was also a loss; much perished which we would gladly have kept. While, however, we mourn the loss, there was also an equivalent gain. The poetry of the past drew its elements only from war, Nature-myths and ancestral heroism. The new poetry or the new poetic feeling drew its elements from the whole of human life, entered into all the outgoings of the human heart, found its subjects in the common doings of daily life. Christianity made all the life of every man and woman interesting and impassioned from the cradle to the grave. No one can read the *Ecclesiastical History* of Baeda without seeing the truth of this statement. The book, in all its stories, is steeped in poetic feeling. Religion, with its ideals, laid its hands of awe or of love on men from the king to the slave, and on all their relations one to another. It made a country of which all were citizens by right; it made a society which knit together all classes into a union in which the various kingdoms of England dissolved their differences and their wars. It brought together all men in one relation; it filled those doings of life which were common to all with one spirit. In this fashion it expanded the whole world of feeling, and though I cannot say that all these new elements were actually worked out in Anglo-Saxon literature, yet the new acre of poetic work was ploughed and sown, and the seed was afterwards to grow into a great harvest.

The Cross was, at first, set up in every village, on every noble's estate. At its foot the missionary stood —the preacher from the Bishop's house or from the monastery — and said mass and baptized and married and recited prayers for the dead. Later on, when Theodore had established a priest in every township or bundle of townships,[1] each of these had its Church, and around it clustered all the main interests and emotions of humanity. The dead were no longer burned, but laid together in the acre of God. The wife and the husband began their mutual life within the walls of the Church; the children were baptized inside its porch. The people maintained it by their offerings, the affairs

---

[1] See Stubbs' *Constit. Hist.* vol. i. p. 227.

of the township were discussed and ordered in its yard, at least wherever the Church occupied the place where the folk-moot had been held. Thus that association of religion with all that was peaceful, with all the beloved emotions of common human life, began, which has formed one of the great motives of poetry. Peace and its powers were made poetical. We have seen how Cynewulf was not ashamed to sing of all the doings of the farm, of the merchant's life upon the sea, of the green grass and the singing birds. Other subjects were also disclosed. The solitary life of the hermit, the victory of the martyr over earthly force, the triumph over temptation, the abjuring of revenge, the sacrifice of this world for the world to come, the conquest won by faith and not by arms, the little children who died for Jesus, the virgin life, the surrender of wealth and fame for the sake of civilising men—all these were a new world; and it was the larger humanity in Christianity which opened it to those who sang, and to those who listened to and loved the singing. The range of poetry was indefinitely extended.

Other figures also than those of men now passed over the scene, and they were not only great queens or stormy-hearted women, but lowlier and gentler creatures of the imagination. Woman took an equal place with man in poetry, and the attributes which ennobled her were changed, at least were modified. The sweet and tender grace, the humility and loving-kindness of the Virgin, her maidenhood, her motherhood, became the most vivid and beautiful image that filled the minds of men after the image of Christ. More than half of the beginning of Cynewulf's *Christ* is dedicated to her exalting. The saintly women who in the days of martyrdom kept their chastity against the tyranny of men and the threats of the Demon, like Juliana whom Cynewulf sang, passed, like the ancient goddesses who brought peace and protection to the faithful wife and the good spinner, from land to land and became dear to every household. When the shepherd, Eoves, in Bishop Ecgwine's legend, told that he saw in a forest glade fair women singing a magic song and thought them, perhaps, heathen haunters of the forest land, the Bishop saw in them a vision of the Virgin Mother and angels, and in the spot where they had sung rose the Abbey of Evesham. It was no longer Choosers of the slaughter or Elf-women that rode in the air and shot deadly spears; but figures of excelling beauty, clothed in light, singing softly, took their place—the Angels of God, whom Caedmon exalts and Cynewulf is unwearied in praising, who brighten the pages of Baeda from legend to legend, whose songs are not of war but of spiritual peace, and who receive the warriors of Christ into the heavenly Hall and to the heavenly banquet. The relations of women to men, which we have seen honoured in *Beowulf*, and which played so large a part in English policy and war while England was yet heathen, received a fresh dignity in Christianity; and this new source of emotion produced many a poetic story. It increased the material of literature. The double monasteries, which afterwards became the cause of scandal, were, while they kept their first purity, the cause of tender and beautiful friendships between grave men and holy women. The relations of Hild and Aidan, of Cuthbert and Ælfleda, of Cuthbert and Verca, of Ealdhelm and the virgins whose praise he wrote and to whom his letters are so gay, of

Boniface and the nuns who wrote to him so lovingly, were charming, full of grace and poetry, though when the men were not Cuthbert and Aidan similar relationships soon degenerated. The great Abbesses were great folk in Northumbria. Heiu, who founded Hartlepool, was noble, so was Verca of Tynemouth. Hild, whom we know, and Ebba, whose monastery at Coldingham, seated on its lofty cape, rivalled its sister of Whitby; Ætheldreda who, amidst the rushy fens, founded Ely on its emerald isle; Ælfleda, as patriotic as religious, who finally brought peace to Wilfrid,[1]— were all princesses, powers in the state, with whom kings and bishops had to count, whose advice was taken in great movements, and whose lives, and all the legends which the emotion of the people for noble womanhood collected round them, became for centuries the material for ballad and song; but more especially for that silent literature which is, as it were, the background of the literature which is written—the popular emotion, the feelings of the mother and father and child in hamlet and town, the memories and prayers in times of distress and joy, which come together, like doves to their dwelling, to the names of the women who have consoled or exalted the world.

These are the main lines of the changes wrought by Christianity in that inner life of imagination and sentiment which collected round the gods and their worship. Other changes which we may allot to the realm of history, rather than to that of literature, will be found in other books. I turn now to changes of another

---

[1] There were many other of these royal and noble abbesses in Mercia and Wessex, as well as in Northumbria and those who would like to read their legends, and to judge of the far-spread influence these had on the imaginative material of literature, will find an enthusiastic account of them, written with a strong monastic bias, in the fifth volume of Montalembert's *Monks of the West*.

kind, to those which belong to that grave and moral view of life which was as steady in the English character in the days before, as in the days after Christianity. There is a picture of this temper of mind in Baeda as well as of the more worldly and gayer temper which in contrast it often creates—even in the same person, a point continually made in *Hamlet*—and the picture belongs to the heathen time and heathen men. This picture is well known, but, even if I did not need it as an illustration of literary matters, it is in itself worth quoting as a piece of noble literature, done with simplicity of touch and delicacy of outline. Each character stands clear, and indeed there were men alive when Baeda wrote it who had seen Paullinus and Eadwine; and were, likely enough, at the meeting he describes.

When, then, we read this story of the year 627, we look, almost with the eyes of one present in the hall, into the judicial thoughtfulness and dignified seriousness of our heathen fathers. In the long-continued consideration Eadwine gave to the question of a change of religion we have that very temper which, in our poets, prevented English verse from being overwhelmed by the *esprit gaulois*. When we listen to the speech of the ealdorman, we have in it one of the motives of that graver poetry which, amid war-lays and stories, existed among the English before Christianity. On the other hand, the scene contains some new elements which were soon to influence English literature. When we look on the aspect of Paullinus and listen to his solemn question to the king, the religious awe which accompanied Rome, the dignity of her great age and yet her undiminished power, the emotion which grew solemn and enthusiastic round the Church as the

Voice of God on earth, are placed before us; and we are compelled to estimate the immense force these new feelings were destined to have in literature. The very aspect of Paullinus is representative of the keenness and power of the intellect of Rome. A personal description, taken by Baeda from the lips of one who had seen him face to face, brings the Latin monk before us. He was "tall of stature, stooping, however, a little. His hair was black, his eyes vivid, his face thin, his nose slender and aquiline, and his air majestic and venerable." It was he who had initiated the scene we are about to describe; for one day he entered the room where Eadwine sat alone, seriously pondering what religion he was to follow, as was his custom for hours together—and, laying his hand on the head of the king, asked him if he knew that sign. Then Eadwine, remembering a vision which had come to him (*Eccles. Hist.* bk. ii. ch. xii.), trembled, and said he would confer with his friends and redesmen. Whereat he called them together in his hall with the doors open east and west. To complete the scenery of the event, we must remember that it takes place in the country, in some rural seat of the king, near a knoll where stood a sacred grove enclosed with a low hedge, and in the shady centre of which was the tree round or near which the wattled Temple was built, and on which was fastened the symbol of the gods to whom the place was dedicated.

Near this grove, in the spring-time, the *witenagemôt* was held by Eadwine which made Northumbria Christian, and two well-marked types of Englishmen are vividly drawn for us in the narrative. The first is that of the grave and experienced Thegn—like the old warrior in Hrothgar's hall who remembered the many questions he had asked in life,—and his speech is entirely contradictory of the traditional notion of a heathen Englishman. "The present life of man," he said, "seems to me, O king, when we put it side by side in thought with the life which is unknown to us, like the quick flight of a sparrow through the hall when you sit at supper in the winter-tide, with your Aldermen and Thegns, when a good fire is burning in the midst upon the hearth, but without are the storms of rain and snow. Then the sparrow, flying in at one door and immediately out at another, is safe from the wintry tempest as long as he is within; but after this short tide of pleasant weather he vanishes out of your sight into the dark winter whence he had come. So is it with the life of man. It is seen only for a moment, but of what went before it and of what cometh after it we know nothing at all. If, therefore, this new teaching tells us anything more sure concerning it, it seems to be right to follow its law." No Roman or Greek of the dignified time could have expressed himself better or with a milder wisdom, and Baeda thinks it was by a divine inspiration that he and the others spoke on this matter.

This king then who sits wrapt up in musing for hours together at a crisis—as much political as religious in the history of his people—this grave assembly of warriors, considering and speaking with poetic and anxious thought concerning the change of their religion —are heathens of the seventh century—and bear no resemblance whatever to the conventional portrait of the English chieftain and his folk that some historians are so fond of painting.

As interesting, and just as modern as the Ealdorman, is the character of the priest Coifi—a type of man who was sure to have made in hall many bold songs. Baeda's sketch of him is itself a piece of English literature. Coifi is the chief of the king's priests. He is the sceptic who has always had his doubts about the gods, who, if he serve them well, demands return from them like Jacob; who has no fear of them and counts his own individuality, like many a Norseman, to be as strong as any god. A rough gay humour, which we scarcely ever find among the English Christians, a sturdy eye, also like Jacob, to the main chance, belong to his character. He also is a clear-hewn type; but he, too, is a gentleman. He is asked, first of all, what he thinks of changing the religion of the kingdom. "O king," he answers, "the religion we have had up to this time has no virtue in it. Not one of your folk has been more diligent than I in the worship of our gods, and yet there are many who receive greater favours from you, and are better off than I. Now, if the gods were good for anything, they would rather forward me who have been so careful to serve them. It remains, therefore, if the new doctrine be likely to do more for us, that we immediately take it up."

Then, after listening to the old warrior's speech about life, he changes from this tone, which is that of the humorous man of the world, to a graver one. "I should like," he says, "to hear Paullinus;" and when he had heard him, he said, "I have long thought that all we worshipped was naught, for the more I sought for truth in that religion the less I found of it. But in this preaching I find the gift of life and happiness for ever. So my counsel is that we burn down those temples and altars which we hallowed of old, but out of which we have got no good." And when this bold speech was accepted, he declared that he himself would profane the temple, and seizing a spear and sword, and mounting a stallion—things unlawful for a priest to do—he rode straight to the sacred grove, and, casting his spear into the temple till it stuck in the opposite wall, commanded it to be burned with fire.[1] In place of the temple grew up, as usual, the Christian Church—the church of Godmundingham—and tradition said that in it was preserved the font in which Paullinus baptized Coifi.

The story illustrates the meeting of two faiths and the meeting of two literatures. It is plain that men like the king, the ealdorman and Coifi, would hold it their duty to propagate the new faith by the spreading of its hymns, but would not neglect their own ancient songs when they dealt with heroes, not with gods. The war-song then would last, but the worship-song would perish. Bishop and priest would not interfere with the first, but would passionately expunge the second. They would be helped by the remarkable, almost unique enthusiasm which, as we see from many a story in Baeda, the English kings and nobles showed for Christianity; and the result is that in no literature are the heathen gods so completely cleaned out as they are in Old English literature. But the other type—the heroic tales—continued. Ealdhelm may have sung them on the bridge, Ælfred had perhaps a book of them, and the story goes that his mother sang them. Part died, part survived, and when Christianity was securely established in England, an effort was made, I believe, in Northumbria, to recover a great deal of what

---

[1] O nimium tanti felix audacia facti,
Polluit ante alios, quas ipse sacraverat, aras.
    Alcuin, v. 186, *De Pont. Ebor.*

had been lost. While the victory of the new over the old is still doubtful, the old is hunted down; but when the kingdom of the new is firmly fixed, then the new rediscovers what was excellent in the old and often falls in love with it. I should not be surprised if that was the case in Northumbria in the eighth century, and that we owe to it the preservation of the heroic lays contained in *Beowulf*.

Now I use this scene, full as it is of the grave and serious temper of which I speak, to introduce and illustrate what I have now to say concerning the elements which, making that temper, appear in English literature, and of the change wrought in them by Christianity.

There was first the belief in the Wyrd—the goddess who presided over the fates of men, and who, as Englishmen thought, was mostly against them, so that their life was a heavy-weighted battle, and sorrow and weariness its chief companions. The Gallic lightness, the Italian contentment, were unattainable in the "welter of care" in which they lived. Wyrd was hard upon them, but her work nourished a steady fortitude in which they found a grim contentment. When England became Christian, this deep-rooted faith, though changed in form, continued. The very name of the goddess was kept. But God was now put above destiny. "The Wyrds change not God," says the Gnomic Verses. But for the most part Wyrd passed into God and was used to express the Deity. "The Wyrd is stronger, the Lord mightier, than any man's thought," is a phrase used in the *Seafarer*, and it might be matched in many of the Anglo-Saxon poems. Then the contest with the ills which Wyrd allots to man, in the noble doing and enduring of which honour was won, changes also its aspect. We have seen the spirit which met the Wyrd in *Beowulf*—

> So shall each of us, every-one abide the end
> Of the worldly life; let him win who may
> Honour ere he die! To the helmèd warriors,
> When their days are done, dearest afterwards is that.
> *Beowulf*, l. 1386.

A different note fills a parallel passage in the *Seafarer*—

> So to every earl this the laud from after speakers,
> This the laud from all the living, this the best of last words—
> "That he worked and wrought, ere he went his way
> On this earth with bold endeavour 'gainst the onset of the fiends
> With his deeds of daring, right down upon the devil."
> So his laud shall ever live among the angels.
> *Seafarer*, l. 72.

The sadness, then, of destiny still remains, but it is now met by the noble consolation of eternal holiness and peace in the world to come; and the temper of the best men and women, as represented in early English poetry, is that of Eadwine and the ealdorman, careful, sorrowful, of quiet thoughtfulness, but no longer grim. It is now mingled with faith and with a certain triumph of joy.

Again, among the old sorrows which continued in Christianity to brood over the English mind, none was deeper than the passing away of the splendour and mirth and fame of men. The note which we hear in the Prince's lay in *Beowulf* is repeated over and over again. It fills the *Rime Song* in later times; it is the subject of the *Wanderer*; it is imported into the *Seafarer*; it is the subject of many moral verses; it is the frequent wail of Cynewulf in the personal passages in his poems. Even Ælfred, full of work as he was, stays his practical advice to make this cry. But it is deepest in the North. It has intensity in the poems of the

Seafarer, the *Wanderer*. In the later poems of Cynewulf, its greater intensity is due, I conjecture, to their being written during the decay or the anarchy of Northumbria. At both periods men looked back on a time of splendour and peace from a time of disorder and destruction. Moreover, these passages are almost always put in the mouth of one who either suffers or has suffered exile; and the personal sorrows of a man who has lost his home and his country deepen the general regret.[1]

Mingled with this sorrow there was the common regret for the loss of youth, for the death of old companions, and for the solitude of an old man's life. The *Wanderer*, in a poem which is almost altogether heathen, thinks that he sees the troops of his ancient friends coming to meet him, and he welcomes them with joy; but they are but phantoms and they fleet away, and sorrow is renewed—

Then his mood goes moving on   through remembrance of his kinsmen,
Greets them with glee-staves—   gazes on them eagerly;
These societies of souls   swim away again.   l. 51.

All these heathen elements of grave sorrow were now changed or modified by the Christian hopes. Cynewulf, for example, feels, as he mourns for a ruined world, the same comfort which a Christian hand has added to the poem of the *Wanderer*. Crying to the Cross for help, he says with all the pathos of Vaughan and with much of his spirit, that few were the friends he had left on earth; that all the rest had gone from the joy of the world to live with the High

---

[1] It is remarkable that the Caedmonic poems are wholly free from this wailing note. Those portions of them, if any, which belong to the seventh century were written in a time of national pride; those of them which were written afterwards are supposed to belong to the time when Ælfred had won his day.

Father in his dwelling; but he waited the call from this fleeting life to unite himself to their pleasure.

It was this consolation which changed the whole tone with which the English, in their grave and serious hours, spoke of life, of its fates and sorrows, and it developed round it a new region of literature. Midst all the passing of the world, the changes and turbulence of war and fortune, one thing was steady. "Well is it for him," says the later epilogue to the *Wanderer*, "who seeks for the Father's grace, for comfort with the Father in Heaven, where the Fortress for us all stands sure." Nor was this the conclusion only of the monk. Baeda gives instance after instance of kings and nobles, weary of wars and change and policy, entering the monastic life to prepare for the better light. The legend of Ine and his queen does not stand alone, and it has enough truth in it to prove how deeply this new sense of the eternal strength and splendour of the world to come, in contrast with the passing of this world, had settled into the English mind. In that high land also were now dwelling all whom in life they had loved and whom they longed to rejoin. The tie between monk and monk, between anchorite and anchorite, between those who were soldiers in the service of Christ, had all the closeness and honour of the ancient bond of war-comradeship, and withal a deeper friendship. A passionate eternity was in it, and the dying looked to be received by those who had entered before them into the other life. Cuthbert, living in his rocky nest at Farne, alone amid the wild sea, thought every day of Herbert his friend, who in equal solitude lived on his isle in Derwentwater; and Herbert, who loved him as disciple loved his master, prayed always that he might die on the same day as Cuthbert. Every year they met for one day, and the last time, at Carlisle, Herbert asked that his constant prayer should be granted; and the gracious legend, which Wordsworth has touched, records that the friends passed away together. When Ceadda died in 672 the natural piety of the time made his brother Cedda descend from heaven to meet and welcome him. "I know a man," said Ecgberht (who had been in Ireland with Ceadda), "who is still in the flesh, and who, when that bishop died, saw the spirit of his brother Cedda descending from heaven with a company of angels, and they took his soul with them and returned back again to heaven," and Baeda, who tells the tale (Book iv. 3), moved by the sweetness of the thing, believes its truth. When Guthlac is dying, as Cynewulf writes, he tells his disciple, "for the sake of the fellowship that they of old had proved together, and lest he should after his death be over-sorrowful,"—the great secret of his life — his converse at morn and even with a "glorious angel"; and bids him seek his sister, most beloved, and call on her to come and deck his body with earth. "I saw her not," he says, "in life, not for lack of love but for greatness of love—that we might see one another in eternal joy when our love should be faithful for ever."

These were new feelings to the English, and I do not think that any one could have predicted that their tenderness and grace were latent in the nature of our warlike forefathers. It is a wholly unexpected vein of feeling, added on to and modifying the serious sorrow of their fatalism. Yet it is one of the foundations of our literature. It is the ground tone of a class of religious poetry which never quite failed in England, and which has continued with its gentle, half joyful, half sorrowing sentiment to the present day. Now and then it was traversed—so modern is early England—by troubled questioning. "Mirk and mysterious is that other world. No one returns from it to tell us of its secret"; and the greedy way in which the dreams of monks and laymen were seized on to prove what was to be found beyond the earth is but the vulgar form of the metaphysical doubt and trouble concerning that undiscovered country which Cynewulf felt, and of which Hamlet is the type in literature.

The sorrows of which I have spoken were common to heathen and Christian times, but there was one sorrow which was entirely new, and which created a new world of poetry. It was the sorrow for sin, for a violent, sensual, or wasted life. There is a well-known passage of Cynewulf's in which he laments his past, and which is the first utterance of that poetry of the regretful soul so much of which belongs to England, and in which so many poets have represented their inmost personality with a vividness which has endeared them to our imagination. It is not so much the religion of it for which we care, nor in which lies the poetry. It is the personal cry which has been wrung out of them by their religion. The source of human love lies deep in our nature. But the source of this religious passion lies deeper still, more profound than any plummet sounds; and when we hear its voice, we hear that which lies at the very bottom of the abyss of personality. Here is the cry of Cynewulf, and it is repeated in three or four different places of his poetry with varying intensity. This, which is the least poetical, is from the end of the *Juliana*, and I translate it loosely; the others I leave aside for a time, because they belong more distinctly to his biography. The single letters (they are runes in the original) are the letters of his name, and it was his habit thus to riddle on his name—

> Much need have I that this holy One should help me ... when out of my body my soul fares on its journey, I know not whither, to that undiscovered shore. Mourning wander then C. Y. and N. Stern is then the King, the Victory Giver; and flecked with sins E. W. and U. await, with anguish filled, the doom He shall allot to them according to their deeds. L. and F. tremble; troubled with cares they linger on. I think of all the sorrow, all the wounds of sin that I in earlier and later life have wrought within the world. Crying "Woe, woe," I shall bewail it all with tears. Far, far too late it was ere I shamed me of my evil deeds. ... Therefore I pray of every man, whoso may sing this song, that he may earnestly bear my very name in mind, and ask of God that the Helm of heaven bring me help, the King of Mights, on that great day; the Father, the Spirit of all comfort, in that awful tide.

When this personal voice is not heard in the religious poetry, that poetry is extraordinarily dull, and the imagination, if the pangs of hell are the subject, is paralysed. Whenever that menacing subject arises, it chokes the literary faculty, except the writer be one of those imperial creatures, like Milton or Dante, who are able to make human passion greater than human pain.[1] Even Baeda, when he relates, and with some gusto, the dreams of those who had visited hell, seems to me to lose his style.

But it was different when triumph over sin and the lovely world of heaven were described; and as the sorrow for sin made a new world of poetry, so also did the rapture that followed the conviction of redemption. Most of the images and legends used to express this were common to Christendom. But the English, like the Saxon writer of the *Heliand*, made this triumphant

---

[1] Ed ei s' ergea col petto e colla fronte,
  Come avesse lo inferno in gran dispitto.—*Inf.* x.
So it was with Farinata, *quell' altro magnanimo*; and so it is throughout the hell of Milton.

joy national; first, by using concerning it phrases and thoughts borrowed from their heathen customs; and secondly, by filling it with a distinctive English rapture, as distinctive as the English melancholy. And it became all the more distinctive since it was expressed by Englishmen in their native tongue. Elsewhere, being only expressed in Latin, it had always, whatever the nation, a Roman note, a classic twang. Elsewhere also this triumph and heavenly joy were sung by monks, but the best of the poems of this class were written in England by Cynewulf, who, as I think, never became a monk.

The triumph over sin was poetically concentrated into the victory of Christ over Satan, and we shall meet hereafter many examples of the delight and excitement with which the poets celebrated it, and of the high and exultant Saga-form which they gave to it.[1] I content myself here with one passage from the *Christ* in which Cynewulf concentrates the victoriousness of Jesus, and which illustrates the early mediaeval love of symbolism. I presume, but I do not know, that the six leaps of Christ were a common homiletic explanation of a phrase in the *Song of Solomon*.[2] But the exultation of the poetry, the applause of the Victor, appear in every line. He quotes the text in this fashion—

> 715. Known shall this become   that the King of angels,
> He of mights the very master,   on the mount shall spring,
> O'er the lofty dunes shall leap!   Lo, the hills and knolls
> Girdles He with glory of Him;   gives redemption to the world,
> Unto all the earth-indwellers,   through that leap exceeding praise.

---

[1] See the *Temptation* in the *Christ and Satan*, the *Descent into Hell*, the *Christ*, the *Dream of the Rood*.

[2] "The voice of my beloved! behold, he cometh leaping upon the mountains, skipping upon the hills."—Canticles ii. 8.

The first leap was when he entered the spotless Virgin and took the form of man. The second leap "was his birth when in the bin he lay, of all majesties the majesty." The third leap was the mounting of the Rood. The fourth was into the rocky grave, when he left the tree for the earth-house. The fifth was when he bowed the multitude of the dwellers in Hell, and in quick torment bound their king. The sixth leap was the Holy One's enraptured play when he stept up into Heaven, to his ancient home, to his house of glittering light; and the angel bands were blithe with laughter and with joy upon that holy tide. The glory of this Conquest, which became the dowry of all sinners who, like Cynewulf, repented and loved the Lord, was as consistent an element in Anglo-Saxon poetry as the personal sorrow for sin.

Prayer and Praise became then two of the vital elements of Early English literature. The piteousness of prayer does not produce fine poetry except when it is exceedingly personal. But praise can create poetry of a high quality. The very first upwelling of English song, after Christianity had come, the dream-beginning of our poetry, was an outburst of praise, and the same note is sounded again and again in the Caedmonic poems. As to Cynewulf, he excels in rushing praise, and the adjective is not too strong to use for many of the passages in the *Christ*. Ea, la! he begins the soaring laudations with that double interjection, the sound of which lured his poetic ear. It was like the shout of praise with which he could fancy the warriors of the Lord went into battle. Indeed, this trumpet voice of the heart belongs to the English nature, and the lofty music of Milton's praise came down to him in legitimate descent from the earliest exultation of English psalm.

Their loud, uplifted, angel trumpets blow

is a line which might have been written by Cynewulf. It was first God as Creator whom they praised; then, as I have said, the victory of Jesus Christ; but with the tendency of the Northern poets towards Nature, they often turned to praise the creation of God and its beauty, and one of the favourite forms of this was in the shape of a riddle. Ealdhelm, following his original, had made a long riddle in Latin—*De Creatura*. This Cynewulf translates with his usual freedom and imagination.[1] But, weary with a succession of phrases which did not hit the point, and like a poet sick for finer form, he flings all the force of his thought into another riddle, and concentrates into its ten original lines the meaning of the one hundred and seven lines of his imitation of Ealdhelm. It is a noble piece of praise. The *Creation* is supposed to speak—

> Than this Garth of Earth   I am greater far,
> Than the hand-worm am I less,   more wide-flashing than the moon,
> Than the sun I'm swifter!   All the sea-floods are
> Folded in my arms,   and the fields so green,
> And the breast of earth!   Down to the abyss I cling;
> Under Hell I bow myself;   and the Heavens I overtop,—
> Glory's Fatherland!   Far and wide I reach
> O'er the Angels' own estate;   and the Earth I fill,
> And the ancient Mid-Garth,   and the ocean streams,
> Spacious, with my Self.   Say what I am called.   Rid. lxvii.

This is the universal grasp of the poet, and we

---

[1] I give one instance. Ealdhelm has one line concerning the Whale—

> Grandior in glaucis quam ballena fluctibus atra.

Cynewulf touches this with fire—

> I am stronger, I am greater than the mighty whale,
> Who upon the ground abyss of the grisly ocean
> Looks with his black eye.

may compare with it lines written some thousand years later to express the same conception—

> A motion and a spirit which impels
> All thinking things, all objects of all thought,
> And rolls through all things.

But there was another poetic element introduced into the North by Christianity which had far-reaching effects, and in Northern England (helped as it was there by the instinct of the Celtic blood for natural beauty) it stimulated a love of fair scenery, and especially of quiet, gentle, summer-tempered scenery. I have spoken of the desperate weather the Northern Englishman endured, and how, when the Viking temper lessened, he suffered from it and expressed his sufferings. He had no escape from it in heathendom. He looked forward, if he looked forward at all, to a world of deeper gloom, of darker weather, than he endured on earth. The realm of Hel, the deathgoddess, was a world of sunless mists. The pain and weariness of the fierce climate he bore upon earth was expressed in his poetry; it was expressed in a sadder fashion when Christianity added to his hatred of it a more sentimental way of looking upon life; and this cry against the wintry world and the suffering it brought, became one of the poetic elements, as it is now, of English feeling. But it had naturally another side. The pain created the desire to be free from it; the evil climate caused men to picture the fairer world. The Mignon feeling—that of the southern child lost in the bitter north—who sings her own longing for the shores where

> Ein sanfter Wind vom blauen Himmel weht,—

that she may wake the same longing, and with it, love,

in the heart of him she loves—arose among the English, but with a religious note in it, immediately after the introduction of Christianity.

This desire, stirred by the iron climate of the North, for the soft wind and blue sky and warm sunlight, has also been a fruitful source of English poetry. It appears first, but scantily, as a pleasant delight in green grass and sunny streams and flowers—a delight the origin of which we need not seek in Christianity, for we may find it in the old Northern joy in the coming of summer. But there is a contemplative quiet of pleasure, a note of differentiated tenderness in the following passage of Caedmon which separates his poetic pleasure from the mere exultation of heathendom in the coming of summer, and which is much more marked in the Anglo-Saxon than it can be in any translation. The words are soft, and softly linked together. He is describing Paradise—

> Winsomely the running water, all wellsprings that be,
> Washed the happy lands; nor as yet the welkin
> Bore above the roomy ground all the rains that are
> Wan-gloomed with the gale; yet with growing blooms
> Was the Earth made fair. *Genesis*, l. 210.

Again, in the *Song of the Three Children*, the original text is expanded to describe the pleasure the translator had in the waters that fell from the pure rock—

> Lord Eternal, all the river springs,
> Laud Thee high exalted! Often lettest Thou
> Fall the pleasant waters, for rejoicing of the world,
> Lucid from the hill-cliffs clean. *Azarias*, l. 134.

Nor did Cynewulf think less of streams than the writers of the Caedmon poems. The Phœnix finds its happiness "in the bubbling streams that run through the woods," in the "fountains that well upwards in the glades through the soft sward."

This love of the gentler aspect of Nature, though nurtured by Christianity or by the temper of mind that Christianity created, does not seem in England to have wholly arisen in monasticism. The Irish preferred to establish their monasteries in the savage lands, or built them near the lonely caves or huts which the anchorite hollowed for his retreat in the most desolate places he could discover. Columba sought, when he reached Scotland, a lonelier and yet lonelier isle. He handed on this feeling for savage places to the English of Northumbria. Nothing could well be more wild than the height of Whitby or the rocks of Lindisfarne. Cedda chose to place the monastery where he died "among craggy and far-off mountains, retreats as of robbers and wild beasts." It is then in spite of this Celtic severity that we find the love of quiet and gentle nature among the English. Baeda's history has a few touches which suggest and confirm this statement. The traveller who, passing over the battlefield at Maserfeld, observed one spot greener and more beautiful than any other, and justly concluded that this arose from some person of unusual holiness being buried there, was one who had a wise and seeing eye. There Oswald's blood was shed, and the gentleness of his dying cry was well symbolised by the softer, greener grass. This is but a slight touch, and perhaps to use it in this fashion is to overstrain the passage, but there are enough phrases in Anglo-Saxon poetry to prove what I say. "Serene," cries Cynewulf, describing the view from the hill where Guthlac lived in hermitage, and forgetting the desolation of the lonely island, "was the glorious plain, fresh his dwelling-place, sweet the song of birds, blossoming the earth and the cuckoos announced the year. In guard of God stood the green plain, for God loved all that He had shaped under the Heaven." "All the birds," for Guthlac was, like Francis, tender to the fowl, "rejoiced in the food he gave them," flitting to his hand for refuge, singing praises to him in their song; and when he dies, Cynewulf can find no better image of the sweet odours that came from his mouth than this: "Such fragrance as in summer's tide blossoming plants, honey-flowing and rejoicing, send forth over the wide plains." The fragrance of the woods was one of the common pleasures of the English poets. The perfume of the panther's breath—the panther is here the symbol of Christ—"is sweeter and stronger than the blooms of plants, and than the flowers of the trees."

The same delight in the tenderer offices of Nature is seen in the translation of the passage in the *Song of the Three Children*, where the coming of the angel of the Lord into the oven is thus translated in our version: "He smote the flame of the fire out of the oven, and made the midst of the furnace as it had been a moist whistling wind." The Anglo-Saxon poet turns it thus—

> Then 'twas in the oven   when the angel came
> Windy cool and winsome,   to the weather likest
> When is sent to earth   in the summer tide,
> Dropping down of dew-rain   at the dawn of day.
>
> *Azarias*, l. 61.

In the *Daniel* the same passage is translated, but another aspect of Nature is added to it. The angel's coming makes the fire like a "warm shower from the clouds." But this is not all. The original comparison charmed the English poet, and he has inserted it elsewhere, but again he changes it, and makes it still more poetical. It was within the fire for them, as when—

In the summer tide   shining is the sun,
And the elf-enchanted[1] dew,   at the dawning of the day,
Winnowed is by wind.   *Daniel*, l. 276.

These are passages full of a mild savour of contemplative pleasure in Nature, such as we neither find in the heathen poems, nor in Icelandic verse. They have a quality of their own, like Jacques' melancholy, and they lead us on, like many other elements in Anglo-Saxon poetry, to the feeling of the nineteenth century, to the sentiment of Wordsworth and Tennyson.

As to the longing their fierce climate gave them for a warmer and brighter land, it appears most fully in the delight of the poets in the Christian conception of Paradise. Nowhere is this clearer than in the famous passage in the *Phœnix*. There Cynewulf, if it was he who wrote that poem, has let loose all his pleasure in soft air and lovely scenery. The thirty Latin lines on which he worked are cold in comparison with the eighty-four verses into which he expands them. It seems as if he could not stay his hand till he had wholly forgotten in his dream the icy seas and the fierce storms, the misery and might of which he has also told so well. The Elysian fields of Homer and Virgil, the Sicily of Theocritus, the Earthly Paradise of Dante, the Eden of Milton, the lovely country where in Shelley's poem Asia and Prometheus wander, are not ill-paralleled by this English poem of the eighth century. Christianity created it in the English heart, and as such I give it in this chapter. But it is a

---

[1] And deáw-drías on dæge weorðeð
Winde geondsáwen.

I was so pleased with "elf-enchanted dew," which is Dietrich's suggestion, that I put it into the translation; but *deáw-drías* really means, I imagine, nothing more than "the dew-fall."

parallel only in its enjoyment of its subject. Its poetry does not approach that of these masters of song. The man who wrote it sought by repetition, not by concentration, to express what he saw in his soul, and this is the weakness of all Art at its origins, as in its decay. This is the passage—

  1. Far away from hence,   I have heard it told—
    Of all lands the noblest is,   in the Eastern parts;
    Known to folk by fame;   yet that fold[1] of earth
    Unto few of the folk-owners   faring over Midgard,
    Easy of access is;   but is far withdrawn
    From the men who mischief make   by the might of God!
    All the land is lovely;   with delights made happy,
    With the very sweetest   of the scents of earth.
    Onely[2] is that island,   ætheling its maker,
    Mighty and majestic,   who its mould has set!
    To its blest indwellers   oft the door of heaven
10. There is clear disclosed,   clear the joy of hymns!
        Winsome is the wold[3] there;   there the wealds are green,
    Spacious spread below the skies;   there may neither snow nor rain,
    Nor the furious air of frost,   nor the flare of fire,
    Nor the headlong squall of hail,   nor the hoar-frost's fall,
    Nor the burning of the sun,   nor the bitter cold,
    Nor the weather over-warm,   nor the winter shower,
    Do their wrong to any wight—   but the wold abides
    Ever happy, healthful there.   Honoured is that land,
    All ablown with blossoms.   Not abrupt the mountains:
    Steep the hills stand not,   and the stony cliffs
    Are not high upheaved,   such as here with us they are!
    Nought there is of dells and dales,   nor of deep rock-gorges
    Heights or hillocks rough;   nor hangs over there
    Any unsmooth thing,   but the noble land
27. 'Neath the welkin waxes   with its winsome joys ablown.
       .   .   .   .
33. Calm and fair this glorious field,   flashes there the sunny grove;
    Happy is the holt of trees,   never withers fruitage there.
    Bright are there the blossoms;   and the (bearing) trees

---

[1] *Sceat*, that which is folded over, as we say, a lap of the land.

[2] Sidney uses this word "onely" (*aenlic*), and I use the word *ætheling*, here as an adjective—that is, *noble*.

[3] *Wong* is the word I have translated "Wold." "Wold" has nothing philologically to do with it, but it means much the same. Had not *wong* been too obscure to be introduced into modern English I would have used it, for it still exists in English dialects. In Lincolnshire it means a marsh, a lowland. Elsewhere it has its Anglo-Saxon meaning of a meadow, a plain, an open space.

Stand forth ever green in it,   as ordainèd God to them.
In the winter, in the summer,   is the wood alike
Hung with blossomed boughs.   Never breaks away
Leaf below the lift,   nor shall low of fire scathe them
Through the ages ever   till the end shall be
40. For the world accomplished. . . .

. . . .

50. In that home the hating foe   houses not at all,
Nought of vengeance nor of wailing,   no woe-token ever.
Nor the narrow death,   misery nor Eld,
Nor the loss of life,   nor of loathly ill the coming ;
Nought of strife or sin,   nought of sorrow-soreness,
Nor the wretchlessness of want,   nor of wealth the needing ;
Neither sleep nor sadness,   nor the sickman's weary bed,
Nor the winter-whirling snow,   nor the wax and wane of
   tempests—
Roughly storming under skies—   nor the savage frost,
With his chill cold icicles,   crushes down the folk !
There no hail or hrime   hurtleth down to earth ;
Never vapours full of wind,   nor rain-water falleth,
Lashed the lift about [1]—   but the liquid streamlets,
Wonderfully beautiful,   from their wells up springing,
Softly lap the land   with their lovely floods.
Winsome are the waters   from the woodlands' middle
Which, at every moon,   through the mossy turf of earth,
Surge up cold as sea-foam ;   seek their path around the trees
Gloriously, from time to time ; —   for 'tis God's behest
That the mirth of river floods,   every month that goes,
All about the fame-fast land   should o'erflow in play !
There with gladsome growths   all the groves are hung,
With the (wildwood) blossoms.   Never wither there,
Hallowed under heaven,   of the holt the lovelinesses !
Never there the fallow foliage   falls upon the earth,
Fairness it of forest trees ;   full of beauty are
Evermore the branches,   bent adown upon the trees,
With a fruitage always fresh,   fadeless day by day !
On the grassy plain,   stands in green array
Brightest-gleaming of all groves,   gloriously enclad,
Through the craft [2] of Holy God !   Never change is there
In the beauty of the holt ;   there its holy fragrance
Wons above the winsome land ;   nor is waning known
Ever through the ages,   till the end He brings
To the ancient work of old   who erst its making had.
   Phœnix, ll. 1-84.

The writer of these verses had lost his youthful

---

[1] Or lashed by the air, by the wind.
[2] I use *craft* in all these translations with its old meaning of *power*.

unconsciousness in art, and, in endeavouring after his Latin original, was not himself quite free; yet his natural originality breaks through his convention. His work is scattered, but he has tried to give it some unity by the use of a refrain. It is also full of repetition, but the repetition is but another instance of the pleasure with which the Northumbrian poet dwelt on that aspect of natural scenery and soft air which the Christian vision of Eden afforded him when the bitter weather froze his bones. Moreover, though the thoughts are repeated, the words used in the repetition are different; and different words, I have already said, for various phases of the same natural phenomenon are a proof that the people and the poet who use them are close and affectionate observers of Nature. I repeat the statement in connection with the subject of this chapter. The poetry of natural description, already slightly touched in *Beowulf*, was developed to a much greater fulness under the influence of Christianity. It is a very remarkable and uncommon thing that at this early time, such a poetry should have existed at all; that the doings of Nature should have been made, by deliberate choice, a separate subject of song. This owes its origin, I think, partly to a special strain in the nature of the Northern English, the cause of which I cannot render definite; partly, I believe, to the reading of Virgil. It was, no doubt, strengthened by an admixture of Celtic blood. Whatever its origins, it is of extraordinary interest when we consider that in the European poetry of the last 150 years there has been no growth of the poetry of natural description so varied or so complete as that which arose into flower in Great Britain. In Germany that poetry was fairly wrought, but it was not, at the beginnings of this century, as full or of so great a range as ours, nor is it now. In France, that poetry has been, of late years, extensive, tender, and minute, but in the fulness of this we preceded France; and I may perhaps be allowed to trace our quicker seizure and more finished development of the subject to the fact that the root of the matter was in us more than a thousand years ago.

CHAPTER XII

MONASTICISM AND LITERATURE

THE monastic life, so largely developed in England both by Celtic and Latin Christianity, increased the force of some of the literary elements on which I have dwelt in the last chapter, added others, and brought to the help and adornment of literature new arts, and new forms of human life. Moreover, it enlarged the material of literature by producing a literary class and by the collection into libraries of the literature of the past. It founded the literature of History, Rhetoric, and Philosophy. It established schools. Laymen attended them, and it actually created in this fashion, and for a time, a small literary class of laymen in Northumbria. By means of the unity, which, independent of diverse nationalities, knit together the monasteries, monasticism opened to Englishmen Rome, Ireland, and the Continent. New thoughts, new scenes, new views thus entered into the life of thought in England. The pilgrimages which it encouraged did the same kind of work; and the movement to and fro of the missionaries whom England sent out to the Teutonic lands brought her into contact again with the original spirit which informed her poetry, and strengthened that spirit. It is worth while to briefly develop these various points, and to bring them, however diverse they may be, into as united a form as possible.

First, those emotional habits of daily life, of custom and thought on which I have dwelt in the last chapter, and which form, as it were, the ground-ooze of poetic literature, grew into a special charm in English monastic life. There was added to them a religious tenderness, a fuller love of quiet beauty, an imaginative heavenliness, which our sacred poetry has never lost. That charm is seen most clearly in the writings of Baeda. It runs like a sweet clear stream through the stories he tells of holy men and women who, while yet alive, heard celestial sounds and saw their convent gardens, the woods and moors and starry heavens irradiated by the "solemn troops and sweet societies" of the angels. A history of literature is bound to quote one of these tales,[1] itself a lovely illustration of the temper I am describing, and told with an ideal grace and innocent simplicity which arise out of Baeda's own delight in that of which he speaks.

When Ceadda, bishop of the Mercians, was near the hour of his death, it happened that a monk, whose name was Owini, was employed in the garden of the monastery at Lichfield, and became aware of a strange thing. The bishop was alone, reading or praying in his oratory, when on a sudden Owini "heard the

---

[1] No history of poetic literature would be in any sense complete which did not draw special attention to the stories contained in the *Ecclesiastical History* and in the *Biographies* of Baeda. I have quoted one of them above, in order to ask those who care for fine literature to read them all. I wish they were collected separately. I think it would be an admirable thing if some Anglo-Saxon professor were to put them into Anglo-Saxon and make a little reading-book out of them ; or were to isolate them in their original Latin, and give them to the Class to reproduce in the manner of the later Anglo-Saxon of the *Chronicle*.

voice of persons singing most sweetly and rejoicing, and the sound seemed to come down from heaven. And he heard the voice moving from the southeast, but afterwards it drew near to him, till, coming to the roof of the oratory where the bishop was, it entered therein and filled it. Owini listened, all attent, and after the space of half an hour the same song of joy ascended from the roof and returned to heaven with an inexpressible sweetness. While he stood astonished, turning seriously in his mind what this might be, the bishop opened the window of the oratory, and clapping with his hand as he was wont to do, bade him come in. 'Make haste to the church,' he said, 'and cause the seven brothers to come hither, and do you come with them.' When they were at hand he admonished them to keep the virtue of peace among themselves and towards all, and to be careful to practise the rules of regular discipline."
. . . "And then he said, 'The time of my death is at hand, for that amiable guest who was wont to visit our brothers has vouchsafed also to come to me this day and to call me from the world. Return, therefore, to the church and speak to the brethren, that they recommend in their prayers my journey to the Lord; and be careful also (for the hour is uncertain) to provide for their own, by watching and prayer and good works.' When he had spoken thus much and more, and they, having received his blessing, had gone away in sorrow, he who had heard the heavenly song came back alone, and, kneeling on the ground, said, 'I beseech you, Father, that I may ask a question of you.'— 'Ask what you will,' answered the bishop. Then he added, 'I entreat you to tell me what song of joy was that which I heard coming upon this oratory, and

after some time returning to heaven?' The bishop answered, 'If you heard the singing, and know of the descent of the heavenly company, I command you, in the name of our Lord, that you tell it not to any before my death. These were angelic spirits who came to call me to my heavenly reward, for the which I have always longed; moreover, they promised to return seven days hence and take me with them.'"

This is but one of many tales, full of so heartfelt a harmony of feeling and style, that it is impossible to ignore them as one of the original sources of English religious poetry. This sweet and well-bred gentleness, this religious fervour, with its tender supernaturalism, its natural dignity, its grave seriousness of life, and its quietude in death, added new and special elements to the Sacred Song of England, which, continued up to the present day, is not excelled in the world for its variety and depth, for the passion of its sadness and joy.

The romantic tone added to it by the Celtic missionaries ministered still further to its endurance. Our island religion—at least in the home of poetry in the North—was first made by the Irish, and was deeply tinged by their nature. Owing to their influence, a more changing colour was given to the religious life, a greater spirit of adventure pervaded it, a freer and more passionate daily life entered into it. Moreover, the life the Irish missionaries lived and the spirit they imposed on religion were alike romantic. These things have been one of the powers of our literature —one of the fires which have burnt in it down to the present day.

We can trace these romantic roots of poetry and the subjects of poetry in the lives of the evangelisers of

Northumbria. They were the eager bringers into life of an imaginative, richly-coloured, natural music. They filled with poetry popular religious emotion. Aidan, with his gentleness and fire thrilled the land he converted. We may even claim the life of Columba as another influence in the same direction, for after his death his romantic soul touches from afar the hearts of English kings. Oswald, who had been in exile at Iona, felt all through his life the spirit of the founder of Iona. The legend runs that on the evening before the battle of Denises-burn, Columba (now dead for thirty-six years) appeared to him, and stretched his glittering robe over the little army, and cried, "Be of good courage and play the man. Join battle at the dawn. I have won victory for you from God, and the death of the tyrants." But the ideal example of this influence is Cuthbert, and the best also to take, for he was not, like Aidan, a Scot, but an Englishman. His very birthplace is one of the homes of our romance, for he grew up on the Lammermoor, in the country of Tweed and Teviot, and kept the flocks of his master on the sheep walks of the Leader. He is bound up with Aidan, as Elisha was with Elijah; for as he was watching the sheep one night in the starry silence he saw Heaven opened, and a host of angels descend on a stream of light, and fly upwards again with a resplendent soul. And he knew afterwards, it is said, that this was Aidan who had just died at Lindisfarne. At fifteen years old, the story runs, he came to Melrose on his horse, like a young warrior, spear in hand, and with an attendant rider, and the picture is like a ballad. No life could be wilder, more impassioned than the missionary life he then undertook, roving from one lonely hamlet to another among the pathless fells, living in the open air from glen to glen, lighting the desolate country with "his angel face," preaching to English and Celts, redeeming them from the remnants of heathenism. For weeks, for months, he was away from the monastery, going from the Forth to the Solway, even piercing northward into the land of the Picts.[1]

Then the anchorite spirit seized him, and he prayed on the dark nights beside the icy waves, and the otters or seals came out of the water, moved with pity, to lie over and to warm his feet, a story which clung to the popular memory. All through his life he had pleasant doings with the animals, as many others had among the early English saints. Cuthbert, in this relation, is the St. Francis of England; and it is agreeable to think, and may have more in it than mere fancy, that the love of Walter Scott and Burns— lowlanders like Cuthbert—for the poetry of animal life had a far-off origin in Cuthbert's affectionate regard for birds and beasts — creatures who, he thought, served God, and ought to love God's minister. To the birds who wasted his barley on Farne he spoke, appealing to their honesty not to injure that which belonged to another; yet they might take the corn, he said, if God had given them leave. One day, hungry and in a waste place, an eagle killed a fish for him. His boy brought him the food. But Cuthbert reproved him. "What have you done, my son; why have you not given part to God's handmaid? Cut

---

[1] The wandering missionary bearing the Gospel from land to land carries on into Christian times, and is in full analogy with the wandering Scôp bearing his sagas from hall to hall. The bishops, like Ealdhelm, who preached from village to village, brought to the people, by the stories and parables in their sermons, even by the old songs they did not disdain to sing or to make in English, something of what we may call literature. The sermon was often the successful rival of the War Tale.

the fish in two pieces, and give her one, as her service well deserves." Two ravens that lived on the rocks of Farne pulled out the thatch of his hut to build therewith their nest. He reproved them, and they fled away in sorrow. At the end of three days one returned, and spread out his wings and bent his head most piteously, asking pardon by his gestures of Cuthbert who was digging in his field. And the man of God gave them leave to return, the which both of them did, and brought a large piece of hog's lard with them, with which Cuthbert always greased the brethren's shoes; and for many years in all humility, penitence, and peace, the ravens dwelt with him in Farne. As I write this, I think of the spirit which fills the *Ancient Mariner* of Coleridge.

But he was not as yet living in this lonely island. It was after years passed at Melrose, at Ripon, at Lindisfarne and in his frequent journeys, that, wearying for loneliness with God, he came at last to Farne, an island opposite Bamborough, ceaselessly swept by the winds and waves of the fierce sea. There he lived a happy, and, when he was visited, a hospitable life for nine years (676-684). Made bishop then of Lindisfarne, he carried, as before, his poetic spirit and the peace of God over the whole of his wild diocese in incessant journeys. When, worn out, he went back, after two years to die at Farne, his last breath was drawn in the midst of the quiet sea, and the bells of Lindisfarne answered the waving candles of Farne which told his brethren on the mainland that their master had departed (687). This was a romantic life, and it sank deep into the hearts of the English people. One beautiful story after another is told of his tender, passionate, daring, and childlike character. Women loved him well in all honour and noble friendship. His life has been called uneventful, but the spirit of it was more longlived than the memory of all the wars and policy of his time. Northumbria chose him for patron. Every valley and fell loved his memory. He gathered round his bones a host of the relics of noble Englishmen. The head of Oswald lay on his breast; the bones of the bishops Aidan, Eadberht, Eadfrith, Æthelwold, the head of the most glorious Ceolwulf, and the relics of Baeda, rested with him in his coffin. The kings of England paid him homage. He edged Ælfred's falchion on the Dane, and the Norman Conqueror honoured him. The great rock of Durham, resting on the curved arm of the Wear, received his bones; the solemn cathedral rose, and the vast bishopric grew into its power under the protection of his name. The battle of the Standard was not unconnected with the insult offered to his lands. It was under his banner, "the holie corporax cloth" with which he covered the chalice, that David II. was beaten at Neville's Cross in 1346. It is said that Surrey carried the sacred talisman to Flodden, and that the Northern earls upraised it in the futile rising of 1569. That sad history drew the pen of Wordsworth, so that Cuthbert, not only in the eighth, but in the nineteenth century, not only in Baeda, but in Walter Scott and Wordsworth, has been the subject or inspirer of literature. Romance, intensity of character, variety of life, impulsive change, a deep humanity, the resolute consistent force of a man, the sentiment and tenderness of a woman, make up an image which has sent its influence throughout English literature from his day unto our own. In lives like this of Cuthbert—how different from the ordered, but no less useful, lives of the Roman missionaries,—lies one of the chief impulses of song in early times. Now the whole of Northern England, which became the special home of poetry, was subject, and far more than Mercia, to the quickening impulses of many men of this kind, of whom Cuthbert is the type. They took the place of the saga-heroes among the people, poetry collected round them, and in their legends took a Christian form. Their lives sent down the materials of poetry from century to century. It would be well if English literature looked far more than it has yet done to the primal rock from whence it was hewn.

On the other side from this wandering life was the retired and workful stillness of the monastic scholar; not the inspirer, but the producer of literature. His was the quiet cell with desk in the window, a single chair at the desk, with cupboard and bed, and a chest full of manuscripts, where the monk lived and worked year after year, looking up now and then to hear the bird sing on the sill, to see the flowers in the paved cloister, or the fruit-trees blossom in the garden—a simple, silent, happy life.

These cells were the nurseries of learned literature. Sometimes they were like that of Mailduf, an Irishman, who in the midst of the untilled forest set up a hermitage, and then a school, and then a monastery. Sometimes they were like that of Theodore or Hadrian, from which a sun of learning illuminated England; and we see, with the eyes of Ealdhelm, Theodore, issuing from his cell, and walking to and fro in the shade of the cloister, with his Irish scholars, arguing like a wild boar surrounded by a snarling troop of Molossian dogs, whom he repulsed with his sharp grammatic tooth. Sometimes they were like that of Ealdhelm, Theodore's finest scholar, where Greek, Latin, and Hebrew were studied and expounded; where first the Latin muse was wooed by an Englishman; where English songs were made, whence he wrote letters to kings and chiefs and virgins on the joys of study. Sometimes, we see, as at Whitby, the poet in his chilly cell, ruminating the song he is to sing at night. At another time the cell is filled with plans for building, with musical scores, with illuminated manuscripts, such as were the daily care of Benedict of Wearmouth. Sometimes the little room holds one who writes a biography of some stirring man like Wilfrid, or records a merchant's tale of travel to the Holy Land. As we look at England, during the eighth century, there was scarcely any monastery which had not at least one literary man who was eager, not only for his spiritual work, but for some special line of literature or of art.

The writing also of history, or rather the collection of the materials for history now began, and in the monasteries. Most of the great foundations jotted down short annals of their growth and expansion, or any remarkable story which belonged to their history. What they did was not literature, but it was one of its infantine beginnings, and it rose rapidly into work like the *Ecclesiastical History* of Baeda. Then books began to be collected and libraries established. The kings and chieftains, the rich earls who joined or founded monasteries, carried into them as gifts the manuscripts they had received or purchased. The monk returning from pilgrimage brought back some treatise of a Roman bishop, some manuscript of a Latin father, some copy of a classic poet. The warrior who wished to gift the monastery which had baptized and educated him, the wandering merchant who wished its custom or its support, the visitor from Ireland or Gaul, brought with them, as their most precious offering, some book which was received with joy, and cherished in the library. We know, through a letter of Alcuin's, the contents of the library at York, and it gives us a notion of what may have been in Jarrow, in Wearmouth, at Hexham or Canterbury. A long list is given of the Latin and Greek fathers, and among them were a few Hebrew manuscripts. Boethius, the supposed Lactantius, Orosius, were also there, and these names are of interest to us, for Ælfred translated Orosius and Boethius, and Cynewulf must have had Lactantius in his hands or heard it translated to him. Among the ancients were Aristotle, Cicero, Virgil, Pliny, Statius and Lucan. Donatus, Priscian, and other grammarians rested also in the chests of that famous library.

When we read Baeda's account of his own works, and know that he spent all his life at Wearmouth and Jarrow, we know also how large his library must have been. Indeed, the founding of that library illustrates the literary excitement of the monasteries of the seventh century. In 671 the Abbot Benedict, whose surname was Biscop, went for the third time to Rome, and passing by Vienne, bought in that ancient capital a number of books which he stored there till his return. On his way back from Rome, with a large cargo of manuscripts and relics, he took up the books he had left at Vienne, with others collected for him by friends, and returned in triumph to England. It was then that he built the monastery of St. Peter's, Wearmouth, in 674, and, moved by the passion of the collector, went a fourth time to Rome, and brought back books, images, relics, and pictures. After his return from this voyage in 679, he founded Jarrow in 682, and made a fifth journey to Rome in order to establish in Jarrow a library as large as that at Wearmouth. He loved his collection like a child, and his love was strong in death. One of his last recommendations to his monks was to keep it carefully, to take care it should not be either injured or dispersed. His influence did not close with his death. It is to his libraries that we owe Baeda, the School of York, Alcuin, and all the continental learning that flowed from the work of Alcuin.[1] His friend and successor, Ceolfrid, was as eager as he in collecting, and still further enriched the two libraries. A pleasant story proves that not only monks but kings were lovers of books in this century. There was a *cosmographorum codex* of marvellous workmanship in the library of Jarrow, and King Aldfrith was keenly desirous of possessing it. Ceolfrid sold it to the king for a land of eight families, and later on sold this land for a larger territory close to Jarrow. Baeda then, owing to the work of these two predecessors of his, had two large libraries at his command when he began to write.

Nor were the women in the monasteries without their books. Barking and Wimbourne were celebrated at the beginning of the eighth century for their literary, even their classic, studies. Ealdhelm, writing to the nuns of Barking, quotes to them Virgil and Ovid. It has been held that some of his phrases presuppose that a few of them knew Greek. The nuns who wrote to Boniface write in an impetuous, incorrect Latin. They send him books and receive them from him. They quote Virgil to him. They

---

[1] See Bp. Stubbs' article on Benedict in the *Dictionary of Christian Biography*.

make Latin verse for him, "in order to exercise the little intellect that God has given them."

Thus, as Roman writing, replacing the runic characters, trebled the creation of literature, so also the collections of books refined and impelled it. For the books were not only manuals of devotion, but some of the masterpieces of the world. The delicate, pellucid style of Virgil, the finished rhetoric of Cicero were unattainable by the English monk, but they supplied him with a model and an inspiration. Nor were Greek books altogether absent. Plato seems to have been quoted by Ceolfrid in a letter to a Scot king, but I suppose Ceolfrid found the passage in some Latin writer. Aristotle was one of the books in the library at York. The story of Andrew and the Mermedonians, the foundation of the *Andreas*, only exists in Greek; and I try, remembering an allusion here and there, and that Theodore studied at Athens, to persuade myself that Theodore or Hadrian brought with them a manuscript of Homer. At least, some of the great models, which whosoever reads has seen the stars, wrought upon the literature of the seventh and eighth centuries.

Along with Roman literature came also through the monasteries the Roman arts; and the arts dance with, inspire, and are inspired by literature. The method of Roman singing taught by James the Deacon filled, we are told by Baeda, with its respondent chants the ancient church at York; and then spreading from Kent in the time of Theodore was soon taught in all the English churches. John, Abbot of St. Martin's at Rome, whom Benedict Biscop set up as teacher of singing at Wearmouth, not only taught the method of singing throughout the year as it was practised at St. Peter's in Rome, but also the reading aloud of the ritual, the writing down of all that was needful for the yearly celebration of all the festivals ; and monks, from the greater number of the monasteries of the Northern province, flocked to hear him and to learn of him. Wilfrid, the story ran, so filled Richmondshire with the Latin music Eddi and Eona taught, that the very peasants mingled the Gregorian chants with their daily work. Bishop Acca, himself a "heavenly singer," who succeeded Wilfrid at Hexham in 709, having "diligently gathered a numerous and noble library together," invited Maban a celebrated singer from Kent to the North, and kept him for twelve years by his side to teach such ecclesiastical songs as were unknown, and to restore others corrupted by neglect."[1]

Not only music but architecture, sculpture and painting ministered to literature and kindled it, and those forms of them which were brought from Rome soon drove out the ruder forms which had come from Ireland and Iona. "Churches of stone, *ex polito lapide*, in the Roman style" rose at Wearmouth, Hexham, Ripon and other places. Wilfrid brought with him from Gaul "builders and teachers of every art." It was he that covered the roof of the church at York with lead, glazed the windows, and whitewashed the walls. The basilica he built at Ripon astonished the Northumbrian world by the height of its porches and its polished stone columns,[2] and on the day of its

---

[1] These things will be found in the *Ecclesiastical History*. Musical instruments, the horn, flute, harp, and trumpet—were used, and Ealdhelm describes in his *Praises of Virginity* the mighty organ, with its blasts and tones, its windy bellows, and golden pipes ; and since this instrument came from the Greeks, it was probably introduced into England by Theodore.

[2] Its vault, called "St. Wilfrid's Needle," still remains.

dedication, standing before the altar, he laid upon it a cross of gold and a splendid Evangeliarium covered with plates of gold and precious stones, and written in letters of gold on purple parchment. Hexham, another foundation of Wilfrid's, was still more magnificent. Its deep and immense foundations, its crypt, its numerous aisles and stories, galleries and high-hung bells, made it for two centuries, till it was destroyed in 875 by the Danes, the finest church on this side of the Alps; extolled, Eddius declares, even by those who came from Rome. The Archbishops of Canterbury had set up a cathedral of stone on the plan of a Roman basilica. The great church of stone at Crowland, built on piles in the marshes of the hollow land of Lincolnshire, is said to have been set up by Æthelbald of Mercia in the eighth century, and it was only one out of many. Ealdhelm placed side by side with Mailduf's small church a great minster, one of the finest in England, which William of Malmesbury saw. At Frome also, and at Wareham, he built churches of stone. Architecture had advanced farther than we think. The common notion was that the parish churches of the seventh and eighth centuries were, like those Baeda describes as built by the Celtic monks, of wood and thatched with reeds. On the contrary, the Roman method was established by the end of the seventh century, the masonry of squared stone was good; carved figures adorned the buildings. They had nave, chancel, and north porch. The style was primitive Romanesque, not Norman. At least, this is the case with St. Laurence at Bradford-by-Avon, which William of Malmesbury believed to be the genuine work of Ealdhelm, and whose continued existence to the present day enabled Mr.

Freeman to make the assertions I have here derived from him concerning the architecture of the late seventh and eighth centuries. This little building, at Bradford, this *ecclesiola* (it is less than forty feet long), is as precious as a gem. "It is the one perfect surviving Old-English church in the land. The ground plan is absolutely untouched, and there are no mediæval insertions at all. So perfect a specimen of Primitive Romanesque is certainly unique in England, we should not be surprised if it is unique of its own kind in Europe."[1]

As to embroidery, it was developed to a high excellence in the female monasteries, not only for the sacred vestments both of altar and priest, but also by the womanly desire to make a show of gorgeous garments. Baeda thought the divine wrath would fall on the nuns of Coldingham, because "Texendis subtilioribus indumentis operam dant"; Boniface denounced this luxury; Ealdhelm warned his sisters against it; the council of Clovesho in 747 prescribed that the nuns should revert to the ancient and simple robes, and the monks give up the fashionable gartering of their legs.[2]

The art of glass-making, of glazing the windows of churches, the Roman and Gallican arts of gold embroidery and of gold work in lofty rood and

---

[1] See *English Towns*, E. A. Freeman, pp. 134, etc.
[2] This Synod discloses the other side of the monastic life. It was not all glittering gold. Pagan observances still prevailed in the country places; the clergy are warned against obscene conversation and drunkenness; the monasteries were to be looked after lest they become full of ludicrous arts, versifiers, harpers, and buffoons; the nunneries not places of junketing and luxury. Baeda, Alcuin, Wilfrid, all protest to the same tune. In fact, many of the monasteries, with lay priors, were like pleasant country-houses, and ended by becoming mere resorts of idleness and dissipation (Hook's *Archbishops of Canterbury*, vol. i. p. 276). And no one can read the scattered allusions to the courts of Æthelbald and Offa, which no doubt had many parallels, without knowing how much morality and simplicity suffered at the courts of kings.

chalice, pyx, missal, and crosier, were soon established in England, and added their fresh impulse to that ancient English art of gold web and golden smithery which, influenced by Celtic art as well as by Roman, nevertheless kept its own spirit and worked from its own invention. Gregory's Bible at St. Augustine's, Canterbury, had leaves inserted in it at the beginning, "some of a purple, others of a rose colour, which, held against the light, showed a wonderful reflection. There is also a Psalter, having on its exterior the figure of Christ in silver, with the four evangelists. Another book, placed on the high altar, has on it a figure of Christ in silver, erect and blessing with His right hand. Another is ornamented with the rays of the Divine Majesty in silver gilt, set round with crystals and beryls. Another has on its cover a single large beryl, set round on all sides with crystals." This Roman work started work of the same kind in England, and was soon equalled, if not excelled. The binding and illumination of books soon became of national importance. The cover of the *Lindisfarne Gospels* is entirely English design and work, and it is only one example out of many. Even painting, perhaps mosaic, followed Benedict Biscop from Rome; and Wearmouth, apse and walls, shone with the precise ascetic figures of the Virgin, the apostles and prophets, with the stories of the Gospel and the imagery of the book of Revelation.

This quiet monastic life, with its musical services, its literature, its gold-embroidered work, its rich ecclesiastical furniture, its books, is not quite unrecorded in English literature. There are passages in the poems of Cynewulf which bring portions of it vividly before our eyes. In his riddles on the sacramental paten or the chalice and the pyx, we are placed in the church; we see the priest " turning and changing the golden ring (perhaps the wafer) round and round"; and the people, "wise in spirit, watching it in mind; praying and naming it the saviour of those who do well; also the ring has glorious wounds in it which speak aloud to men" (Riddle lx.) We see the pyx of red gold held up before the congregation, and though tongueless, it spoke well and cried for men, "Save me, helper of souls!" Mysterious was its speech, its charm; let men bethink them of it (Riddle xlix.) Then we are brought into the monastery. There, in the cell, is the book-chest (Riddle l.) "standing firm on the ground, deaf itself and dumb and witless, that swallows things more costly than gold." We watch the "dark and swarthy-faced thegn (some Celtic noble) stowing away under its lid manuscripts that kings and queens desire." There, too, we see the missal or a Bible codex in the library, and trace the parchment from the skin to its illumination and its binding. It is "dipped in water, set in the sun, stripped of its hairs, cut with a knife, ground down with cinders, folded with fingers. Then the delight of the bird (the wing feather—the pen) wandered o'er my dusky surface when it had sprinkled me with healing water (this refers to the illuminations which preceded the writing). Then the wing swallowed the dye of a tree mixed with water (the ink) and stepped over me, leaving black marks behind. Afterwards men covered me with protecting boards, drew a skin round me, decked me with gold, adorned me with the fair work of smiths, encased me with (gold and silver) wire; and my ornaments and my red purple, and the glorious possessions in me are famous far and wide. Shield I am to nations, if the children of men will use me. I helpful to men; great is my name; healing to heroes and I myself holy!" And lastly, we see the monk wonder-stricken to find the moth eating his books. "'Tis a marvellous wyrd," he thinks, "that a worm should devour the speech of men, and that this thief in the dark, this robber-guest, should be no whit the wiser for his eating."

When we pass from the arts as ministers of literature in the monasteries, and return to the influence of monasticism upon literature, we find that its indirect influence was very great on the variety and the development of letters. The great extension of the seventh and eighth century monachism and its corporate union spread the literature of each monastery to the others. Books and unique manuscripts were naturally exchanged between connected monasteries, and the copying of these was part of the employment of the monks and of the literary hacks at the court of kings. That which belonged to one, it was felt, ought to belong to all. Irish monks borrow books from Ealdhelm; he himself sends his treatise on Versification to Aldfrith, the King of Northumbria, and dedicates his *Praise of Virginity* to the learned nuns of Barking. Baeda and Acca, Boniface and Ecgberht interchanged books, and these are only two instances out of a multitude which might be given. Even between the nunneries and scholars there was, as we have seen, an interchange of literature, of manuscripts, of criticism.

Baeda's friendship with Trumbert and Sigfrid, with Acca and Benedict Biscop, with the men of Canterbury, enabled him to master the learning of the Irish, the Roman, the Gallican, and the Canterbury Schools. The account he gives of the authorities he used for his

Ecclesiastical History illustrates this literary interchange still further. It was Albinus the abbot, educated by Theodore and Hadrian at Canterbury, who persuaded him to write the book, and who sent him through Nothelm (who also gathered materials for him in the archives of Rome) all his information about the Church in Kent and the adjacent parts. He speaks of consulting all the writings of his predecessors. Daniel, Bishop of the West Saxons, sent him materials for the history of the West and South Saxons and of the Isle of Wight. His story of Christianity in the province of Mercia and among the East Saxons was gained from the brethren of Lastingham. The writings and traditions of "our ancestors," and the relation of Abbot Esius informed him concerning the East Angles, and letters from Cunibert, Bishop of Sidnacester in Lincoln, told him of the sacerdotal succession in the province of Lindsey. All he wrote about Cuthbert was taken from the records kept at Lindisfarne. It is plain there was a literary intercommunion over the whole of England at the time of Baeda, and this was due to the corporate brotherhood of the monasteries.

Nor did this interchange of learning and discussion exist only within the bounds of England. One of the chief advantages which Roman monasticism brought to literature was that it opened out communication with the Continent, and increased thereby the means of literature. England extended its arms beyond itself. Every one has heard of the incessant movement to and fro of English and Irish scholars in the seventh century, and I need not dwell upon it. In the first half of the same century we know from Baeda that the intercommunion between Gaul and England was frequent;

"Many fared, since few monasteries were as yet established among the Angles, to the monasteries of the Gauls, and they also sent their daughters to be there instructed"; and the story of the schools set up by Sigeberht of East Anglia on the model of those he had seen in Gaul, goes to prove this intercommunion. This was still further developed when the voyaging to Rome through Gaul began. Ireland then and Gaul, two different nations of distinct types, added at least some of their elements to the rise of literature in England, and did this through monasticism. Then also, through the same channel, the mighty influence of Rome—so many traces of whose ancient greatness the English saw in their own land with awe and curiosity—bore not only on the bishops who felt themselves in union with a greater tradition than that of their own nation, and members of a universal power; but also on the whole crowd of English clergy, secular and regular; on the women of rank and the nuns who cared for letters; on the kings and nobles, who, weary of war and turmoil, sought the monastic shades in England or in Rome.

This communication with the Continent, with the new ideas it brought into all the spheres of intellectual labour, was largely increased by the craze for pilgrimage which seized on England. Kings shared in it; Caedwalla, Coenred, the East Saxon Offa, Ine and others took their journey to Rome. "Noble and ignoble," says Baeda, "laymen and clerics, men and women, outdid one another" in eagerness. Through Gaul, over the Alps, down through Italy, and over divers paths and provinces, the pilgrims went, enlarging that knowledge and quickness of reception which give men interest in literature and desire to make it; seeing men and cities different from their own, having adventures, touching many divers peoples and manners, becoming conscious of a larger world—things which add new materials to the feelings and thoughts, which are the roots of literature. The English missionaries, on the other hand, under Willibrord at the end of the seventh century, and under Boniface in the beginning of the eighth, converted Friesland and Germany, brought Englishmen into touch with folk related to themselves, re-animated and strengthened in this way their original temper of soul; and carried the fresh rough impulse and the new interests of the Franks into England.

The conversion of Friesland and the Saxon realms by Englishmen had, it is believed, a much larger influence on our literature than was till lately suspected, and there are theories which connect portions of the "Caedmon poems" with old Saxony. The closer bond with the Franks which arose from Charles Martel's sympathy with the mission work of Boniface continued after his death, and the literary connections between England and the great kingdom which was growing into the empire became extensive and important. This was one reason of the far-reaching influence of the School of York. Nor must we forget, though it is not directly connected with monasticism, that Charles the Great was in constant correspondence with English kings and with the seat of learning in York, at a time when he was collecting into a series, now unfortunately lost, the old war-sagas and the adventurous tales of the Germanic nations.

Monasticism, out of which many of these missions grew, and in extending which many of them ended, was thus one of the roots of the closer connection of

England with Rome, Germany, and Gaul; and this connection added no slight impulse in various ways to the literary development of England in the eighth century. It was unfortunate that this impulse tended to weaken or to destroy vernacular literature, and to replace it by Latin; and it was characteristic of the national genius of Ælfred that he felt this misfortune, and strove to remedy it. It was still more unfortunate, if anything in history can be called unfortunate, that just as England reached this point, and under the supremacy of Ecgberht might have won the peace which literature requires for her steady growth, the Danes broke in and swept away a harvest which might have ripened to a full ear.

NOTES

A.—(CHAPTER I)

WIDSITH

THE introduction may have been written on the continent by a poet of the Angles, for "the poet clearly refers to the old country under the title of *Ongle*." The country of Eormanric was, he says, "east from Ongle." This is the view of Dr. Guest, and he thinks that this part of the poem belongs to the time after the Ostrogoths had left the Vistula, probably between the years 480 and 547, the date of Ida's occupation of Bamborough. This would put the original poem, which begins at line 10, back into an earlier part of the fifth century, between the years, as Guest conjectures, 433 and 440. If we take, with him, the poem as genuine, the poet was contemporary in his youth with Eormanric, and must have sung in his court before the year 375, when this King of the Goten died. But the poet also mentions Ætla (Attila) as king. But Attila was not king till 433. The poem then, to include these two dates, must have been written in Widsith's old age, and after 433. Moreover, Guest continues. "the Goths appear in the poem as the enemies, still independent, of Attila"; and he makes a criticism which, coming from so careful an historian, must not be omitted. "Eormanric and his generals are spoken of in the poem in a sober manner. We see none of the fable which afterwards enveloped their names; they are still the mere creatures of history."

But all this is subject to other explanations, and we can come to no certainty about it. The most that critics can dare to suggest is, first: "That the theory which maintains the genuineness of the poem is the theory which is beset with the fewest difficulties" (Guest); and secondly, that the kernel of the poem, from verse 10 to verse 75, and from verse 87 to the close (verses 131-134 being excepted) is very old, the oldest English poetry we possess.[1] Originally

---

[1] This great age is agreed to by Leo, Müllenhof, Ten Brink, Möller, and Wülker, to speak of the Germans alone.

written by a Myrging, it was adopted by the Angles, to whom the Myrgings, if we may conjecture this from a passage in the poem, were tributary in the days of Offa of Ongle.

The poet represents himself as contemporary with Hermanric, Attila, the Visigoth Wallia, the Burgundian Gibica, and these kings range from the year 375 to 435. He also speaks of Offa of Ongle, Ongentheow, Hrothgar, Finn and Hnaef as known of by him, and as historical rather than legendary personages.

But this theory of the genuineness of the poem is not so easily settled. In the midst of the list, other kings are mentioned whose reigns extend beyond 440, and whose names, if we accept the visit to Eormanric as genuine, must have been afterwards interpolated. This is certainly the case if we are to take Ælfwine, whom Widsith says he met, as identical with Alboin, who was not king in Italy till the year 568. Guest avoids this difficulty by making the Ælfwine of the poem one of the chiefs who followed Alaric in his inroad, 401 A.D.

The editors of the *Corpus Poeticum Boreale* assume at once, without expressing a shade of doubt on the matter, that the Traveller's Song was written after the death of Alboin, 572 A.D. They quote a passage concerning Ælfwine's (Alboin's) fame from Paul the Deacon, and say, "This passage is strikingly confirmed by the fame of Ælfwine having reached even the English author of the Traveller's Song." This opinion makes the poem to be written in our England, and probably not earlier than the seventh century, a view which is not without its critical supporters. Maurer, referring to the mention of the Cæsar in it, places it still later, after the time of Charles the Great, and suggests that the name Vikingas which occurs in the list of tribes, points to a time when the English had made acquaintance with the northern rovers.

On the other hand, it has been held, and by a number of commentators, that the insertion of names later than the fifth century is due to the work of an interpolator, who probably lived in England in the seventh century, and that the total absence of any mention of our England as England goes far to prove—independent altogether of the directness and simplicity of the personal portion—that the body of the poem was composed upon the continent. The English editor of the seventh century would then have used the ancient poem as a frame into which he inserted what men had come to know (a hundred years let us say after the death of Alboin), of other countries and their rulers, introducing also, from his own knowledge, the passage concerning the Picts and Scots and the Armoricans. We should then have a poem, the body of which was composed by a man who in his youth may have been a contemporary of Eormanric in the fourth century, but who did not write his verses till the fifth century, 435-440, and which, brought to

Britain by the Angles, was taken up, added to, and produced in its present form in the seventh or eighth century.

A word remains to be said about some names interesting to us. The poet stays his hand in the middle of his list to speak at some length of Offa who ruled Ongle, as if Offa's history were specially bound up with his own tribe. "Offa," he says, "set up, while yet a youth, the greatest of kingdoms. With his sword alone he widened his marches against the Myrgings, by Fifeldor. And as Offa fixed it, so Engle and Swaefe held their place." We only know Offa as a legendary hero, whose story gets mixed up afterwards with that of Offa of Mercia. But this sober mention of him has the air of history rather than of legend, and the fight at Fifeldor, which in after saga is clothed with imaginative details, is here wholly free from them. We seem to touch a piece of reality concerning a king who was in ancient days, one of ourselves, a great Englishman who fought the battles of the Angles in the lands about the Elbe. Whether this is really so will, I suppose, be discussed till every possible theory is exhausted. The reference to the Engle and Swaefe as neighbouring nations is also to the point. "It is clear from this," says Guest, "that the latter had not as yet left the shores of the Baltic. This is one of the many circumstances which prove the great antiquity of the poem."

Another passage of interest is that in which the writer also interrupts his mere catalogue of names to tell a piece of history or of what seems history. It contains names well known to us from the poem of *Beowulf*. He speaks of Hrothgar, and of his famous Hall, Heorot, and he speaks of both without any allusion whatever to the legend of Beowulf and Grendel. It seems as if this poem had been written before the legend of Beowulf had been connected with Hrothgar and Heorot. So also he speaks of Finn and Hnaef, who occur in one of the episodes of *Beowulf* and in the fragment we have in English of the *Fight at Finnsburg*.

Still more curious is another coincidence which I have already noticed. In one of the episodes introduced into *Beowulf* there is an account of a feud which arose between Hrothgar and Froda, and of the way the feud was healed by the marriage of Hrothgar's daughter Freaware to Ingeld, the son of Froda. But the slayer of Froda comes as attendant on Freaware to the hall of Ingeld, and Ingeld slays his father's murderer. In the trouble that follows, his love for his wife grows cold. There the episode ends, but the hero Beowulf, who tells the story, prophesies that evil will flow from it, that war will arise between Hrothgar and Ingeld. We hear nothing of the result in the poem of *Beowulf*. But the result is given us in the Traveller's Song. Widsith tells us that Heorot was attacked by Ingeld, and that he was beaten back and slain. "They" (Hrothgar, and Hrothulf his brother) "bowed down at Heorot the sword of Ingeld, hewed down at Heorot the host of the Heathobeards."

This is what Paley would have called an undesigned coincidence, and it seems to bring Hrothgar and Heorot and Ingeld, that is, some of the names in *Beowulf*, into the realm of history.

B.—(CHAPTER I)

THE LAMENT OF DEOR

Weyland, Egil, and Slagfin entrap three swan maidens who came flying through the mirkwood. Of these Lathgund clasped the white neck of Weyland. But when nine winters had gone she left him, and he stayed in Wolfdale hammering the red gold, for he was the first of smiths. Then Nidad, King of the Niars, came on him by stealth and bound him and bore him to the palace, and the queen, seeing him and his eyes like the flashing snake, was afraid, and said, "Sever the might of his sinews and set him down at Seastead"; and there Weyland, lame as the Greek smith, wrought many treasures, and thought of vengeance. And the sons of Nidad, young boys, came to Wolfmere in Seastead to see the red gold and jewels, and Weyland seized them and made cups for Nidad out of their skulls, and out of their eyeballs gems for the queen, and out of their teeth brooches for Bodwild (Beadohild). And Bodwild broke her ring and came to Weyland to get it mended, and he gave her a drink and took his will of her. And when he had so wrought his wrath he made himself wings and flew over the palace and mocked Nidad, and crying out all that he had done, rose laughing into the air, but Nidad and Bodwild sat behind with many sorrows.

This is the drift of the version in the Edda. It is the most poetical of all. The version in *Deor* is perhaps older, and it is not apparently derived from Scandinavia, but from German saga; from sagas "of which the Edda knows nothing." The names are not names of the Edda, but of German saga. England, France, and Germany know the old Scandinavian smith. *Beowulf* mentions him; Ælfred translates, by a pleasant mistake, Fabricius by his name; he appears in the "Weyland smithy" of the O. E. Berkshire charter, in the "Weyland's houses" or labyrinths of northern Europe, and in the *Galant* of the French Chansons de Gestes. His son by Bodwild is the Wade of the Wilkina Saga whose magic boat *Wingelock* was known till almost modern times in northern England.[1]

The legend of Geat and Maethhild—or of Hild and Geat, if we

---

[1] See the "Lay of Weyland" and notes thereon in the *Corp. Poet. Boreale*, vol. i. p. 168.

translate with Wülker's reading—exists only in this Anglo-Saxon song; but I would like to suggest that it may be from the same root as the story which is told in Iceland of Frey and Gerda in the lay of Skirni. Frey sits all day alone in the hall, with heavy heart-sorrow, for he saw a maid in Gymir's croft whose arms beamed so brightly that sky and sea were lit by them. Skirni, Frey's page, goes to giantland to win Gerda and bring back her consent. In three nights' time she will meet Frey at Barra, a peaceful copse, and grant her love; and Frey, when he hears, cries out, "One night is long; two nights are longer, how can I endure three? A month has often seemed shorter to me than this half bridal night." This is a close parallel of circumstance—but infinite has been such circumstance. Yet there is no reason why Geat should not have the same mythical origin as Frea (as an Angle, if he knew of him, would call Frey); though Grimm has said that he is Woden. We know Geat was one of our ancestral deities, and if his name be derived from *geotan*, "to pour," it harmonises with the character of Frey who was the bounteous summer god — the God of Love and Fruitfulness.

But who can decide aright concerning the first line of the stanza? There are at least six conjectures concerning the words *maeð hilde*. Is it a proper name, Maethhild; or is it the "dishonour, or the miserable ill-fortune of Hild" (I have left it *meed*, that which was measured to her); or are both the words to be taken as simple substantives—"this reward, or this shame, of battle"—no proper name being there?

I am myself inclined to think that there may have been a full stanza about Hild, and another about Geat, and that these two persons are not connected at all, but have here got together by the loss of four or five lines. The dishonour or the dreadful fate of Hild would then be, I suggest, an allusion to that story which afterwards, in Icelandic saga, became the tale of Hogni and Hedinn, in which Hild, the daughter of Hogni, is basely ravished away by Hedinn, to the fearful travail and torment of the two heroes, who fight together and slay one another night after night for a hundred and forty-three years, while Hild sits still in a grove hard by and looks upon the play. But this is a guess and no more.

The passage about Theodric may refer to the fable of his thirty years' exile among the Huns, but it may also refer to something which is not contained in the later myths about Theodric, and of which we have no knowledge. In explaining this and other historical and mythical allusions in Anglo-Saxon poems, Guest says, "That we must not pay too much attention to the later myths of the Icelander and the German." There is, however, a fragment which is assumed to concern Theodric and the Maerings which is quoted in the *Corp. Poet. Bor.*, vol. i. p. 59. "It was found on an ancient

Runic stone (early tenth century?) known as the Rökstone, in East Gothland, Sweden. This stone stands in the same relation to the Deor lay as does the Ruthwell Cross to the Lay of the Rood. The identity we assume from the correspondence of the name Theodrick and the Maeringa with the Maeringa-burg where, according to the old English Deor's Lay, Theodric ruled." "Theodrich the daring in mood, the lord of seamen, ruled Redmere's strand. He, the Prince of the Maerings, sitteth now in full war-gear on his steed, shield-girt."

Waiting like Barbarossa and all the other heroes who sit armed in caves—in that frequently recurring folk legend!

C.—(CHAPTER IV)

WALRUS OR SPERM WHALE?

The common explanation of the *Hronaes ban*—the *Whale's bone* in the text—is that (since the casket is of ivory) it belonged to the walrus which was hunted in the North Sea at and before the time of Ælfred. Ohthere mentions its ivory, but calls the animal the *Hors-hwael*. But the walrus, unless the weather was much colder than now in earlier times, did not come below the North Cape, and our hunter may have slain his quarry in the icy seas beyond Archangel. However, I see no reason why the walrus should not, in the eighth or the tenth century, have haunted the Shetlands or the Faroes, or the northern coasts of Norway or Scotland. If the reindeer was hunted in Caithness, the walrus may have visited the Shetlands in winter; and whether or no, as the ivory tusk of the walrus was, to our knowledge, an article of commerce in Ælfred's time, it is the most natural supposition to make our hunter's *Hronaes ban* a walrus tusk.

I have, however, made the guess (at p. 84), that it was the ivory jaw of the sperm whale, and the guess is not devoid of probability. First, I am not sure that the word *Hron* is ever used in the loose generic sense in which *Hwael* was used. *Hwael* meant any great beast that tumbled about in the sea,—a whale, a porpoise, or a seal; but when the walrus was meant, *Hors* was added to it to distinguish it from the rest. *Hron* may have been kept for the whales, as apart from the seals.

Then the whole description suits a whale-hunt better than a walrus-hunt. The mountain of water the huge head makes as it moves through the sea, the groaning of the ocean under the monster, the great distress of the beast in the shallows (a walrus would have been much more at ease among the rocks), belong to a whale driven ashore or caught in a bight of land.

Moreover, it was as easy to meet a sperm whale as to meet a walrus. If the writer, who describes the way he got his ivory, was an English sea-rover in a Viking galley, as I think very likely to be the case from the runes about Egil and Siegfried, he might come across sperm whales in the Mediterranean, or outside the Straits of Gibraltar; nor is it at all impossible that some gipsy of a sperm whale might have wandered northward as far as the west coast of Scotland. There are at least two instances known of this whale being killed on the coasts of the British Isles within the last century.

When Spenser uses *Whale's-bone*, he is said to certainly mean the walrus tusk. It does not follow at all. The ivory jaw and teeth of the sperm whale were certainly known to the Elizabethans,—and the Norsemen must have also met and killed it.

D.—(CHAPTER V)

ON THE WORSHIP OF WODEN BY THE ENGLISH, AND ON SCEAF

It is a remarkable thing that there is no mention whatever in the whole of Anglo-Saxon literature before Ælfred of Woden being the god of the English. This is scarcely accounted for by the desire of Christian writers to suppress the name of heathen gods. In the seventh century, when many suppose that the legends of *Beowulf* were given, on the whole, their present form, a Christian poet would not be so particular; and it is astonishing that not the faintest allusion is made to Woden in *Beowulf*, if his was the name of the supreme god of the English. Baeda himself has no objection to speak of two heathen goddesses by name, and to trace the name of Easter to Eostra. Moreover, if Woden had been ever of the same importance in England as he became in Germany proper, in Scandinavia in later times, or in England after the Danish invasion, some hint of his existence, some words derived from his attributes, would, we should think, have stolen into the large body of poetry which we owe to Cynewulf; or into poems like the *Wanderer* or the *Wife's Complaint* and a few others, the bulk of which seems either pagan or semi-pagan, written on the border-line between Christianity and heathendom. But not one word appears; and Baeda and Ealdhelm are just as silent. When Grimm tries to get Woden into early English poetry, all he can do is to say that *woma* ("clamor, sonitus") is connected with *Omi*, which is, he thinks, another name for the Norse Odinn. There is not much in that; and this absence of the slightest allusion to Woden as a god suggests the question—"Whether the Angles, when they came over, worshipped Woden, whether he was ever their god in England before the Danish invasion?" and the further question, "whether any of the tribes north of the Elbe—Danes, Angles, Jutes, or any of the Scandinavians, *at the time of the invasion of England*—worshipped the Heaven under the name of Woden, or even thought of him as one of their ancestor-gods?" I do not think, though I speak with great diffidence, that there is any sure proof of the affirmative, and I think that there is a good deal to be said on the side of the negative. Nevertheless, I put forward the following considerations only as a guess, a conjecture. If they are worth nothing, they may at least amuse the reader.

It is plain enough that Woden (Wuotan) was the name which the tribes of Germany proper came, in process of time, to give to the supreme being. "Wodan," says Paul the Deacon, "qui ab universis Germaniae gentibus ut deus adoratur!" Jonas of Bobbio, Paul's elder countryman, also mentions him—"illi aiunt, deo suo Vodano, se velle litare"—testimonies which, however, belong only to the seventh century. It is also plain from the Abjuration of idolatry and declaration of faith imposed by Boniface on his converts in Thuringia that Woden was worshipped in these forest regions in the eighth century. Here is the phrase in the Abrenuntiatio: "I forsake all works and words of the devil, the worship of groves, Woden and Saxnote, and all evil spirits that are their companions." None, however, of these and kindred passages proves that in the fifth century the English worshipped him as God; or that even when Boniface was writing in the eighth century, Woden was remembered as an English god by the Englishmen with whom Boniface corresponded. It is most probable, I think, that the central German tribes did worship Woden as their tribal deity in the fifth century, and if so, he would have been known as such to the Saxons who came to England; but the Wessex genealogy which goes back to Sceaf through Woden does not suggest that Woden was supreme in the West Saxon mind, and Æthelweard, himself a West Saxon, knows nothing of his godhead. Even if those Saxons who came to England from the inland of Saxony worshipped him as an ancestor, it does not prove that the Angles did so; and all the vernacular literature we have before Ælfred is Angle. In that literature there is not a trace of Woden-worship. Whatever we may say then of a certain element of Woden-worship existing among some of the Saxon invaders, it may be conjectured that this worship had not extended northward among the Angles, Jutes, or Danes at the time of the English migration. After their departure, and a good time after it, I conjecture that Woden-worship got to the North, seized on the Danes, on Sweden and Norway: and I have often thought that the late legend of Woden's wandering from the East and taking refuge in the North contains in it some faint record of this Northern drift of his worship.

These are the matters I think probable. After all, it is only an inference that Woden was the English god, and an inference based on somewhat shadowy arguments. If we do not make that inference, much which is strange in the silence concerning Woden in Anglo-

Saxon literature is explicable. Have we any right to make it at all? That is the question.

There is the argument for Woden's worship derived from the place-names in England compounded with his name, a number of which, more or less certain, are given by Kemble;[1] and from the trees, stones, and posts which in the charters bear traces of his name. But this is no proof of his worship, unless we first assume that he was worshipped. Those names may have been given by the Danes ; and those which existed before the Danish invasion only prove that Woden was a name known to the English as one of their ancestors, or as one of the heroes of their kinsmen—and this nobody denies— but not that he was believed to be the supreme god. Place-names only prove that the name they take was famous.

Secondly, the mention of Woden as a god occurs in Anglo-Saxon poetry and prose. In every case this mention of his divinity is confined to writings which are subsequent to the invasion of the Danes, a time when it is plain that Woden-worship had become extensive ; and when English writers would not hesitate, for the sake of clearness, to give his name to the supreme being whom their ancestors worshipped as the Heaven. We see this custom fully carried out in the Norman chroniclers who, one and all, call the English god by the name of Woden. But we do not see it done by the Latin writers before the Conquest, as I shall afterwards make clear.

To return however to the poetry, Woden's name is mentioned in one of the *Gnomic Verses*: *Woden worhte weos; wuldor-alwalda rume roderas*—"Woden made altars, but the glorious Allwielder the spacious skies"; but I suppose no one will maintain that this is one of the early sentences in that various collection. He is also mentioned by Homilists after Ælfred ; and in one metrical homily Mercury is said to have been honourable among all the heathen, "and to be called Odinn in Danish," but the identification of Mercury with Woden,[2] whether here or in the Norman chroniclers, does not prove that the English worshipped him before they were Christians. It only proves that when the homily was made, and

---

[1] *Saxons in England*, vol. i. p. 344, etc. The whole question of Woden's worship in England is debated in those pages, and what does it come to ?

[2] The Mercury of Tacitus has been identified with Woden, but if the identification be correct, it is evidence that the dwellers in Germania worshipped him, but not that his worship went north of the Elbe. When Tacitus comes to speak of the divine ancestors of the Germans, he speaks of them under their native names, ancient gray-haired personages—Tuisco, Mannus—ancestral gods, and when he gets more north, the worship of Nerthus swallows up the rest. She is Mother Earth, and is the only divine Being of whom we have any direct evidence in Anglo-Saxon literature. Whether in the line *Erce, Erce, Erce, corþan modor*, mother of Earth—we have a goddess who is an older Being even than Earth herself, we cannot tell, but at least the phrase suggests a primeval deity older far than Woden. Moreover, there is a kind of bidding prayer for or to the Earth in the same Charm in which the enigmatic *Erce* occurs—"Hale be Thou, Earth,

the Chronicles written, Woden was considered as the supreme god of the pagans, and this is not denied.

When we look however, and this is a third point, at earlier writings, at Nennius, at Baeda, at the *Anglo-Saxon Chronicle*, even at the Chronicle of Æthelweard in the tenth century—that is, when we consider writings nearer to the times of English heathendom—we find nothing which should make us suppose that the English pagans adored Woden as their great god. I take Æthelweard first. He wrote after Woden-worship had certainly entered into England with the Danes; and he knew that the *Chronicle*, from which he took his history, looked on Woden as one of the ancestors of the English kings. It seems almost impossible, if he was aware that the English had once worshipped Woden as the supreme god, or as a god at all, that he should speak as he does. "Woden was king," he says, "of a multitude of barbarians. But the unbelievers of the North are overwhelmed with so great a delusion that they even now worship him as a god—the Danes, the Northmen, and the Suevi." "Hengist and Horsa," he says again, "were the *nepotes*"—he means the descendants, for, according to his own genealogy of them, they were the great-great-grandsons of Woden—"of Woden, king of the barbarians, quem post, infanda dignitate, ut deum honorantes, sacrificium obtulerunt pagani, victoriae causa sive virtutis." And again—"Woden, king of the barbarians, whom some pagans now still worship as a god" (Books i., ii.) No doubt a Christian chronicler of the tenth century would be glad to leave out Woden's name, but, having used it, the way in which the phrases about him are put is not the way in which a writer would naturally speak who was aware that in old times Woden was the supreme god of his folk. He knows Woden as one of the ancestors of the English kings, whose worship in after years became prevalent among the Northerns. And this is the very thing I conjecture to be true.

Now as Æthelweard is of the tenth, so the book compiled under the name of Nennius is probably of the eighth century. Its materials were then gathered when the traditions of the English heathendom were fresher than in the tenth century, and before the Danish invasion. What does Nennius say? Does this book know anything about Woden's deity? Nothing at all! It speaks of Woden as one of the ancestors of Hengest and Horsa, but when it comes to talk of the god of the invaders, it is of Geat and his divine father it tells,—Geat, who, *as they say*, was the son of a god." I have

---

mother of men!" *Hal wes þu, folde, fira modor;* but I doubt whether this is more than the conventional phrase of a farmer. "Earth, be in good fettle for me"—and the *fira modor*, may also be a mere phrase, and have nothing to do with any conception of the Earth as divine.

italicised *as they say*, because this phrase gives the quotation about Geat an importance it would not have otherwise had in so loose and corrupt a compilation as Nennius. It marks this passage as one of those he collected "de scriptis Scotorum Anglorumque, et ex traditione veterum nostrorum"; from the ancient registers of our history from which Baeda also learned the facts of the English story before the entrance of Christianity—"ex priorum maxime scriptis, hic inde collectis." It is Dr. Guest,[1] who says that when Baeda states a fact on the apparent authority of these ancient chronicles, he sometimes adds, "ut perhibent," "perhibetur"; and the phrase "as they say," used here in this book of Nennius, isolates into importance the statement about Geat.

Asser seems to take up the same view. In his history of Ælfred Woden is not an English god. He is the great-great-great-great-grandson of "Geat whom the pagans long worshipped as a god." Geat, who is in Nennius the son of a god, is here a god of the English—the ancestor-god, as I should say, of the Geatas, just as Taetwa, Beaw, Sceldi—who are the father, grandfather, and great-grandfather of Geat in the Wessex genealogy—may be ancestor-gods of other Northern tribes who one by one separated from the original tribe ruled by Sceaf from whom they all descended. But, leaving this aside, it is at least a little curious that neither Asser nor Nennius, who founded their special statement about the English god on ancient documents, knew anything at all about Woden as an English deity.

Now take Baeda; does he seem to be aware of Woden's importance? When he does mention two of the goddesses of his heathen ancestors, Rheda and Eostra, he is wholly silent about him who is declared by so many to have been the supreme god of the English. When, on the other hand, he does speak of Woden, it is not as a god, but as the ancestor of English kings. "Hengest and Horsa," he says, "were the sons of Victgilsus, whose father was Vecta, son of Woden, from whose stock the royal race of many provinces deduce their original."

Baeda got this, no doubt, from the same ancient sources from which the similar entry in the *Anglo-Saxon Chronicle* is derived, and I appeal now to the witness of the *Chronicle*. "From this Woden," it says (adding, however, one generation more than Baeda contains to Hengest's descent from Woden), "sprang all our royal" (*i.e.* West Saxon) "families and those of the South-humbrians also." A little farther on and the Northumbrian princes are also traced back to Woden, and afterwards the Mercians Penda and Offa. But nothing that the *Chronicle* or Baeda says would suggest to their readers that Woden was a god of the English, much less their supreme god. This might, however, be a possible inference if the

---

[1] *Origines Celticæ*, vol. ii. pp. 157-163.

other full genealogies in the *Chronicle* ended with Woden, but this is not the case. The complete genealogies given in the *Chronicle* of 855 or 891 are those of the Northumbrian, Mercian, and West Saxon princes. The two Mercian genealogies, those of Penda and Offa, go back to Woden, and no farther. The two Northumbrian genealogies, those of Ida and Ælla, both go back to Woden, but in Ida's genealogy, Woden has five ancestors, the last of whom is Geat, and in Ælla's genealogy, Woden has one ancestor, Friduwulf. The Wessex genealogy, made either after Æthelwulf's death or in Ælfred's reign, goes back beyond Woden for twelve generations to Sceaf. The genealogies are also, with differences, given in Nennius, Asser, and Æthelweard during Anglo-Saxon times, and they attribute many ancestors to Woden. Many of the Norman chroniclers give them also; and Woden never closes their lists. He has, variously, four, eight, or even sixteen ancestors. Generally speaking, Sceaf is the oldest heathen name in any of the pedigrees. It is so in the Wessex genealogy, which, for many reasons, may be looked on, as Grimm allows, "to be the complete and correct thing." It is so, also, in Æthelweard, who repeats the *Chronicle*, but was also a special authority on this matter, for he was of the house of Ælfred, and knew his own lineage. Except in Mercia then (in, that is, the full genealogies, for there are several incomplete ones which only go back to Woden), Woden does not take the closing place; and though in the *Chronicle* he does close the Mercian line, he does not close it in the Mercian genealogy of Matthew of Westminster, who gives thirteen ancestors to the Woden of Mercia. Woden's position then is not of first-rate importance in the genealogies. He is one only of a host of ancestors. Had he been the supreme god of the English, he would, I conjecture, have been more isolated. Nor, if we take the generations which lead up to him from Cerdic, in the Wessex genealogy, does he get back into any remote antiquity. Cerdic died in 534. Woden precedes him by nine generations, which (if we give thirty years to a generation) proves that the West Saxons thought that he lived in the midst of the third century—not a very ancient lineage for their supreme being! In fact, if we are to take the genealogies as any evidence of the way in which the English thought of Woden, it is difficult to give Woden any other place than that of an ancestor, whose force and heroism had made him important. A nation would scarcely imagine that their supreme god had twelve or fourteen ancestors. Of course, the lists have no backward historical value beyond the names of Cerdic, Ida, or Penda, but they have a value as showing how the English thought about personages like Woden or Sceaf. They do show that Woden did not occupy a supreme position in their minds.[1]

---

[1] Grimm, who is somewhat collared by his belief that Woden was the name

If we are to choose any name as of first-rate importance in the English mind, not as a great god like Heaven or Earth, but as an ancestral divine Person, the name we ought to choose is Sceaf— the father of the Scyld of *Beowulf*—the name of the boy who came out of the deep to Scania, and became, in the myth, king of all the folk round about Sleswick. And, independent of the story told of him by three of the Norman chroniclers, we have the best witness to his importance in the West Saxon genealogy given in the *Chronicle*, and in the pre-eminence which his story takes in Æthelweard. It is scarcely possible to doubt but that Ælfred himself drew up or carefully superintended the account of the West Saxon lineage in the *Chronicle*. We have, if this was the case, his own view, in the genealogy, of the question, Who was the root, the founder, the remotest ancestor of the West Saxon folk, and indeed of all the English; for the place Ælfred elsewhere brings the English people from is the very place where this remote ancestor was said by tradition to have set up his capital town, Sleswick, which the Danes called Haithaby. This primeval ancestor of the English, according to Ælfred, was Sceaf. (The derivation of Sceaf from Noah, and so from Adam, has plainly nothing to do with the question.) Through twelve generations then, anterior to Woden, Ælfred looked back to his origins. Moreover, it seems also pretty plain that Ælfred knew of the legend of Sceaf, though he took care not to introduce such a matter into the *Anglo-Saxon Chronicle*. The legend is told by Æthelweard, and with remarks attached which, considering who Æthelweard was, force us to believe that the house of Ælfred knew the tale. Æthelweard was extremely particular about

---

of the god whom all the Teutonic races adored as supreme and naturally identifies him with the Mercury of Tacitus, declares that because Woden is in the centre (which he is not always) of the Anglo-Saxon genealogies, his pre-eminence is evident. This is a curious argument.

Troubled too with the statement that the English worshipped Geat, he says that Geat is another name for Woden. This is mere assertion. Geat was probably the semi-divine tribal father of the Geatas, and worshipped as such by that tribe and its emigrants; and Wuotan, as it seems to me, occupied the same position among the Central German tribes, and especially, I conjecture, among the Franks, whose great influence would tend to make the name of their tribal deity the name of the supreme god, and send his worship all over the Teutonic peoples, but not till long after the English migration.

A memory, a tradition, of these different tribal worships lingers in the phrase used in the St. Olaf Saga—" Thor is the God of the Englishmen, Odinn of the Saxons, Skiold of the Scanians, and Freyr of the Swedes." " I wonder," says Grimm, " why the writer gives Thor to the English, who were votaries of Woden." He may well wonder why.

As to the names of the days of the week which are alleged as proving the English worship of Woden and the rest, these names were made long after the English migration, and prove nothing at all as to whom the English worshipped before Christianity. "Their very forms," Vigfusson and Powell say, "prove them to be loan words."—*C. P. B.*, vol. i. p. 428.

his lineage, and he wrote his Chronicle not only to tell his cousin Matilda the story of the English in England (it is taken chiefly from the *Anglo-Saxon Chronicle*), but also, as he says, to make her thoroughly acquainted "with the origin of our family, who were our relations, and how and where they came from, as far as our memory can go, and as our parents taught us." He and his cousin were both of the royal West Saxon line. Æthelred, son of Æthelwulf, and brother of Ælfred, was his direct ancestor, and Ælfred himself was the direct ancestor of his cousin Matilda. Being thus connected with the West Saxon kings, and himself an eager genealogist, he would be sure to preserve carefully the views held by his ancestors as to their origin, and we hear from him—and the testimony is of worth—that Æthelwulf, Ælfred's father, traced his descent to Sceaf, as we infer from the Chronicle that Ælfred also did. There is then, I think, clear evidence that the West Saxon House—and at the time of its greatest importance, when it would be most jealous of its ancestry, from the time of Æthelwulf to that of Eadgar—held that Woden was but one in a long series of their ancestors, and that Sceaf was their most ancient and venerable father. Here is the passage in Æthelweard. He has brought King Æthelwulf back through Ina and Kenred to Cerdic, and Cerdic through eight generations to Woden—"And Woden was son of Frithowald, son of Frealaf, son of Frithuwulf, son of Finn, son of Godwulf, son of Geat, son of Taetwa, son of Beaw, son of Sceldi, son of Sceaf. This Sceaf came with one bark to an island of the ocean, named Scani ; surrounded with arms, and he was a young boy, and unknown to the people of that land ; but he was received by them, and they guarded him as their own with much care, and afterwards chose him for their king. *It is from him that King Æthelwulf derives his descent.*" If we are to choose then the oldest ancestor-god of all the English tribes, the one whom the consistent English tradition lodges in Sleswick whence Ælfred derives the original English ; if we are to select the mythical ancestor, through Cerdic, of our own Royal House, we look back beyond Geat or Beaw or the rest (who may have been worshipped by separate tribes), and far beyond Woden, in a straight line to Sceaf, who, fatherless, motherless, came out of the mists of myth, out of the unknown deep, out of the secret hiding-places of the gods, to Scania ; and whose story—inserted into the poem of Beowulf—we possess under the name of his son Scyld, in perhaps the most ancient song in the English language.

I put forward these considerations with no impertinent assertion. They are no more than a conjecture which seems to have enough support to render it perhaps worthy of being called a theory. They are considerations which account for the silence of early English literature on the gods who have been transferred to the English from the later Viking creed, and whom Kemble and others discover hidden away like shadows in allusive words and phrases. They mean to suggest that the worship of Woden as the supreme being had not reached the older England of the mainland at the time of the migration; that it did not get into the lands about the mouth of Elbe, or into Denmark and Sweden until a good time after the fifth century; that then it did drift northward and seized on the Danes, and was brought by them to England; that the Vikings took it up, mingled it up with Christian myths, and sent it over other regions of Europe than Germany; and that then Woden's name became of so much importance that writers in England transferred it backwards to the supreme god whom the pagan English worshipped, but that the pagan English did not use that name for their god. Woden was no more to them than one of the heroic ancestors of their kings.

I repeat that this is only a suggestion; but that the religion of our fathers was a simple and homely affair, and had nothing to do with the complicated theology of the Norsemen, is not a theory. It was a nature-worship of father Heaven, and mother Earth, and of their benignant summer children, and to these we may perhaps add a war-god of some kind. Underneath these deities there were semi-divine ancestors of the folk who were worshipped, and each family had probably their own household spirits as well. The rites of these worships were conducted partly in the households, and partly in temples belonging to the tribe or the royal house, and without idols. Below these venerable personages, reverence, founded on fear, was given to the destroying and dark powers of nature, embodied as giants, elves, and monsters, and also to the elements, places, and things in which the gods, the ancestors, and the lower order of beings were supposed to take up their dwelling—the air, the fire, the great water, the burial barrows and howes, the hills, the islands in the river, the groves, the great trees, the wells, the ancient pillars of stone they found on plain or moor.[1] Around these latter things, and round the evil forces of nature, superstitions, evil and innocent, gathered; but the foundation of the religion —the worship of the semi-divine spirits of the forefathers of the tribe or the family, and of the great nature-deities from whom they sprang—was at once homely and noble, reverent and simple. I may add that this simplicity of religion would account for the comparative ease with which Christianity was introduced among the English, and for the wisdom and tolerance with which, for example, Æthelberht and Eadwine considered and carried out the change of religion.'

---

[1] I am sorry that some of this has been already said in the chapter to which this note is attached, but the repetition seemed to be necessary in this place.

E.—(CHAPTER IX)

THE CHARMS

The *Charms*, of which some are here given, were kept in the mouths of the people, and, after the introduction of Christianity, their heathen elements were modified by Christian elements. They are like an ill-rubbed Palimpsest. The old writing continually appears from under the new; the new is blurred by the old, and the old by the new. Sometimes they both mingle into the strangest jumble, in which the heathen superstitions have Christian clothing, and the Christian heathen. This is true concerning the charms mentioned in the chapter on the *Settlement*. Those which follow here are more decidedly Christian, and are partly prose and partly verse. I translate such portions of them as have some poetical value. They have the literary interest which belongs to rude folk-rhymes. The first is the *Nine Herbs' Charm*. In Sweden nine sorts of flowers made the midsummer nosegay for a maiden to sleep and dream upon. Nine is the mystic number (rather three or a multiple of it) which is most popular in Britain, but of course this is not peculiar to Britain. The charm starts with the Mugwort—[1]

Remember thou, Mugwort, what thou declaredst,
What thou preparedst at the great declaration!
Thou art called Una, oldest of worts,
Thou hast might against three, and also 'gainst thirty;
Thou hast might against poison, and against flying things,
And against the loathly ones which through the land are faring.
Thou, too, Waybroad,[2] mother of worts,

---

[1] The Mugwort is the Artemisia, the German *beifuss*. The tradition that whoso wears it does not weary on the way comes down from Pliny. But among all German tribes it is good in a house against fiends and diseases, "against poison and flying things," that is, fevers; and "against the loathly things that fare through the land" that is, against witches and their congeners. Grimm quotes a Galloway song which a mermaid sings to the sorrowful relations of a girl dying of consumption—

Wad ye let the bonnie May die i' your hand
And the Mugwort flowering in the land!

As to the "loathly things," compare Grimm's quotation, which is too amusing to leave out, and illustrates the transference of disease: "God the Lord went over the land and there met him 70 sorts of Gouts and Goutesses. Then spake the Lord, Ye 70 Gouts and Goutesses, whither would ye? Then spake the 70 Gouts and Goutesses, We go over land and take from men their health and limbs. Then spake the Lord, Ye shall go to an elder bush and break off all his boughs and leave unto this man his straight limbs."

[2] Waybroad—the *plantago*—(A. S. *wegbraede*; German, *wegerich, wege-*

> Open to Eastward, inwardly mighty,
> O'er thee ran the Chariots, over thee queens rode,
> O'er thee Brides have brided, o'er thee bulls have panted;
> All hast thou withstounded, all hast thou withstood,
> As thou now withstandest venom and the ills that fly,
> And the loathly kin that o'er the land are faring.

The next four lines are full of questions for critics. The lines which follow, and which have more interest, belong to the plant which is afterwards named *Attorlað*—

> This is here the wort that against the Worm fought,
> This has power 'gainst the poison, it prevails 'gainst flying ill;
> It prevails o'er loathly things that the land are faring through!
> Flee thee, Attorlath, less flee from the greater,
> Greater from the less, till a boot from both arrive.
> Thou, remember, Mayweed, what thou didst declare,
> What thou didst end up, at Alorforda.[1]
> So that ne'er for flying ill was there life e'er taken,
> Since a man did make Mayweed to himself for meat.

The next herb, *Wergulu*, does business which is very curious—

> This is the wort that is Wergulu called;
> This sent the seal o'er the ridge of the sea,
> Of other poison to better the hurt.

Then some strange lines occur about Woden, concerning which I have nothing to say except that they seem to put the charm forward into times after the Danish invasion. The *wuldor-tanas*, the "magic-twigs," sound far more Norse than English—

> These nine herbs did work nine poisons against.
> A worm came sneaking, and with teeth tore the man!
> Then Woden in hand took nine wonder-twigs;
> There he slew the adder, that it flew in pieces nine.

There are three charms to bring back lost or stolen cattle, one of which I have already used. The other two are almost identical, and contain each three verses—

> Bethlehem the Burg was hight, where was born the Christ,
> It is famous far over all the middle Earth!
> So this deed be known in the sight of men.

---

warte) has its Latin name from being exposed to the tread (*plantae*) of passengers, and its English name from growing on the wayside. I wonder if the legend Grimm speaks of (chapter on Herbs)—of the herb being once a maiden that awaited her lover by the wayside—has anything to do with the strange lines 9 and 10?

[1] What she did at Alorforda and what Alorforda is, it is almost too distressing not to know. Cockayne says there is an Alderford in Norfolk?

"*Per crucem Christi.* So pray three times to the East, and say thrice, 'May the cross of Christ bring it back from the East;' then to the West and say, 'May the cross of Christ bring it back from the West;' and to the South, etc.; and to the North and say, 'The cross of Christ was hidden, and has been found.' The Jews hanged Christ; they did the worst of deeds to him. They hid what they could not hide; so may this deed never be hidden. *Per crucem Christi.*" This is curious enough, but the next is more curious. "If cattle be privily taken away; if it be a horse, sing this over his foot-shackles or over his bridle; if it be another kind of cattle, sing over the hoof-track, and light three candles and drip the wax three times into the hoof-track. No man will be able to conceal it," *i.e.* the stealing.[1]

The next three are, like that against the Stitch, against illness. The first is against the *Dweorh*, that is, "against the Dwarf" (or we may read *Weorh*—a warty eruption). If it be the Dwarf,[2] this charm takes us into heathendom. The Dwarf's breath and touch may bring sickness and death. Cattle bewitched in Norway are *dverg-slagen*. Blowing, puffing beings they are, wind spirits of harm, full of mischief, who tangle the hair in knots (Grimm, chapter on Dwarfs). They were thought by the English to tangle the body in knots, to be the source of agues, of convulsions, of all diseases which seem to leap suddenly on a man. Or they took possession of the body and went roving about therein.

"One must take seven little wafers, such as one offers with, and write these names on each wafer—Maximianus, Malchus, Johannes, Martinianus, Dionysius, Constantinus, Serapion; then must one afterwards sing the charm hereafter mentioned, first into the left ear, then into the right, then above the man's head. Then let a maiden go *and hang it on his neck*, and let one do this for three days: he will soon be better."

---

[1] This belongs to the sphere of the ancient superstition that the footprints were so far bound up with the man or animal that made them that an injury done to them is transferred to the man, or that some meddling with the spoor of an animal detains it. The Australian blacks put hot embers in the track of the hunted beast; the Ojibway Indians place "medicine" on the prints of the deer and bear, supposing that this will bring them within reach. The Zulus (and this is a curiously close parallel to the text) resort to a similar device *to recover strayed cattle*. Earth, taken from the footprints of the missing beasts, is placed in the chief's vessel, etc. Then the chief says: "I have now conquered them. These cattle are now here. I am sitting upon them. *I know not how they will escape*."—Frazer, "Popular Superstitions of the Ancients," *Folk-Lore*, vol. i.

[2] Every one knows that in all folk medicine the most frequent source of disease is the anger or the mischief of an external spirit; and the several diseases had each their own spirit. Grimm quotes a Finnish Song which condenses this opinion: "Einen alten Frau neun knaben geboren werden: werwolf, schlange, risi? eidechse, nachtmar, gliedschmerz, gichtschmerz, milzstechen, bauchgrimmen."

>   Here a spider wight   came a-ganging in,
>   He his hands had laid   hard upon his belly.
>   Quoth he then that thou   now his Haencgest wert :
>   *Lay thyself   against his neck.*
>   Now began they then   off the land to sail.
>   And as soon as they came off the land   they began to cool ;
>   Then came in a wild beast's sister—   then she ended all,
>   And she swore her oaths   that never this should harm the sick,
>   Neither him who could   of this charm get hold,
>   Nor the man who knew   how this charm to sing.[1]
>   Amen. *Fiat.*

The charm for a pregnant woman which follows is full of folk fancies, but none of them, save the allusion to the fairy changeling, has more than a passing interest. And the charm against a Wen [2] is another instance of the transference of the disease to some inanimate object, and the passing away of the disease as the object decays.

The last charm of importance is that sung on departing for a journey. Many of the lines have an air of antiquity, but even these, as the whole body of the poem, are Christian or have been made so. The *gyrd*, the rod of the beginning, and its works of defence, is very like an ancient rune-stick, and the phrases *sige-gealdor* (" a victorious charm "), *sige-gyrd* (" a victorious rod "), seem to me also heathen. So also the evils from which the charm guards the traveller belong to the indefinite terrors of heathendom, the nameless horrors of elves and wandering sprites and gangers of the night, or of the bloodthirsty river-spirits that spring upon the traveller. Here is the Spell—

---

[1] The verses from 5 to the end read like a nonsense song, like the wise men who went to sea in a sieve. *Haencgest* appears nowhere else. Cockayne translates it "hackney."

The spider is imprisoned in a bag and hung around the swollen part. This is a common form of cure.

> Only beware of the fever, my friends ! Beware of the fever !
> For it is not, like that of our cold Acadian climate,
> Cured by wearing a spider hung round one's neck in a nutshell.
>   *Evangeline.*

Elias Ashmole, May 11, 1681, writes in his diary : " I took early in the morning a good dose of elixir, and hung 3 spiders about my neck, and they drove my ague away. *Deo gratias !* " In Worcestershire the same remedy is good for toothache. In Norfolk a spider, tied up in muslin and pinned over the mantelpiece, is good for whooping-cough. When the spider dies the cough will go. It is inferred from these instances either that the spider, being poisonous, is supposed to draw the poison of the swelling into itself, or, which is most likely, the disease is transferred to the spider and dies with the spider. Toads are often used in the same way.

[2] It is given in full by Mr. de Grey Birch who discovered it, in the *Transactions of the Royal Society of Literature*, vol. xi. p. 29.

> In this rod I guard myself, and to God's grace trust myself,
> 'Gainst the stitch that sore is, and against the sore blow,
> And against the grim, 'gainst the grisly terror,
> And against the mickle horror that to every one is loathly;
> And 'gainst all the loathly things that into the land may come!
> A victorious spell I sing, a victorious staff I bear,
> Word of victory, work of victory, so may this avail me!
> May no spirit mar me nor the mighty man afflict me.

Then he calls on the Trinity to keep him hale; on holy men and women and the angels to guard him against the fiends, to keep him in peace, to give him the hope of glory of the hall of Heaven!

> Matthew be my helm, Mark my byrnie be;
> Of my life the shining strength; let my sword be Luke,
> Sharp and edged sheer; and my shield be John.

Winds be smooth and light to me, and in God's peace may I dwell, guarded against the loathly One who my life afflicts.

This seems the place for the *Rune Song*, in which, midst of a general Christian form, many heathen elements appear. Moreover, the Runes themselves have a close connection with charms, spells, and magic.

Each rune is taken—and there are twenty-nine—according to the meaning of the word given to it as name. Two, three, or four lines are given to each subject. The poem is, in fact, a poetical alphabet, like "A was an Archer that shot at a frog; B was a Butcher that kept a big dog." Here, for example, are the first and second runes—

> ᚾ Bull is a fierce beast and broad are his horns,
> A full-furious deer; and fighteth with horns!
> A mighty moor-stepper! 'Tis a high-mooded creature.

> ᛁ Ice is over-cold, immeasurably slippy;
> Glistens bright as glass, unto gems most like:
> 'Tis a floor frost-wrought, fair unto the sight.

Most of the verses are of the same type as these. They can scarcely be said to belong to literature. A few, however, which describe natural objects, like hail and the birch-tree, have some poetical feeling. There are one or two, also, which seem to come down from ancient, even heathen times. Of these there are three. The first is the fourth Rune ᛟ Os; the second is the sixteenth Rune ᛋ Sigel; the third is the twenty-second ᛝ Ing.

Os, called in the poem the beginner of all speech, the upholder of wisdom, is not an Anglo-Saxon word. The late editor of the poem did not understand it. Grimm explained it by the Latin *os*. Grein, Rieger, and others make it the equivalent of the Gothic *ans*, and the Northern *as* = "God"; but it is still doubtful whether the word *os*, in the sense of God, ever occurs independently. If it have that meaning the verse is heathen, and the editor did not understand it—a supposition which puts the Christian redaction of the poem forward to a late period.

The same kind of mistake seems made about *sigel*. Sigel is used metaphorically for the sun. But the editor of the verse uses it as if it were *segel*, a "sail."

These two errors induce the critics to conjecture that this was an old Northern alphabet of Runes with explanations, probably Danish; and that it was translated and greatly changed by an Anglo-Saxon in the eleventh or twelfth century.

A verse, the 22nd, on the Rune *Ing* is much more clearly ancient. "Ing" is the divine ancestor of the Ingaevones, one of the names of the many-named hero from whom the Northern tribes of Scandia and Angeln sprang. The verse is the only one in the whole poem that seems to belong purely to the original document—

> *Ing* was the first   amid the East Danes,
> Of heroes beheld,   till Eastward he then
> Went over the wave ;   his wain followed him !
> Thus by the Heardings   this hero was named.[1]

In the explanation of this given by Grimm, *Ing* and the *Wain* (a distinctive mark, he says, of ancient gods, heroes, and kings) are mixed up with the Norse gods. Ten Brink says the chariot was the emblem of the god Ing, or Frea, as well as of the goddess Nerthus. But the passage puzzles them, and their explanation is vague. V. Rydberg, in his *Teutonic Mythology* (English translation, p. 180), claims to have solved the difficulty, and he makes the *waen* of the third line not a waggon, but the proper name of the hero Vagn, Hadding's giant foster-father, who is also called Vagnhofde. He is so called by the Haddings, the Heardings of the Anglo-Saxon text. The lines will now read, and the difference is great—

> Ing was first seen among the East Danemen ;
> Then he betook himself eastward over the sea.
> Vagn hastened to follow ;
> Thus the Heardings called this hero.

This strophe then is said to enshrine an episode in the first Northern Epic, broken fragments of which only remain scattered

---

[1] I insert the Anglo-Saxon—

> ᚷ (Ing) waes aerest   mid East denum
> gesewen secgun,   oþ he siððan est
> ofer waeg gewat,   waen aefter ran !
> ðus Heardingas   ðone haele nemdun.
>
> *Rune Song*, ll. 67-70.

here and there in Sagas, the epic of the "first great war in the world," as it is called by the seeress in Volospa.

That mythic war began between the Asas and the Vans, the two great god-clans, and had its counterpart in a war between the three great Teutonic races, but the main contest is between Ing (Yngwe or Swipdaeg) and Hearding (Hadding). In this contest, as in the Trojan war, the gods join. All the Vans who have now driven the Asas into exile favour Ing, but Odin, Thor, and Heimdal are on the side of Hadding. In his early youth Hadding has been carried to Jötunheim by Thor, and brought up there by Vagnhofde, one of the giants; and during his stay is saved again from great danger by Odin himself, who rides away with him over sea and land on Sleipnir. When he grows up he becomes the chief of the tribes of Eastern Teutondom, and makes war on the tribes of Northern and Western Teutondom. Ing comes forth from Asgard on the Scandian peninsula, and calls on all the dwellers and on the Danes to follow him against the Eastern Teutons over the sea. "Ing was first seen among the East Danemen, and then went eastward over the wave." The Danes and Swedes thus go across the Baltic with Ing to the seat of war. A great battle takes place with Hadding, and Hadding is on the point of perishing, when Odin suddenly brings Vagnhofde to Hadding's help, and places him in the battle beside his foster-son. This is expressed in the Rune strophe by the phrase "Vagn made haste to follow. So the Heardings (the followers of Hadding) called the hero." Hadding, all the same, is utterly defeated.

This is V. Rydberg's explanation, and, if we may accept his upbuilding of the myth out of Saxo and the Northern Sagas, it sounds well, and is a literary curiosity. It is as strange to find this single verse lost as it were in an Anglo-Saxon poem, and referring to a mythic epic which concerns the Teutons, as it is to find the equally ancient piece about Scyld in the beginning of *Beowulf*.

END OF VOL. I

www.ingramcontent.com/pod-product-compliance
Lightning Source LLC
Chambersburg PA
CBHW020239240426
43672CB00006B/583